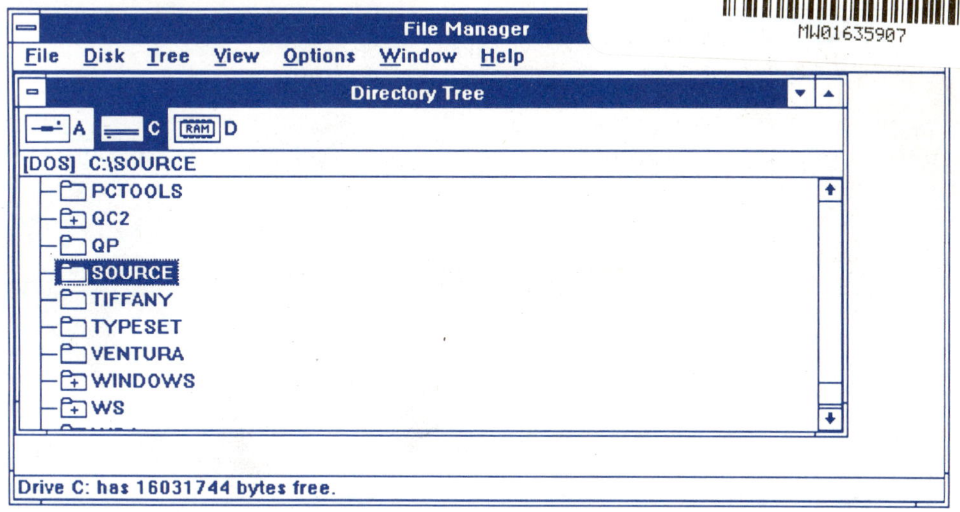

File

Open	Enter
Run...	
Search...	
Move...	F7
Copy...	F8
Delete...	Del
Rename...	
Create Directory...	
Exit	

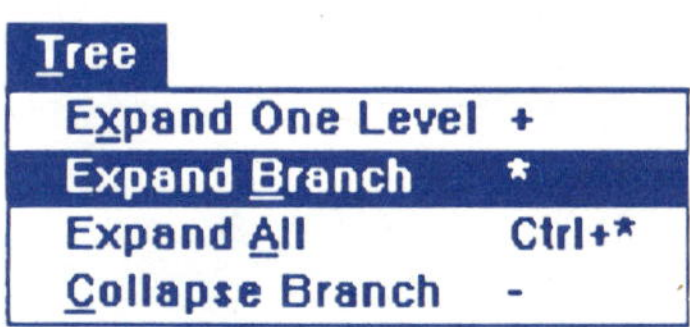

View

✓ Name
File Details
Other...
✓ By Name
By Type
Sort by...
Include...
Replace on Open

Window

Cascade	Shift+F5
Tile	Shift+F4
Refresh	F5
Close All Directories	
✓ 1 Directory Tree	

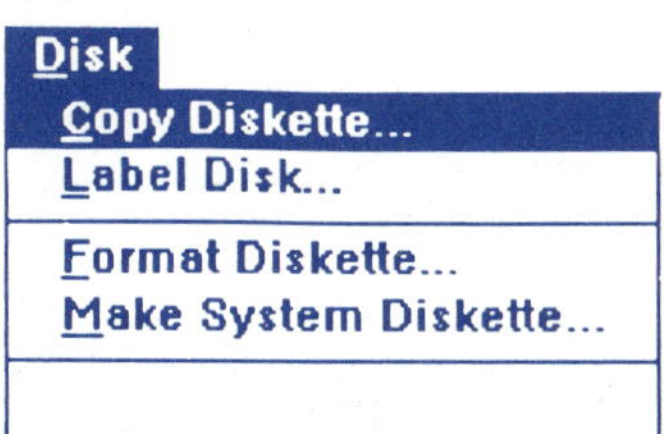

Options

Confirmation...
Lower Case
✓ Status Bar
Minimize on Use

Help

Index
Keyboard
Commands
Procedures
Using Help
About File Manager...

The ABC's of Windows 3.0

The ABC's of Windows™ 3.0

Kris Jamsa

San Francisco • Paris • Düsseldorf • Soest

Acquisitions Editor: Dianne King
Developmental Editor: Christian Crumlish
Copy Editor: David Krassner
Technical Editor: Daniel A. Tauber
Production Editor: Carolina Montilla
Word Processors: Scott Campbell, Ann Dunn, Paul Erickson, Lisa Mitchell
Series Designer: Suzanne Albertson
Chapter Art and Layout: Suzanne Albertson
Technical Art: Delia Brown
Screen Graphics: Cuong Le
Typesetter: The Typesetting Shop, Inc.
Proofreader: Hilda van Genderen
Indexer: Anne Leach
Cover Designer: Thomas Ingalls + Associates
Cover Photographer: David Bishop

The text of this book is printed on recycled paper.

Library of Congress Card Number: 90-71332
ISBN: 0-89588-760-6

Manufactured in the United States of America
10 9 8 7 6 5 4

Windows

Contents at a Glance

Table of Contents

Introduction

WINDOWS IS A VERY POWERFUL SOFTWARE PROGRAM that turns your computer into a natural extension of your desk. With its user-friendly interface, Windows will quickly make new computer users productive while letting experienced users access their computer's full potential.

The ABC's of Windows will get you started with Windows immediately. Using its 64 short lessons, you can quickly master the essentials of Windows, reading the advanced lessons as your needs require.

What You'll Find Inside

The ABC's of Windows contains short lessons that let you concentrate on specific aspects of Windows. By focusing on one concept, each lesson requires only a few pages of text and a few minutes of your time! As you read the first few lessons, you'll agree that there is no faster way to learn Windows.

New to Computers?

If you are new to computers, or new to powerful software programs like Windows, don't worry. Each lesson teaches you how to accomplish a specific task in a step-by-step manner. None of the steps presented will hurt your computer. In most cases, the book shows you how your screen will appear after each step, to help guide you to your success.

A Word on Commands

Most of the functions discussed in this book can be performed using either your mouse or keyboard. Therefore, when a command is described in the text, both the mouse and keyboard steps are listed. For clarity, they are highlighted in the text by their own special icons.

This is the mouse icon:

This is the keyboard icon:

PART I

Getting Started with Microsoft Windows

LESSON 1

What Is Windows?

Featuring

- Point-and-shoot interface
- Multitasking
- Information sharing

TO SIMPLIFY YOUR TASKS, YOUR COMPUTER SYSTEM USES hardware and software. Hardware consists of the physical components, such as your keyboard, screen, and printer. Software is computer programs, such as word processors that let you type letters and reports or database programs that let you store and retrieve information. Before you can use these programs, your computer must run a special program called the operating system. For personal computers, the operating system used most often is DOS.

The operating system serves as your interface with the computer. When you turn your computer on, the computer loads the operating system from disk into its memory. Once in memory, DOS displays its prompt for you to enter commands (the DOS prompt normally contains the drive letter, such as **C**>).

From the DOS prompt you can start your word processor or other application programs by typing in the correct commands. Unfortunately, the number of programs you use increases the number of commands you must memorize. As a result, many users find computers intimidating and hard to use. To simplify computer use, Microsoft developed Windows.

Windows Is a Software Program

You can start Windows from the DOS prompt, like all software programs. Once Windows is running, you can invoke your other applications from within Windows without having to recall difficult command lines. Users often refer to running programs from within Windows as *point and shoot*. Using your mouse or keyboard, you simply point to the program you want to use and double-click with your mouse to select it. Point and shoot is not only fast, but its consistent interface makes running new programs easy, making you more productive.

Windows Lets You Run Several Programs at Once

When you run programs from the DOS prompt, you can execute only one program at a time. For example, if you are typing a letter with your word processor and need to look up information stored in a spreadsheet, you must exit the word processor to DOS, invoke the spreadsheet program to look up the information, exit the spreadsheet program to DOS, and then run the word processor once again. This continual leapfrogging between programs can be time-consuming and frustrating.

Unlike DOS, Windows lets you run several programs at the same time. Running several programs simultaneously is called *multitasking*. Having multitasking capabilities is much like having two computers on your desk. If you are writing a report with a word processor on the first computer, you could look up spreadsheet figures for the report on the second computer. By switching from one computer to the other, you can perform two tasks without laboriously opening, closing, and re-opening programs.

Windows performs its multitasking in a similar way using only one computer. Because you do not have unlimited screens to display each program's output individually, Windows divides your one screen into separate areas for each program.

A Window Is a Region on the Screen

The program is called Windows because it lets you view programs on your screen through rectangular regions called windows. If you are running only one program, your screen will contain a single window, as in Figure 1.1. If you are using Windows' multitasking capabilities, your screen will contain a window for each program, as in Figure 1.2.

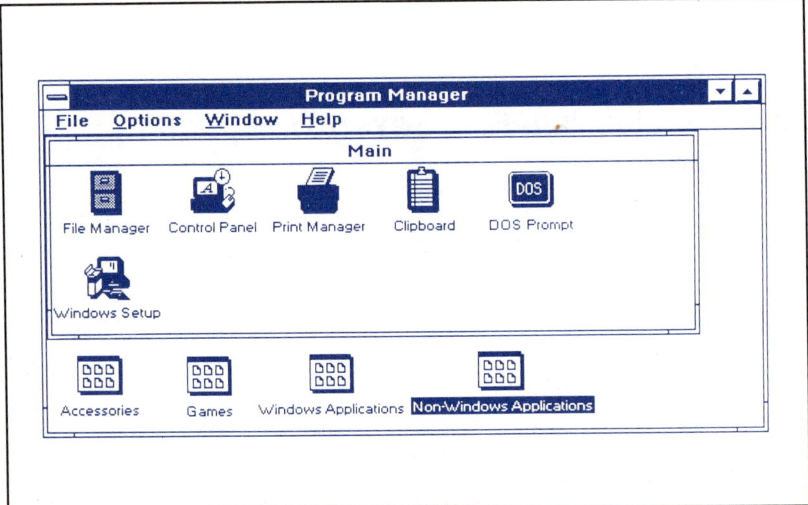

Figure 1.1: *One program running under Windows*

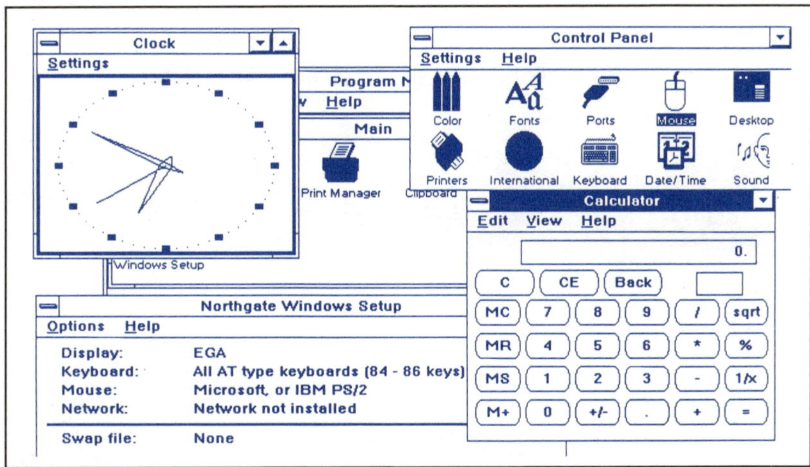

Figure 1.2: Several programs running within individual windows

Unlike the windows of a building, where size is fixed, you can change the size, shape, and location of every window on your screen. Using the point-and-shoot method discussed earlier, you select the program window where you want to work. Best of all, every Windows program behaves the same way. After you learn the simple steps to open and close a window, you can access any Windows program quickly.

Windows Lets Programs Share Information

One of the strongest advantages to running several programs at the same time is allowing those programs to exchange information. This could simplify, for example, a memo you have to write describing employee office assignments in a new building. Using the Write word processor, provided with Windows, you can type the memo's text, as in Figure 1.3. Next, using Windows' Paintbrush utility, you can draw the office layout shown in Figure 1.4. Finally, using Windows' Clipboard, you can copy your drawing into the memo to obtain Figure 1.5. By allowing you to share information between programs, Windows gives you tremendous power and versatility at the touch of a mouse button.

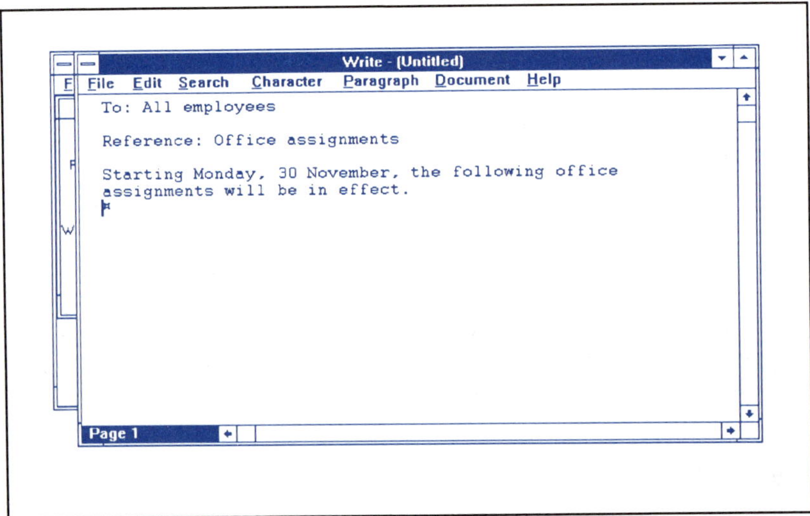

Figure 1.3: Creating a memo using Windows' Write word processor

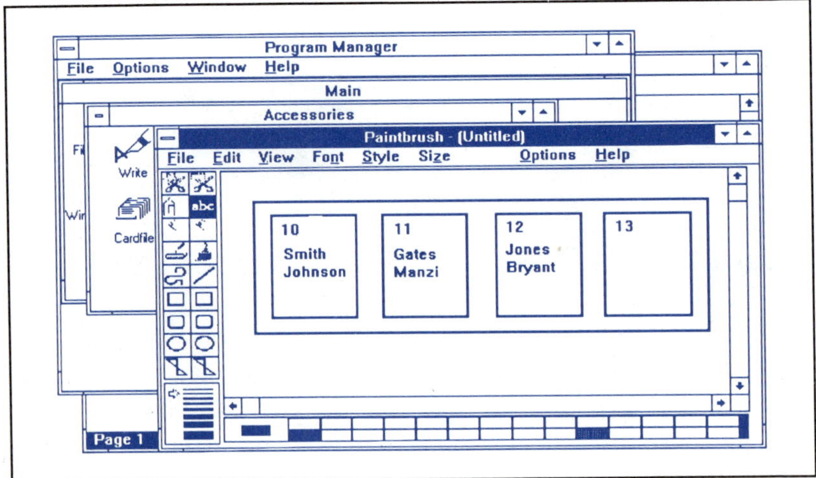

Figure 1.4: Creating an illustration using Windows' Paintbrush

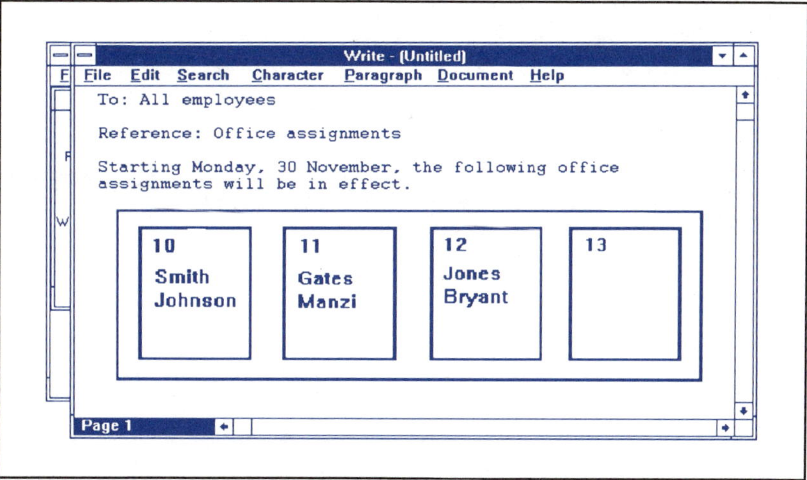

Figure 1.5: Combining text and graphics to complete a memo

Windows Increases Productivity

If you have ever struggled with difficult DOS commands, you will appreciate how Windows' point-and-shoot program execution and consistent window interface can greatly increase your learning curve, making you much more productive.

Windows is more than just a way of executing computer programs. Windows is a working environment that makes your computer feel less like a computer and more like an extension of your work space. Best of all, Windows is very flexible. By customizing your screen colors, you can personalize your work setting, putting an end to tired eyes and headaches. Windows lets you control your computer.

LESSON 2

What You Need to Run Windows

Featuring

- Windows' modes of operation
- Required hardware

AS DISCUSSED IN LESSON 1, WINDOWS IS A SOFTWARE program you can run from the DOS prompt. Depending on your computer's processor (CPU) type—8088, 80286, or 80386—and the amount of random access memory (RAM) in your computer, Windows will run in one of three modes. If you are using an original IBM PC or PC compatible that uses an 8088 processor, or an IBM PC AT with only 640K of memory, Windows will run in *Real mode*. If your computer uses an 80286 processor, such as the PC AT does, or an 80386 processor (or higher) but has only 1Mb of RAM, Windows will run in *Standard mode*. Lastly, if your computer uses an 80386 processor (or higher) and has 2 or more Mb of RAM, Windows will run in *386 Enhanced mode*. Depending on its mode of operation,

Windows' capabilities will differ. (We will cover the actual differences in Part VI.) Windows determines your system type and selects the correct mode of operation automatically. Table 2.1 summarizes Windows' three modes of operation.

Table 2.1: *Hardware Requirements for Windows' Three Modes of Operation.*

HARDWARE	MEMORY	MODE
8088, 80286	640K	Real
80286 (or higher)	1Mb	Standard
80386 (or higher)	2Mb	386 Enhanced

Required Hardware and Software for Windows

Regardless of your computer's processor type, Windows requires the following hardware and software:

At least one floppy-disk drive

A hard disk with 6 to 8Mb of unused disk space

A Windows-compatible graphics adapter and monitor

A Windows-compatible printer

DOS 3.1 or higher

To determine if a hardware device is Windows-compatible, refer to the list of compatible hardware provided with your Windows documentation or contact Microsoft Technical Support.

Optional Hardware for Windows

In addition to the hardware listed above, users who want to make extensive use of Windows' point-and-shoot capabilities should purchase a Windows-compatible mouse. Also, to use Windows' communications program Terminal to access other computers and bulletin boards over telephone lines, you will need a Hayes-compatible modem.

LESSON 3

Starting Windows

Featuring

- Windows' Program Manager
- Solutions to start-up problems
- Introduction to Windows icons

LIKE ALL PROGRAMS, YOU CAN INVOKE WINDOWS FROM the DOS prompt. If you have not installed Windows on your hard disk, turn to Appendix A and do so now. If you have successfully installed Windows, type **WIN** at the DOS prompt and press Enter.

C:\> WIN

If the Windows installation was successful, your screen will display the *Windows' Program Manager*, similar to the screen shown in Figure 3.1.

What if Windows Does Not Execute?

If Windows is not correctly installed, DOS will display the following error message.

Bad command or file name

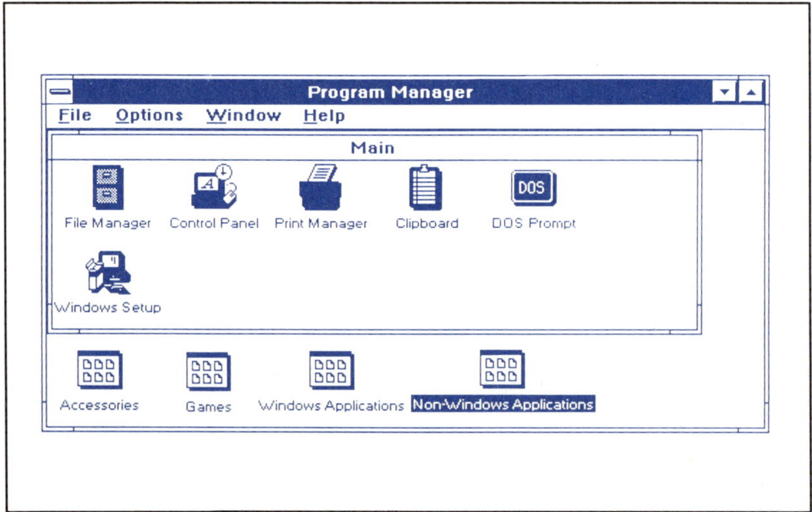

Figure 3.1: *Windows' Program Manager*

Should this error message appear, perform the following steps to correct the problem.

① Verify the subdirectory WINDOWS exists on your hard disk by issuing the following DIR command.

C:\> DIR \WINDOWS

If DOS displays the message **File not found**, Windows has not been installed on your disk. If you get this message, perform the Windows installation as discussed in Appendix A.

Note that if your hard disk contains multiple partitions (drives D, E, and so on), Windows may have been installed on a different partition. Also, it is possible to install the Windows files in a directory other than Windows'. Search your disk's root directory for a directory with a name similar to Windows, such as WIN3.

② Edit the file AUTOEXEC.BAT and make sure the DOS PATH command contains an entry for the WINDOWS subdirectory similar to the following.

PATH C:\DOS;C:\WINDOWS

The Windows installation procedure should place a correct PATH command in AUTOEXEC.BAT for you. Your command path definition may contain more entries than just DOS and WINDOWS. Make sure, however, that an entry for WINDOWS is present.

3. Select the subdirectory WINDOWS as the current directory and invoke WIN as follows.

C:\> CD \WINDOWS

C:\WINDOWS> WIN

If Windows executes, the problem lies in your command path definition. If Windows does not execute, perform the installation again as discussed in Appendix A.

Screens May Differ

The small figures that appear on your screen are called *icons*. One use of icons in Windows is to represent graphically the different programs you can execute. Depending on your hardware configuration and the application software programs you have on your disk, the actual icons that appear on your screen may differ from those previously shown in Figure 3.1.

Standard Icons

Regardless of your computer type and available software, you will see the icons listed in Table 3.1.

Other Common Icons

In addition to the standard icons, your screen may contain one or more of the icons shown in Table 3.2, based on your hardware configuration and application programs on disk.

Table 3.1: *Standard Icons.*

ICON	NAME	FUNCTION
	File Manager	Provides access to the Windows File Manager for file and directory manipulation.
	Control Panel	Lets you select screen colors, configure printer and communications ports and other hardware devices.
	Print Manager	Lets you control the Windows print spooler and the files Windows has placed in the printing queue.
	Clipboard	Lets you share information between Windows programs.
DOS	DOS Prompt	Lets you temporarily exit Windows to DOS. To return to Windows, type EXIT at the DOS prompt.
	Windows Setup	Allows you to modify your system's hardware devices without having to reinstall Windows.

Table 3.2: *Other Windows Icons.*

ICON	NAME	FUNCTION
	Accessories	Provides access to Windows' desktop accessory programs, such as Clock and Calculator.
	Games	Provides access to the games Reversi and Solitaire.
	Windows Applications	Provides access to all Windows-based application programs identified during the system installation.

Table 3.2: *Other Windows Icons. (cont.)*

ICON	NAME	FUNCTION
	Non-Windows Applications	Provides access to commonly used programs that were not specifically developed to run under Windows. These are identified by Windows during system installation.

Invoking Windows from within AUTOEXEC.BAT

Many users want Windows to start automatically, each time they turn on their computer. To do so, place the WIN command at the end of your AUTOEXEC.BAT file.

LESSON 4

Understanding the Basic Parts of a Window

Featuring

- Window titles
- Window sizing capabilities
- Pull-down menus
- Controlling a window
- Scrolling information in a window
- The Windows desktop
- Dialog boxes

WINDOWS INCREASES YOUR PRODUCTIVITY BY LETTING you run several programs at one time, each in its own window. To make it easy for you to learn to use different programs, all Windows applications behave in a similar manner. In this lesson you will examine several basic features of window operation.

As discussed in Lesson 3, when you start Windows, your screen will display the Windows Program Manager, shown in Figure 4.1.

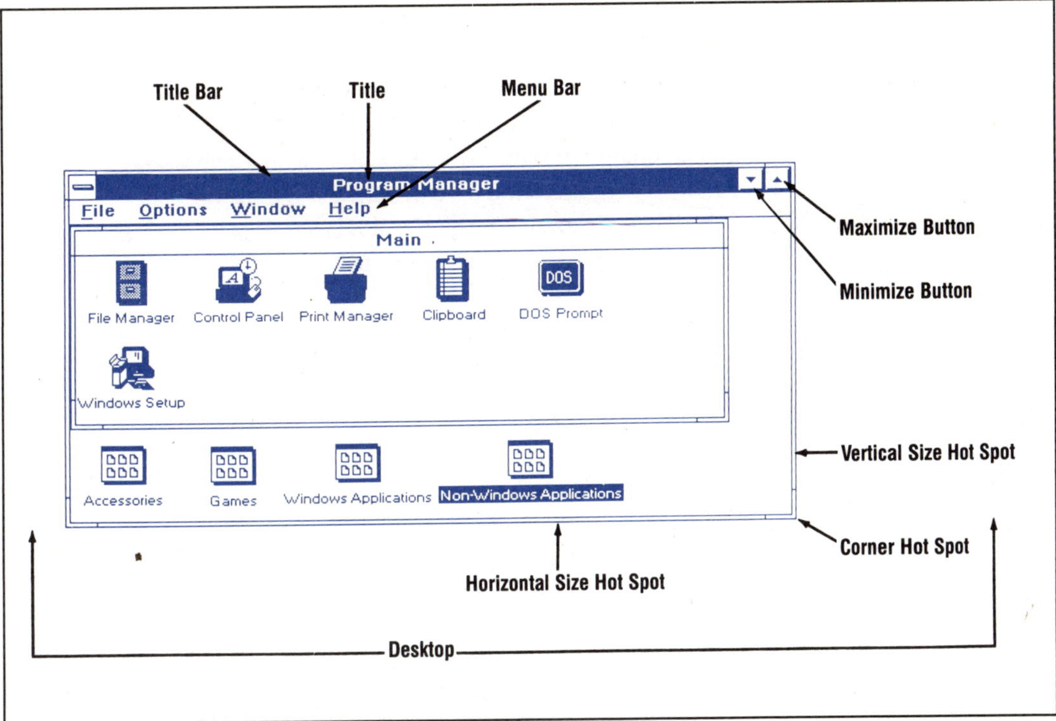

Figure 4.1: Standard window parts and their names

This screen actually contains two windows. The first is called Program Manager and the second Main. Like all of the windows you will encounter, these two windows share basic parts. Figure 4.1 identifies these parts.

Title Bar and Title

When you run several programs simultaneously, you need to know which window on your screen corresponds to which program. Therefore, Windows assigns a *title* to each window it creates. (You will find the title in the title bar at the top of the screen.) In Figure 4.1, for example, the window titles are Program Manager and Main.

Minimize and Maximize Buttons

Each time you run a Windows program, the program itself determines the starting size of its window. Depending on the programs you are running, you may want to change a window's size. In the upper-right corner of each window, you will find two triangles, one pointing up and the other down. These triangles let you quickly compress a window into an icon (*minimize* the window), or expand a window to use the entire screen, hiding all other windows (*maximize* the window). You can use your mouse to perform these operations by aiming the mouse pointer at the minimize (triangle pointing down) or maximize (triangle pointing up) button and clicking. If you don't have a mouse, you can maximize and minimize windows using the Control menu, to be discussed later in this lesson.

Window Size Hot Spots

If you look at a window closely, you will find a thin frame surrounding it. This frame, called the *size hot spot*, allows you to make your windows any size you desire. By positioning your mouse pointer in one of the vertical hot spots and holding down the mouse button, you can increase or decrease the window's width by moving the mouse left or right. Likewise, by selecting the window's horizontal size hot spots, you can change a window's height. Lastly, by selecting one of the window's corners as your size hot spot, you can change the window's height and width at the same time. Size hot spots and the maximize/minimize buttons serve a similar purpose, with the size hot spots giving you more control over the proportions of your window. Lesson 10 discusses sizing your windows in detail.

Menu Bar and Pull-Down Menus

Many of the programs you will run under Windows provide a *Menu Bar* of options. In Figure 4.1, for example, the Program

Manager window has a Menu Bar while the Main window does not. Depending on the program you are running, the options appearing in the Menu Bar will differ. In all cases, however, when you select a Menu Bar option, Windows will display a pull-down menu. Using your mouse, you can select Menu Bar options by pointing to the option and pressing the select button. Using the keyboard, you can select an option by holding down the Alt key and pressing the key corresponding to the underlined letter in the option. If you choose the Menu Bar File option, for example, Windows will display the pull-down menu shown in Figure 4.2.

Pull-down menus are so named because Windows appears to pull the list of menu options down from the menu bar. You can select pull-down menu options by clicking on an option with your mouse, by typing the underlined letter that appears in the option, or by highlighting the option with your keyboard arrow keys and pressing Enter. You can cancel a menu by pressing Esc or clicking your mouse with the mouse pointer outside of the menu.

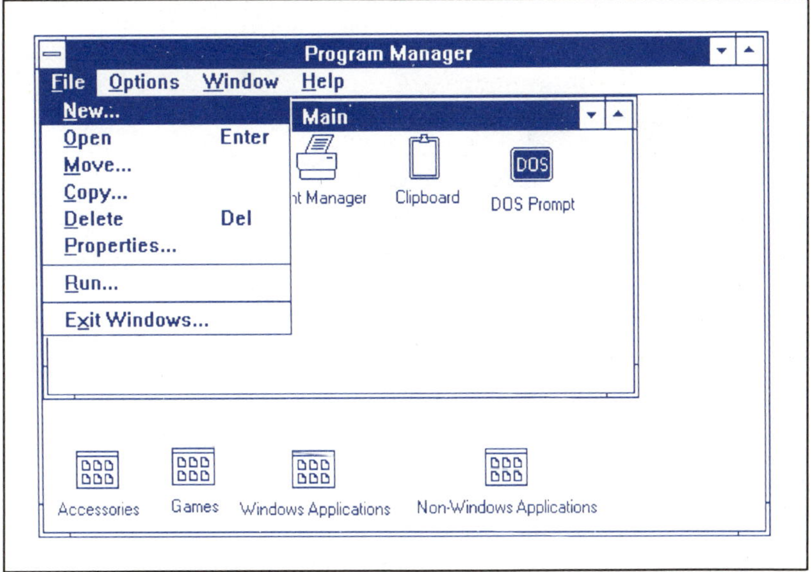

Figure 4.2: *The Program Manager's File menu*

Control Menu Selector

Windows assigns every window you open a Control menu. Using the Control menu you can move a window, change its size, convert it to an icon, or close the window to quit the application. In the upper-left corner of every window, you will find a box containing a dash or space character. This character is the *Control menu Selector*. To select the Control menu using your mouse, aim the mouse pointer into the box and click. To select the Control menu using your keyboard, examine the contents of the Control menu Selector box and press the Alt+Hyphen or Alt+Space accordingly. When you select the Control menu, Windows will display the pull-down menu shown in Figure 4.3. Note the words Alt+F4 and Ctrl+Esc next to the menu options. These words correspond to hot-key combinations you can select as a shortcut to selecting an option, even when the menu is not displayed on the screen. Using the Alt + F4 hot-key combination, for example, you can exit the Windows Program Manager to DOS.

As you run different applications, whether individually or at the same time, you will use the Control menu extensively.

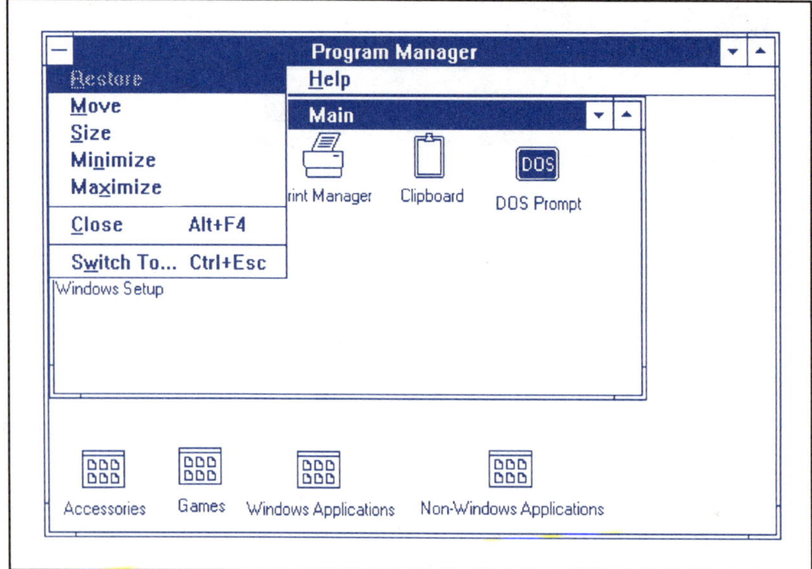

Figure 4.3: The Control menu

Horizontal and Vertical Scroll Bars

As you run your programs, there will be times when an application cannot display all of its information within the window's boundaries. In such cases, the window may have horizontal and vertical *scroll bars* as shown in Figure 4.4.

There is a small box within each scroll bar. By moving the box up and down or left to right along the scroll bar with your mouse or keyboard arrow keys, you can scroll the window's contents into view.

Desktop

One of the purposes of Windows is to automate your desktop, placing items commonly found on your desk such as a calendar, clock, calculator, or note pad at your fingertips while you work with your computer. As such, Windows refers to the area of your screen

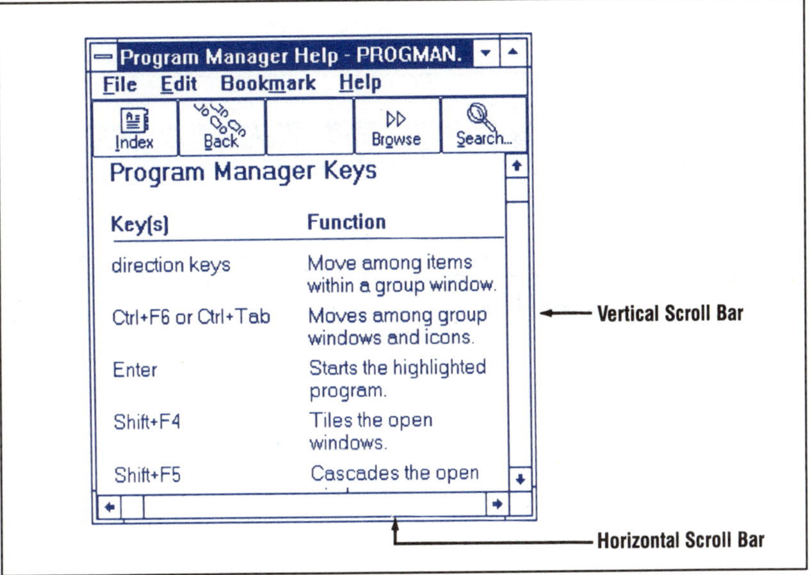

Figure 4.4: *Horizontal and vertical scroll bars*

bordering your open windows as the *desktop*. In later lessons you will learn to customize your desktop by setting screen colors or even placing your company logo in the background.

Dialog Boxes

Although Windows tries to simplify as many operations as possible by letting you point and shoot with your mouse, there may be times when Windows needs to verify an operation or obtain additional information before it can continue. In such cases, Windows will display a box on your screen requesting the information desired. Because this box lets you communicate with Windows, it is called a *dialog box*. For example, each time you exit Windows, the dialog box shown in Figure 4.5 is displayed.

You can select a dialog box option by pressing the Tab key and pressing Enter or by simply pointing and shooting with your mouse. As you work with more Windows applications, you will use dialog boxes to select files, assign window colors, and even configure your computer's hardware.

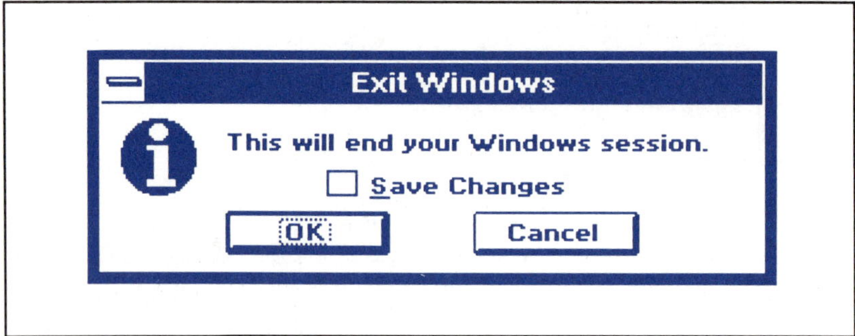

Figure 4.5: Windows' exit verification dialog box

LESSON 5

Using Your Mouse and Keyboard

Featuring

- Mouse select button
- Double clicking
- Keyboard hot keys

AS YOU HAVE SEEN, EACH WINDOW ON YOUR SCREEN contains the same basic parts. Once you learn to work with a window, you can quickly master new Windows programs. Lesson 4 briefly discussed several window operations, such as sizing, moving, and closing a window. Much of this discussion centered around using the mouse to perform these tasks quickly. As you will learn in later lessons, you can also perform all window operations with your keyboard. Unfortunately, using your keyboard often requires several steps to accomplish the same tasks a simple point-and-shoot operation can accomplish in one. In this lesson you will learn several essential keyboard and mouse techniques.

Adding a Mouse to Your System

If you don't have a mouse now, you may wish to consider purchasing one—especially if you plan to work with Windows on a regular basis. If you purchase a mouse after installing Windows, you must use the Windows Setup program discussed in Lesson 46 to inform Windows of your mouse.

Using Your Mouse

Each time Windows starts, it determines whether your system has a mouse present. If you have a mouse, Windows will display the pointer, as shown in Figure 5.1. By moving your mouse, you can aim the mouse pointer at specific objects on your screen, such as a menu option or an icon. Your mouse should have at least two buttons. The leftmost button is often called the *mouse select button*. When you aim the mouse pointer at an object, you can normally select the object by pressing (or clicking) the mouse select button.

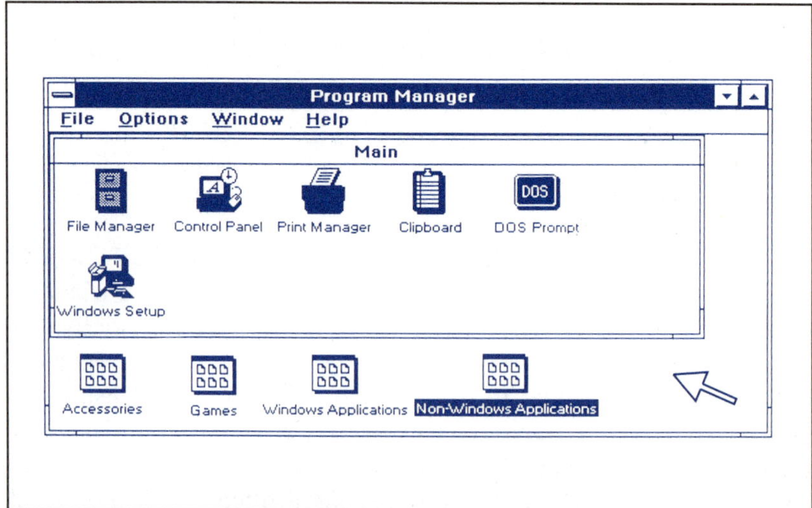

Figure 5.1: *Windows' mouse pointer*

Some Windows options will require you to *double-click* your mouse select button. To double-click, you must press the mouse select button twice very rapidly. As each lesson of this book discusses different Windows options, the lesson will note whether you need to single-click or double-click.

Using Your Keyboard

As discussed, Windows lets you perform every window operation with your keyboard as well as your mouse. As each lesson discusses a different Windows option, the lesson will note both the mouse procedure and the keyboard combinations you must use to perform the option. However, there are several common keyboard combinations you should know.

Selecting the Control Menu (Alt + Hyphen) or (Alt + Space)

Every window has a Control menu that lets you size, move, and close the window. In the upper-left corner of each window is the *Control menu selector*, which appears as a box containing a hyphen or dash (slightly larger than the hyphen). To select the Control menu using your keyboard, hold down the Alt key and press the hyphen key, located at the top row of your keyboard, or the spacebar.

Canceling Menu Options and Dialog Boxes

Windows makes extensive use of pull-down menus and dialog boxes. If you invoke a menu and decide not to select an option, you can cancel the menu simply by pressing the Esc key. Likewise, if Windows displays a dialog box you can press the Esc key if you don't want to respond to the dialog box options. Try selecting and canceling the Control menu now.

Traversing Dialog Box Options (Tab)

Many Windows dialog boxes prompt you to press simply Enter to continue an operation or Cancel to abort it. For example, each time you exit Windows, the dialog box in Figure 5.2 appears. If you press Enter, thereby selecting the default option OK, your Windows session will end, returning control to the DOS prompt. If you don't want to end your Windows session, press the Tab key to highlight the Cancel option and then press Enter. Depending on the dialog box, you may be able to Tab through several different options.

Figure 5.2: *Windows' exit dialog box*

Cursor Movement Keys

Windows supports your keyboard's cursor movement keys such as the Up and Down Arrows, PgUp, PgDn and so on. When Windows displays a pull-down menu, for example, you can select menu options using these keys. Likewise, when Windows displays horizontal and vertical scroll bars, you can use these keys to scroll through text or options within the window.

Using Hot Keys

To simplify your keyboard selection of commonly used options, Windows defines several *hot-key* combinations you can press as shortcuts to an option selection. When you invoke different pull-down menus, pay attention to the optional key combinations specified to the right of each menu option. These key combinations define hot keys that you can press at any time to select the option without having to use the pull-down menu.

After you work with one or two Windows programs, these key combinations will become second nature to you.

LESSON 6

Ending Your Windows Session

Featuring

- The exit dialog box
- Saving changes to open files

AS A RULE, NEVER TURN OFF YOUR COMPUTER WHILE Windows is running. Always exit Windows to DOS first, turning your computer off at the DOS prompt. When running several programs at the same time, you may have made changes to files in one or more programs. If you turn off your computer without ending each program individually, you risk losing some or all of the changes you have made. Worse yet, exiting without saving may damage a file's contents, rendering it unusable. Again, to avoid possible damage, always exit Windows to DOS before turning your computer off.

Exiting Windows

To exit Windows, you must invoke the Program Manager's Control menu and select the Close option. Depending on whether you are using a mouse or your keyboard, the steps you will take to exit Windows differ.

To exit Windows using your mouse, aim the mouse pointer at the Program Manager Control menu selector and single-click. When Windows displays the Control menu, aim the mouse pointer at the Close option and single-click.

You have two options when using your keyboard to exit Windows. You can use the Alt+Space keyboard combination to invoke the Program Manager's Control menu and then select the Close option. Or, simply press the Alt+F4 hot-key combination.

Responding to the Windows Exit Dialog Box

Regardless of the method you use to end Windows, your screen will display the *exit dialog box* shown in Figure 6.1. Simply press Enter or click on the OK option to end Windows, returning you to the DOS prompt. If you don't want to end your Windows session, select the Cancel option.

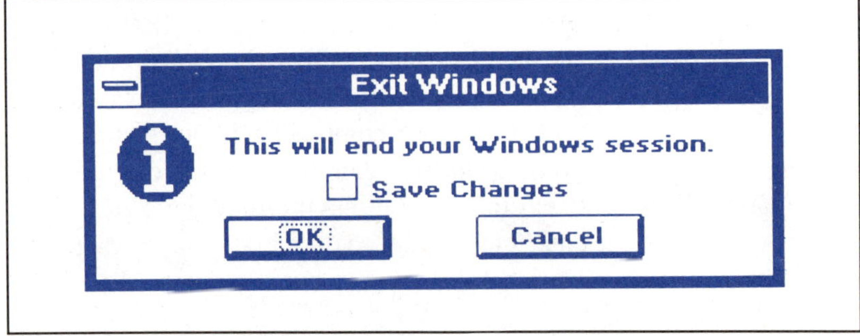

Figure 6.1: *Windows' exit dialog box*

As you become familiar with Windows, you may want to reconfigure the Program Manager's work space to better suit your needs. You must select the Save Changes option in the Exit dialog box to save such changes to disk. Then, the next time you invoke Windows, the work space will appear as you left it. For now, so you will always start Windows with a familiar screen, disable the Save Changes option by removing the X from within the check box. To do this, click on the option with your mouse or use the Tab key to highlight the option and press the spacebar. Next, either press Enter or click on the OK option. Your Windows session will then end. Try exiting Windows now, using either your mouse or keyboard.

Responding to File Save Dialog Boxes

As a safeguard against losing changes to a file when you exit a program, Windows will display a dialog box that asks you if you want to change the contents of each updated file that has not been closed. In cases where you haven't yet named a file, you may need to type in a new file name. Depending on the programs you are running, the dialog boxes that appear may differ. The dialog box in Figure 6.2, for example, asks you to type in a file name for a drawing created with Windows' Paintbrush program. In this case, if you select the Yes option, Windows will display a second dialog box prompting you to choose a name for the new file. If you select the No option, Windows will discard the file's changes.

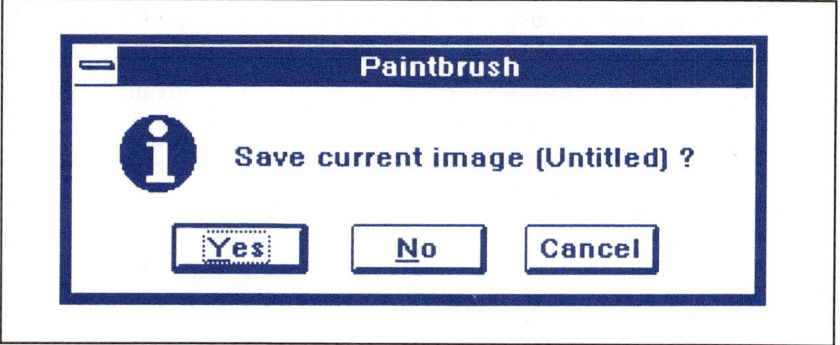

Figure 6.2: *File save dialog box*

LESSON 7

Running Your First Windows Programs

Featuring

- Windows application groups
- Running and ending Windows programs

EACH TIME YOU START WINDOWS, A SPECIAL PROGRAM called the Program Manager runs. In fact, the Program Manager runs the entire time you are in Windows. In most cases, you will run your Windows programs directly from the Program Manager. You also exit Windows from the Program Manager.

To help you organize your programs, simplifying their execution, Windows lets you place programs in *application groups*. Programs within a group appear as icons in a window with the name of the group in the title bar. For example, if you have several programs you need for business, you can collect them into a group named Business. Likewise, programs for school can be grouped in School.

Windows defines several groups for you. For example, the Main group contains Windows' six primary programs. When Windows starts, it displays the icons associated with the programs in the Main group as in Figure 7.1. At the bottom of the screen, Windows displays the Accessories and Games groups and possibly the groups Windows Applications and Non-Windows Applications, depending on the other programs you have on your disk. When you select these groups, each will display a set of icons corresponding to the programs they contain.

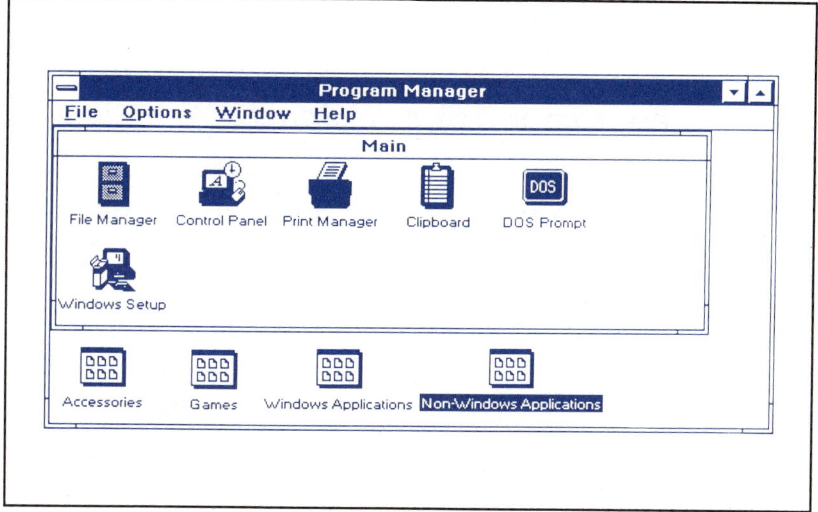

Figure 7.1: Windows' Main group icons

A Windows group, therefore, is simply a collection of related programs. In Lesson 59, you will learn how to create your own custom groups.

Selecting an Application from within a Group

By default, Windows selects the group Main as the active group. When a group is active, you can select one of its programs for execution.

To select (highlight) a program with your mouse, aim the mouse pointer at the program icon and single-click. Windows will highlight the icon selected. To execute a program with the mouse, aim the mouse pointer at the program icon and double-click.

To select (highlight) a program using you keyboard, press your keyboard arrow keys to highlight the desired icon. To execute a program from your keyboard, select the icon using your arrow keys and press Enter.

Running the Windows Control Panel

Using either your mouse or keyboard, select the icon corresponding to the Windows Control Panel and execute it. Your screen will display the window shown in Figure 7.2 if your computer is connected to a local area network. If you are running in Windows' 386 Enhanced mode, the window may contain additional icons. As you can see, each time you invoke a Windows program, Windows opens a window specifically for the program. In Part IV of this book, you will

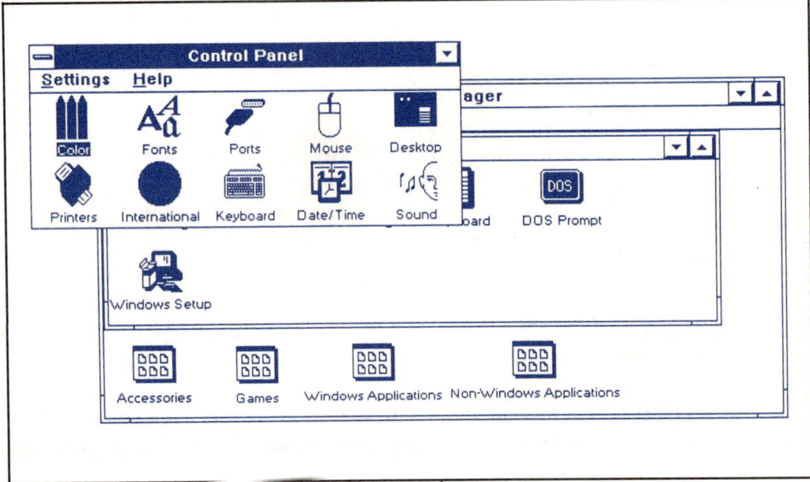

Figure 7.2: The Windows Control Panel

learn to use the Windows Control Panel to customize Windows by defining screen colors, configuring printers and serial communications ports, and so on.

For now, close the Control Panel window by selecting its Control menu with your mouse or pressing Alt+Space on your keyboard. Next, select the Close option. Windows should redisplay the Program Manager screen. If your screen displays the Program Manager as an icon, simply click on the icon with your mouse or press Alt+Tab.

Running the Windows Setup Program

Using the techniques just discussed, select the Windows Setup icon and invoke it. Your screen will display a window containing the Setup program, as shown in Figure 7.3. The Windows Setup program lets you change your system's hardware configuration without having to reinstall Windows each time you add or change a piece of hardware. You will learn more about the Setup program in Part IV, but for now, simply close the Setup window.

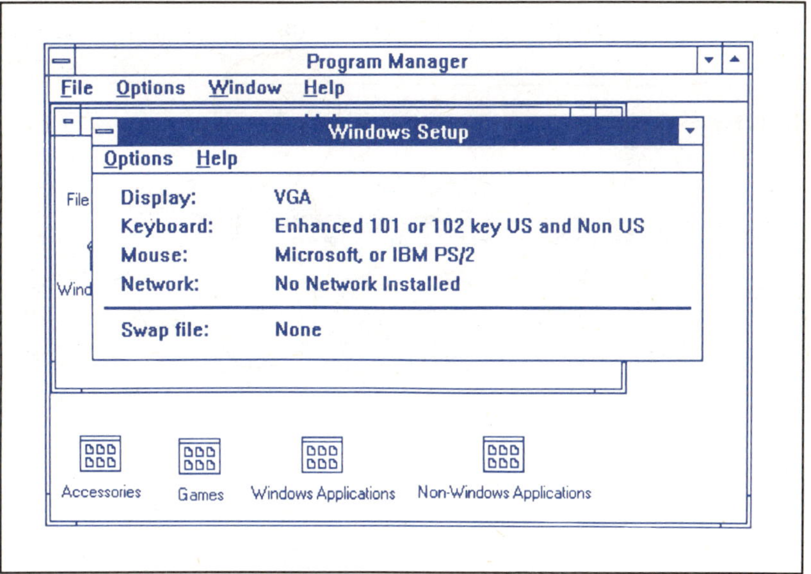

Figure 7.3: *The Windows Setup Program*

Selecting a Different Group

Windows provides you with several predefined groups and lets you create your own. As a result, you need a way to access the programs each group contains.

To select a group with your mouse, aim the mouse pointer at the group icon desired and double-click.

To select a group using your keyboard, press the Ctrl+Tab keyboard combination. Each time you press this keyboard combination, Windows will highlight a different group. After you highlight the desired icon, press Enter.

Selecting the Accessories Group

Using either your mouse or keyboard, select the Accessories group. Windows will display the set of icons shown in Figure 7.4.

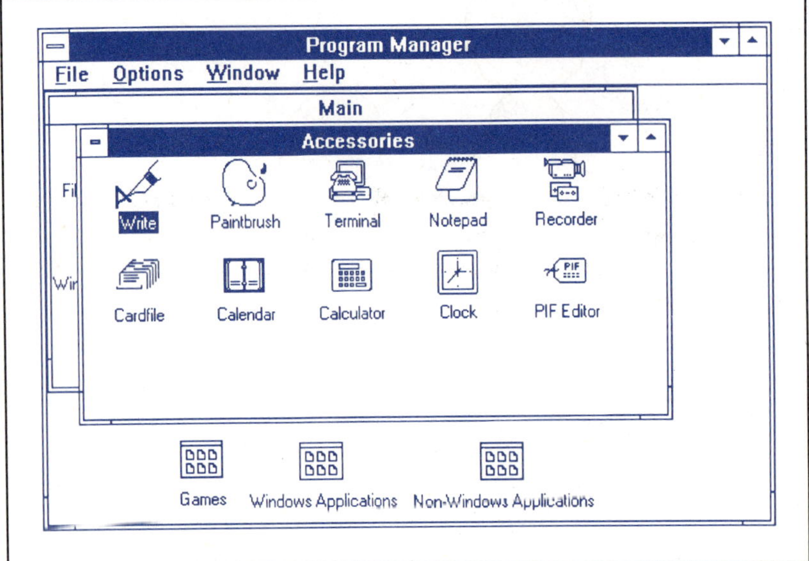

Figure 7.4: Windows' Accessories group icons

The Accessories group contains several desktop programs, including a clock, calendar, and calculator. Invoke the Clock program now. Windows will open a window for the Clock program as in Figure 7.5. Part III of this book examines the Windows accessory programs in detail. For now close the Clock window.

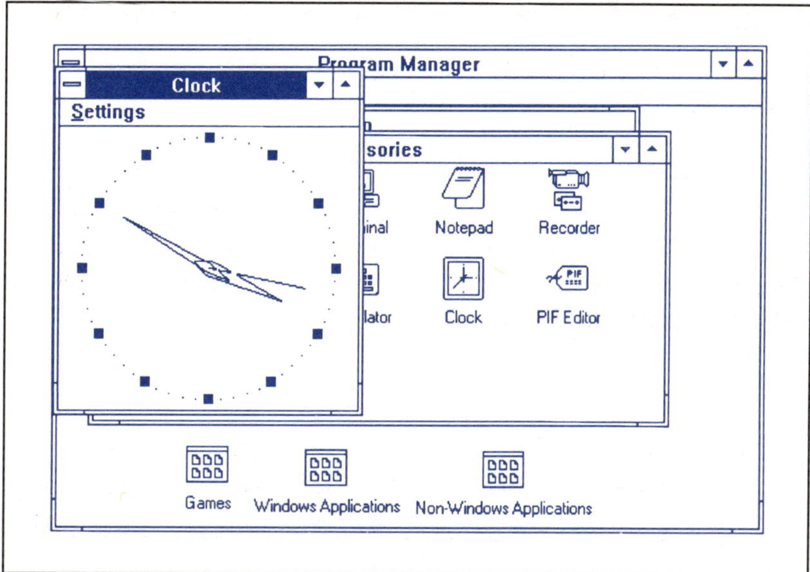

Figure 7.5: The Windows Clock program

Closing a Group

Just as Windows creates a window for every program you run, Windows also opens a window for each group you select. To close a group, select the Close option from the group's Control menu.

LESSON 8

Opening and Managing Several Windows at One Time

Featuring

- Multitasking
- Ending Windows with programs active

AS YOU KNOW, WINDOWS ALLOWS YOU TO RUN SEVERAL programs at one time—*multitasking*. In several of the previous lessons, you have actually had two or more windows open at the same time. In this lesson you will invoke several of the Windows accessory programs and switch from one program to another to practice multitasking.

Running Several Windows Programs at One Time

To begin, select the Windows Accessories group and invoke the Clock program. Windows will open a window for the Clock program, as shown in Figure 8.1. When you invoke a program, Windows opens a window for the program and selects the new window as active. To take advantage of Windows' multitasking capabilities, you need a means of switching from one window to another.

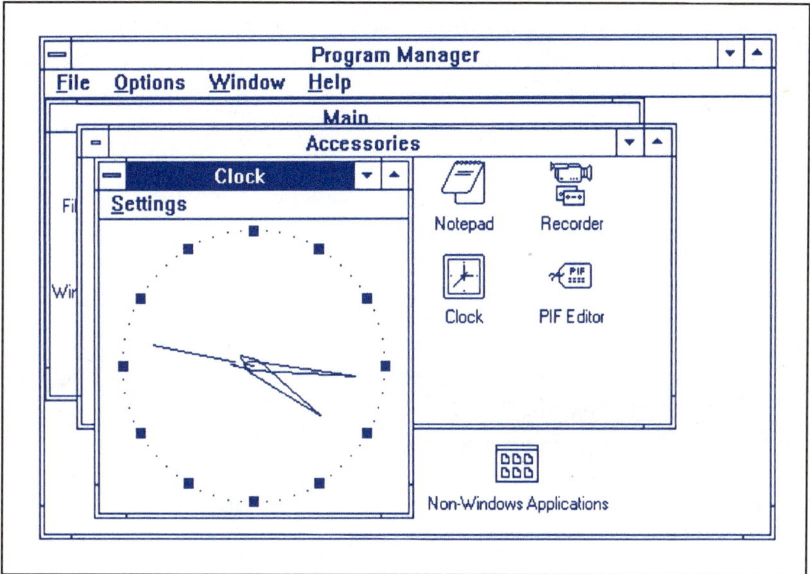

Figure 8.1: *The Windows Clock program*

To select a new active window using your mouse, simply aim the mouse pointer into the desired window and click.

To select a new active window using your keyboard, press the Alt+Esc keyboard combination to cycle through available windows until Windows selects the desired window.

Invoking Additional Applications

Select the Program Manager window as active. Next, invoke the Windows Calculator. Your screen will display a window containing the Clock program and a second window containing the Calculator, as in Figure 8.2.

As you can see, when you run multiple programs, Windows displays portions of each window on the screen, with the active window on top. As before, select the Accessories window and invoke a second copy of the Clock program. When Windows displays the Clock, invoke the Clock's Settings menu using Alt+S or your mouse. The Clock program will display the pull-down menu shown in Figure 8.3. Select the Digital option, and Windows will display the digital clock shown in Figure 8.4.

Using either your mouse or your keyboard, cycle through each of the open windows. As before, you can quit a program by making the program's window active and then selecting the Close option from the Control menu.

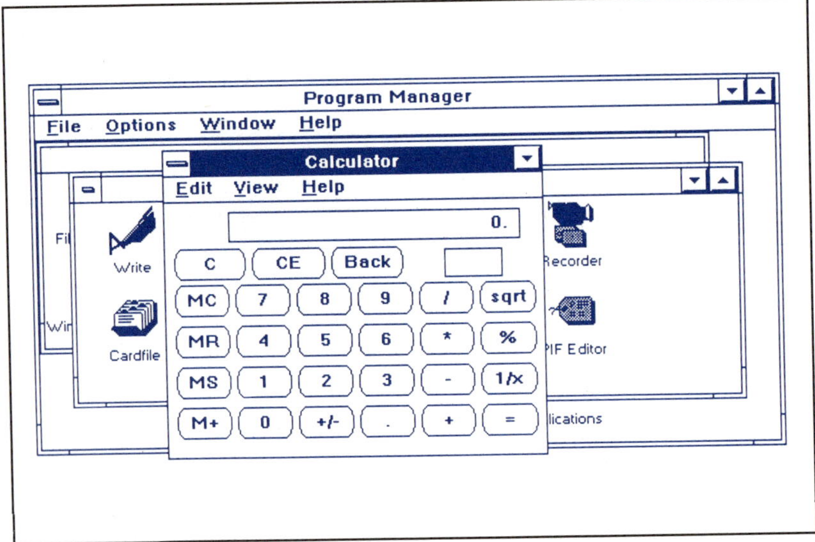

Figure 8.2: Multitasking the Windows Clock and Calculator

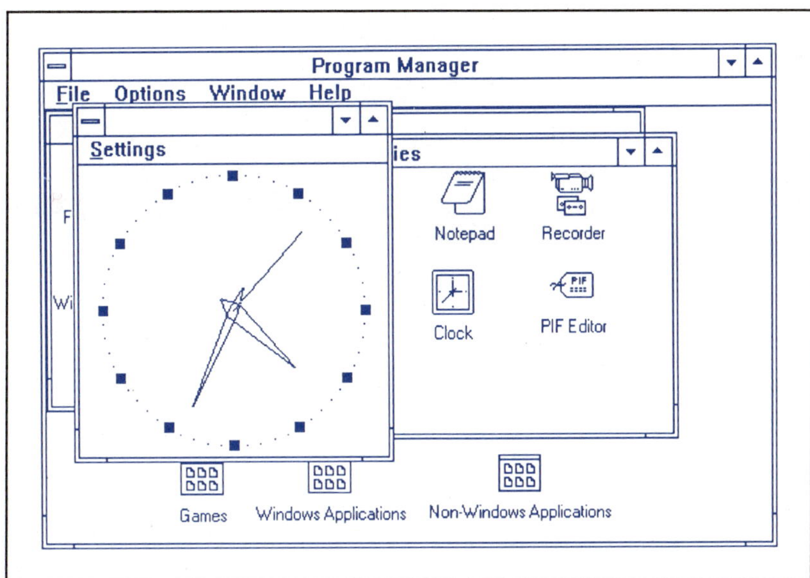

Figure 8.3: *The Clock Settings menu*

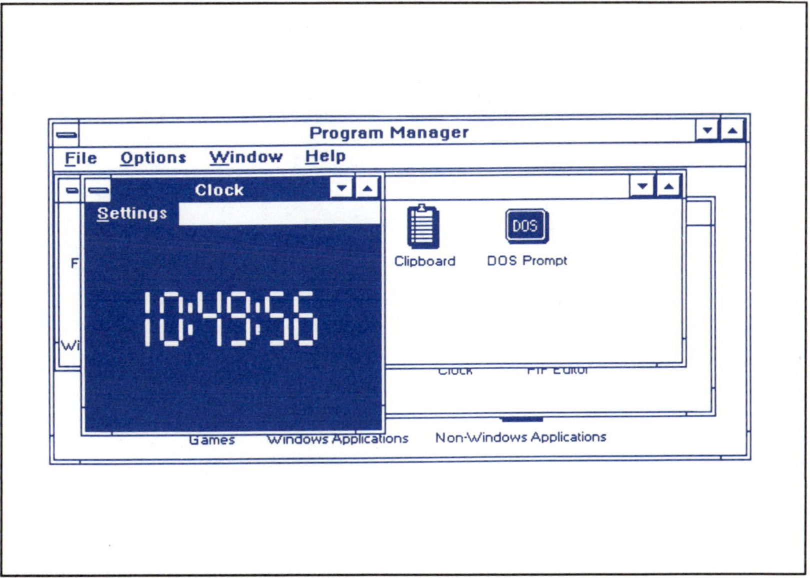

Figure 8.4: *Windows' digital clock*

Ending Windows with Several Applications Running

You don't have to stop each program individually before you end Windows. Instead, you can simply close the Program Manager window. If any applications have files open, Windows will prompt you to save or discard file changes.

LESSON 9

Shrinking a Window into an Icon

Featuring

- Reducing a window
- Expanding an icon
- Closing an icon

WHEN YOU RUN SEVERAL WINDOWS PROGRAMS AT THE same time, your screen may become cluttered with all the open windows. To reduce the number of windows on your screen, you can "shrink" a window you don't presently need into an icon. When you later need to work in the window, you can expand the icon back to the window's original size.

How to Shrink a Window into an Icon

Just as there are times when you temporarily move things to the side of your desk, there will be times when you want to get a window "out of the way" without having to close it. To do so, you *reduce the window* to an icon. Note that when you shrink an application to an icon, you are closing the window, but not the application that owns the window.

As discussed, to the right of every window's Title Bar is a set of Minimize and Maximize buttons. To reduce a window to an icon, select the window as active and then click on the Minimize button (the downward triangle).

To reduce a window to an icon using your keyboard, select the window as active, invoke the window's Control menu, and choose the Minimize option.

Reducing the Windows Clock to an Icon

If the Windows Clock program is not running, invoke it. If the Clock is running, select it as the active window. Next, using either the Minimize button or the Minimize option on the Control menu, shrink the Clock window to an icon. As you can see in Figure 9.1,

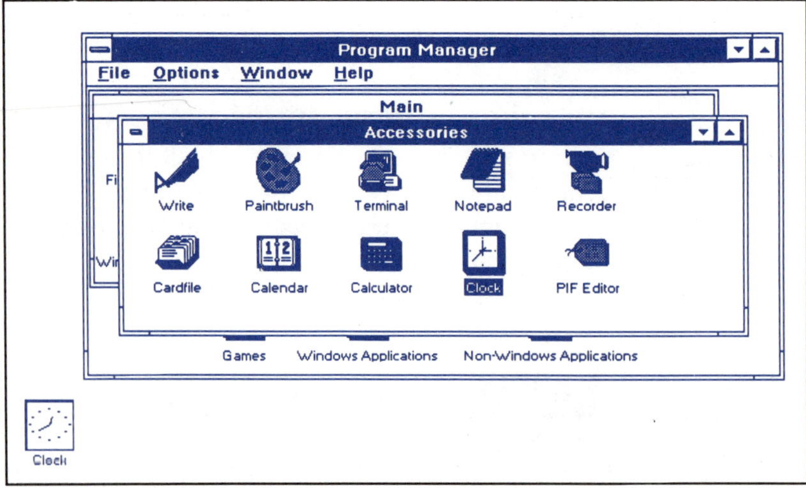

Figure 9.1: Windows' Clock program as an icon

Windows places the icon at the bottom of your screen. Note that this icon differs from the Clock icon that appears in the Accessories group. An icon at the bottom of your screen represents a program already loaded into memory, which you can expand into a window. A group icon represents a program you can execute, for which Windows will create a new window.

If you shrink other windows into icons, Windows will line them up along the bottom of the screen. Try invoking the Windows Calculator and then reducing it to an icon to obtain Figure 9.2.

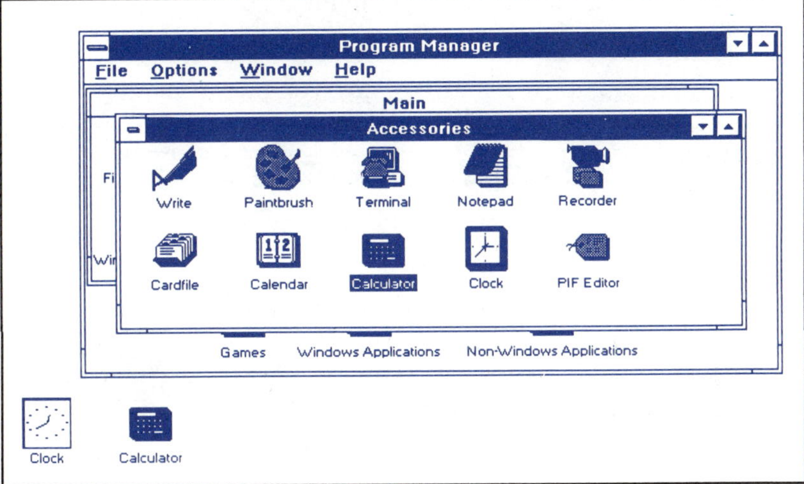

Figure 9.2: Multiple icons

How to Expand an Icon into a Window

As discussed, reducing a window into an icon lets you move the window aside temporarily. When you are ready to use the window, you simply *expand the icon.*

To expand an icon into a window using your mouse, aim the mouse pointer at the icon and double-click.

To expand an icon into a window using your keyboard, you must first select the icon. To do so, press Alt+Esc to cycle through the open windows and available icons. When the desired icon is selected, access its Control menu by pressing Alt+Space. Then choose the Restore option from the Control menu.

Expanding the Calculator Icon

Using either your keyboard or mouse, expand the Calculator icon into a window. Your screen will display the Calculator program within its own window once again, as in Figure 9.3.

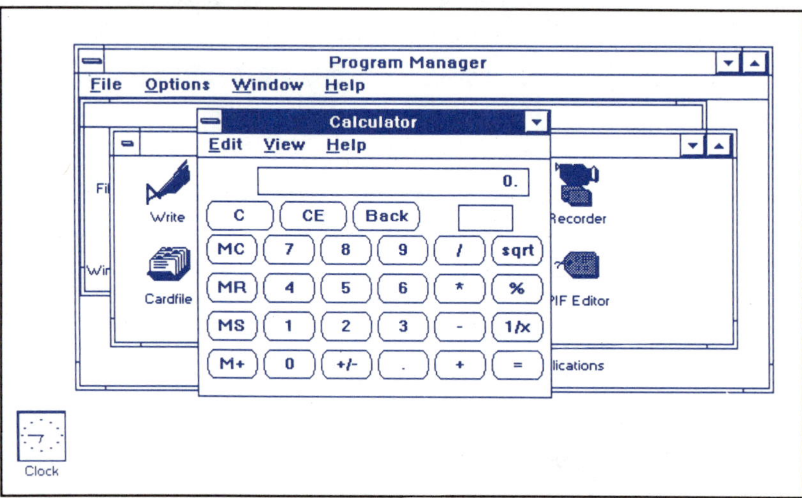

Figure 9.3: *Expanding the Calculator icon into a window*

How to Close an Icon

In some cases you may choose to *close an icon* rather than restore it. To do so, you must access the icon's Control menu and select the Close option. To close an icon using your keyboard, you first must use the Alt+Esc keyboard combination to select the icon. Next, invoke the icon's Control menu by pressing Alt+Space. Select the Close option from the Control menu.

Closing the Clock Icon

Using either your keyboard or mouse, select the Clock icon's Control menu and close the icon. As you can see, working with icons is very much like working with windows.

LESSON 10

Sizing and Moving Windows

Featuring

- Full-screen windows
- Incrementally changing a window's size
- Positioning windows

IN LESSON 9 YOU LEARNED HOW TO REDUCE AN ACTIVE window to an icon and later to expand the icon when you need to access the window. In this lesson you will learn how to size and move your windows. As you have seen, Windows treats every window individually. Using Windows' sizing techniques, you can expand a window to use the entire screen or change the window's size in small increments.

How to Expand a Window to Use the Entire Screen

In Lesson 9 you used the Minimize button and Control menu Minimize option to reduce a window to an icon. Expanding a window to use the entire screen (called a *full-screen window*) is similar, except you are now using the Maximize button or the Control menu Maximize option.

To maximize a window to use the entire screen, aim the mouse pointer at the Maximize button to the far right of the window's Title Bar and click.

To maximize a window using your keyboard, invoke the window's Control menu and select the Maximize option.

Expanding the Clock

Invoke the Windows Clock program. Then, using either your keyboard or mouse, maximize the Clock window. When you do so, your screen will fill with the Clock as shown here in Figure 10.1.

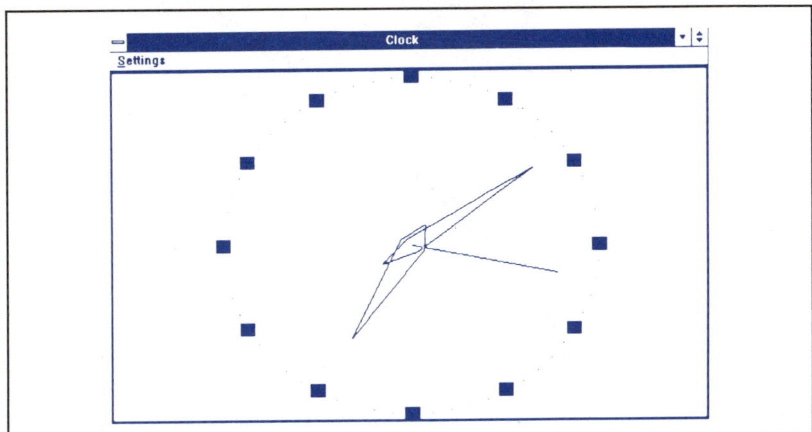

Figure 10.1: *Expanding the Windows Clock to a full-screen window*

Note the change in the Clock window's Maximize button. When the Maximize button contains upward- and downward-pointing triangles, you can use the button to reduce the Window to its original size. Likewise, by selecting the Restore option from the window's Control menu, you can restore the window's original size using your keyboard.

How to Change a Window's Size Incrementally

Depending on the program you are running, there may be times when you simply want to increase a window's size enough to view a program's output better, without using the entire screen. To do so, you can change the window's size in small *increments*.

Windows surrounds every window it creates with a size frame, which you can grab with your mouse pointer to increase or decrease the window's size. To do so, aim the mouse pointer into the size frame. When the pointer is within the size frame, it will change from an arrow to double arrows indicating the directions you can move the window's frame to size the window, as in Figure 10.2.

While holding down the mouse select button, move the pointer in one of the possible directions. Windows will respond by moving the window's frame in the same direction. When you have moved the frame to the desired location, release the mouse select button and Windows will expand or decrease the window to its new size.

The vertical size bars along the right and left sides of the window let you change its width. Similarly, the horizontal size bars at the top and bottom of the window let you change its height. The corners of the size frame are unique in that aiming the mouse pointer into a corner lets you change the window's height and width at the same time.

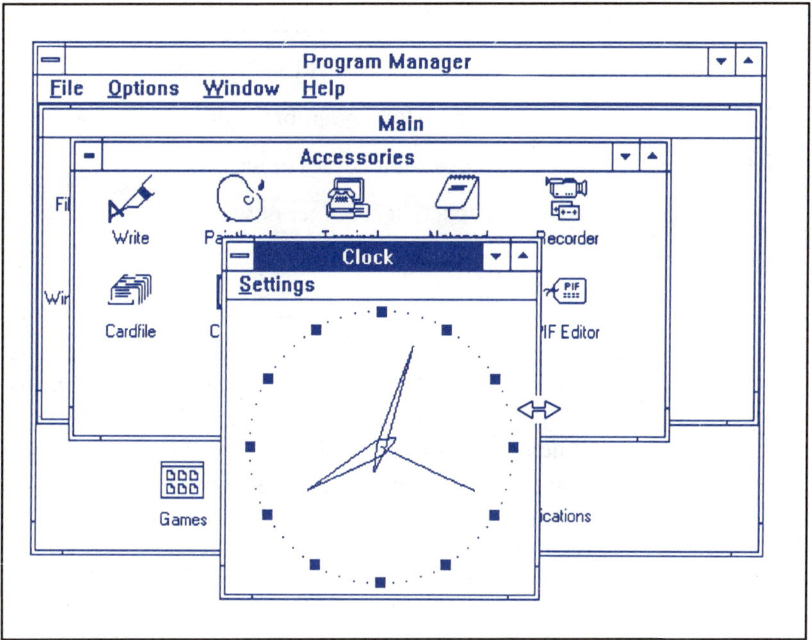

Figure 10.2: Windows' mouse pointer illustrating possible size directions

To size a window using your keyboard, invoke the window's Control menu and select the Size option. Windows will display a pointer with four arrowheads. To change the window's width, press the Right or Left Arrow key. Windows will move the pointer to either the left or right side of the frame as specified. Next, using the Up or Down Arrow key, you can increase or decrease the window's height. When you are satisfied with the window's size, press Enter. To change the window's height, follow the same steps, using the Up and Down Arrow keys. To select the window's corner hot spot, simply press either the Right or Left Arrow key followed by an Up or Down Arrow. Windows will move the direction pointer to a corner as described in Table 10.1.

Sizing the Windows Clock

Invoke the Windows Clock, or select the Clock as the active window if it is currently running. Next, either use your mouse to

Table 10.1: *Arrow Key Combinations for Window's Corner Size Hot Spots.*

KEY COMBINATION	SIZE POINTER LOCATION
Left, Up	Upper-left corner of window
Left, Down	Lower-left corner of window
Right, Up	Upper-right corner of window
Right, Down	Lower-right corner of window

select one of the window's size hot spots or use the window's Control menu Size option and increase the Clock's size, as in Figure 10.3.

Take a few moments to increase and decrease the Clock's size. When you are working with several windows at one time, the ability to size a window is essential.

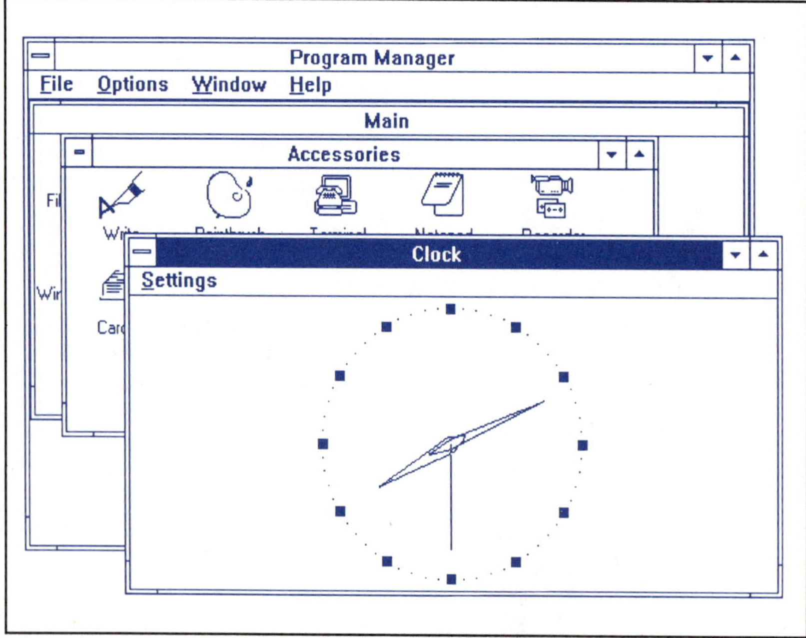

Figure 10.3: *Incrementally sizing the Windows Clock*

How to Move a Window

When you open several windows on your screen simultaneously, you will eventually want to move a window to a new location so you can view the output of two or more windows at the same time.

To move a window using your mouse, simply click the mouse pointer in the window's Title Bar, holding down the mouse select button. As you move the mouse, Windows will move a hollow frame the size of the window you are moving, to show its new position on your screen. When the frame is in the desired window location, release the mouse select button and Windows will relocate the window.

To move a window using your keyboard, invoke the window's Control menu and select the Move option. Windows will display a hollow frame the size of the window you want to move. Using your keyboard's arrow keys, you can move this frame around the screen. When the frame is in the desired window position, press Enter, and Windows will move the window to its new location.

Moving the Windows Clock

Select the Windows Clock as the active window. Using either the mouse or the window's Control menu, move the window to a new location on your screen (Figure 10.4).

Moving and sizing windows are very important capabilities. Take time now to experiment with them.

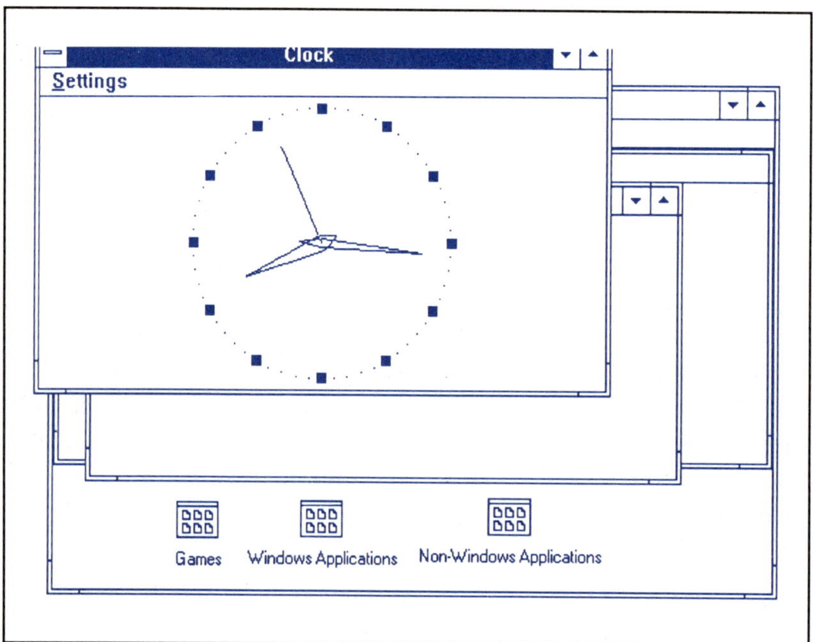

Figure 10.4: *Moving the Windows Clock*

LESSON 11

Tiling All Open Windows on Your Screen

Featuring

- Cascading windows
- Tiled windows
- The Task Manager

EACH TIME YOU RUN A PROGRAM, WINDOWS OPENS A new window for the program, placing it on top of existing windows. To help you select other active programs, Windows always tries to display each window's Title Bar. The overlaying of one window on top of another is called *cascading windows*. If you invoke several of the Windows accessory programs, Windows will cascade the windows, as in Figure 11.1.

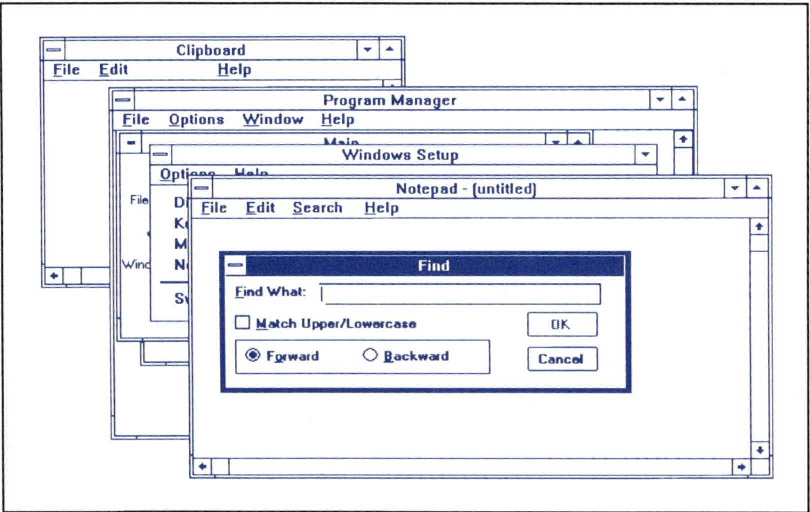

Figure 11.1: Cascading multiple windows

How to Tile Your Windows

Depending on the programs you are running, you may want Windows to display a small window with a portion of each program on the screen as opposed to only the Title Bars. In such cases Windows lets you "tile" a portion of each program on your screen, as in Figure 11.2.

Tiling gets its name from the mosaic tile design on the screen, made up of the different program sizes and shapes. To select *tiled windows*, or to revert from tiled windows back to cascading windows, you must use the Windows Task Manager.

The *Task Manager* allows you to change quickly from one program to another or to end a specific program. Lesson 45 examines the Windows Task Manager in detail. For now, you will simply use the Task Manager to tile and cascade your windows.

When you invoke the Task Manager, your screen will display the box shown in Figure 11.3 listing the available windows.

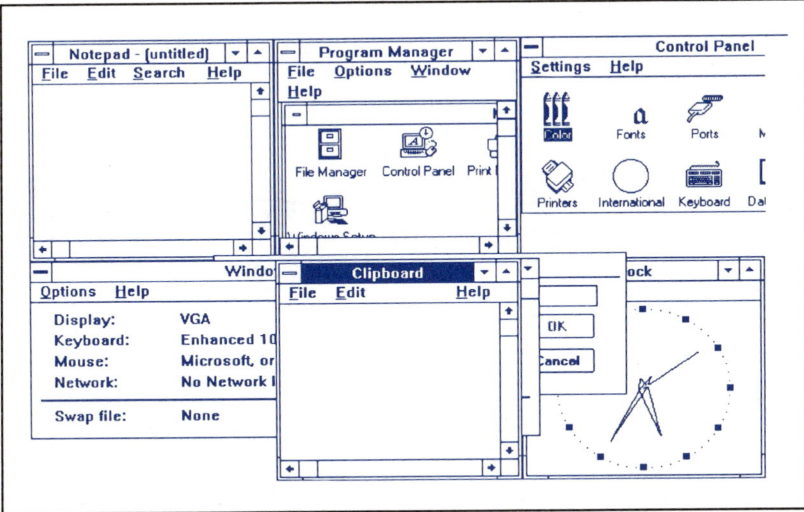

Figure 11.2: Tiling multiple windows

Figure 11.3: The Windows Task Manager window

As you can see, the Task Manager lists all current windows. The Task Manager Tile option tiles your windows, while the Cascade option cascades your windows.

As discussed in Lesson 4, Windows defines the area surrounding your windows as the desktop. To invoke the Task Manager, aim the mouse pointer at the desktop and double-click. When the Task Manager window is displayed, aim the mouse pointer at either the Tile or Cascade option and click.

To invoke the Task Manager with your keyboard, press the Ctrl+Esc keyboard combination. When the Task Manager window is displayed, press the Tab key until either the Tile or Cascade option is highlighted. Press Enter to select the option.

LESSON 12

Using Windows' On-line Help

Featuring

- On-line help
- Windows Help buttons

PART I OF THIS BOOK HAS TAUGHT YOU MANY ESSENTIAL steps you will need to use Windows regularly. Because you won't use each of these techniques on a daily basis, you may not always remember the exact steps required to perform a specific task. For such cases, Windows provides an extensive *on-line help* package. Using Windows Help you can quickly find the answers to your Windows questions.

Windows Help is extensive, providing many advanced features. This lesson will familiarize you with the essential features you will need each day. Using the help package, you can quickly learn the more advanced features. Since most of the Windows programs you will run support the Help package, you can get help on all your programs once you have learned to traverse the Help menus.

How to Start Help

The easiest way to invoke Help is by selecting the Help pull-down menu from the Program Manager window, as shown in Figure 12.1.

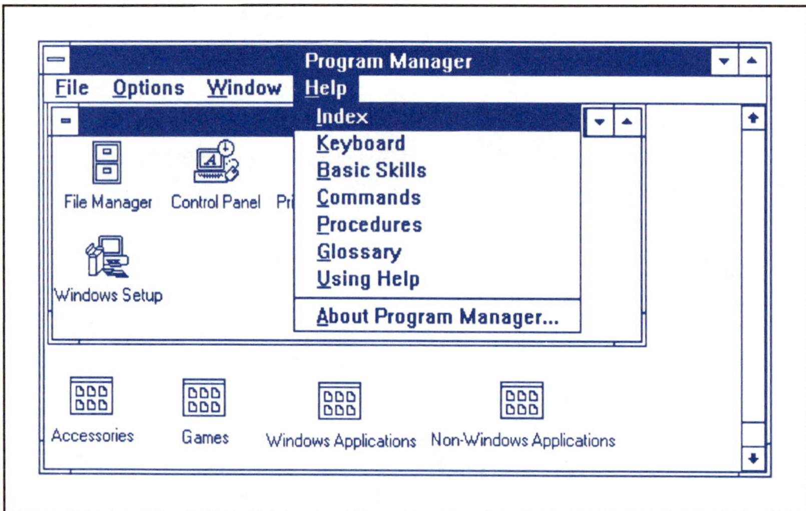

Figure 12.1: Windows' Help menu

Each Help menu option takes you into a different Help topic. Table 12.1 briefly explains each menu option.

Table 12.1: *Summary of the Windows Help Menu Options.*

MENU OPTION	DISCUSSION
Index	Displays an alphabetical listing of each available topic, letting you display help on your topic of interest.
Keyboard	Displays a listing of the keyboard hot keys defined for the current application.
Commands	Displays a listing of each option available in the pull-down menus for the current program and lets you display specific help text for each.

Table 12.1: *Summary of the Windows Help Menu Options. (cont.)*

MENU OPTION	DISCUSSION
Procedures	Displays a detailed description of the steps you must follow to access each feature of the current program, such as printing a file, or selecting a specific option.
Using Help	Displays a description of the Windows Help program and Help's user interface.
About Program Manager	Displays copyright information for the Windows Program Manager.
Basic Skills	Displays a list of the Windows skills you will need on a regular basis, such as closing or opening a window.

To begin, select the Index option from the Help menu. Your screen will display the window in Figure 12.2.

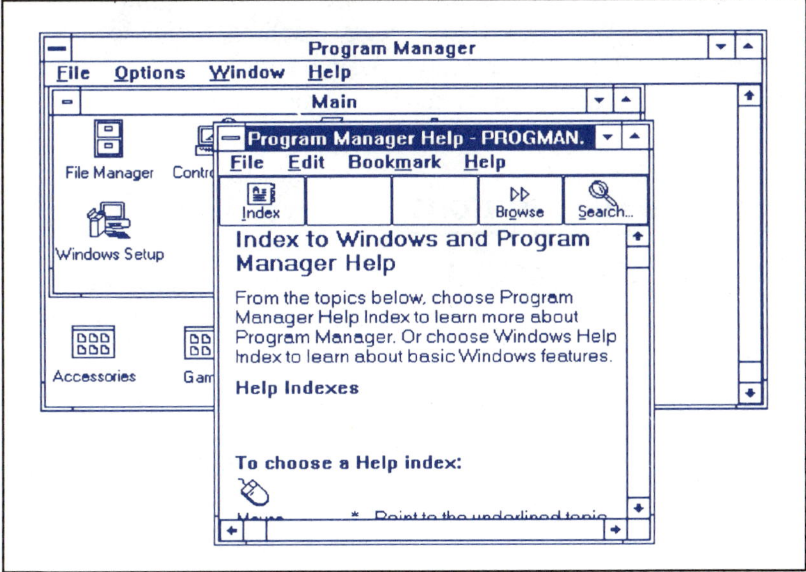

Figure 12.2: *Windows' Help Index*

The first step you will want to perform in Help is to maximize the window. Using either the Maximize button or the Control menu Maximize option, expand the Help window. As you examine each Help screen, note that several items are underlined. An item with a solid underline will display information, while a dotted underline pops up a dialog box.

To display information on an underlined Help topic using your mouse, simply aim the mouse pointer at the topic and click.

To display information on an underlined Help topic using your keyboard, you must first highlight the topic by pressing the Tab key. Then press Enter.

Displaying the Program Manager Help Index

The initial Help window has two underlined topics: Program Manager Help Index and Windows Help Index. The Program Manager Help Index displays a list of topics specific to the Program Manager. The Windows Help Index displays topics consistent throughout all Windows programs. Using either your keyboard or mouse, you can select different underlined topics for display.

How to Use Help Buttons

At the top of each screen of text, Windows displays five *Help buttons* that assist you in traversing through Help. Table 12.2 describes each button's function.

To select a Help button with your mouse, simply aim the mouse pointer at the button and click.

Table 12.2: *Functions of Windows' Help Buttons.*

BUTTON	FUNCTION
Index	Returns you to the first Help Index screen.
Back	Returns you to the previous Help screen.
Browse Browse	Lets you page forward and backward through a long topic.
Search...	Lets you select Help on a topic from a list of key words.

To select a Help button using your keyboard, type the underlined letter that appears in the desired button. For example, to select the Index button, type I.

Using the Index Button

The Help Index button always returns you to the first Help Index screen. Even if you are several layers deep in Help text, you can always quickly return to a familiar place by selecting the Index button.

When to Use the Back Button

As you descend from one level of Help to the next, Help keeps track of not only where you are, but also where you've been. By selecting the Back button you can redisplay the previous screen, backing your way out of the current Help topic.

When to Use the Browse Button

A Help topic can be quite long. As discussed, Windows lets you use the scroll bars to scroll line by line through the topic's text. For more rapid scanning, the Browse buttons let you quickly page forward and backward within the text.

Using the Search Button

The Help Search button assists you by displaying a list of available topics for you to choose from. When you select the Search button, your screen will look like Figure 12.3.

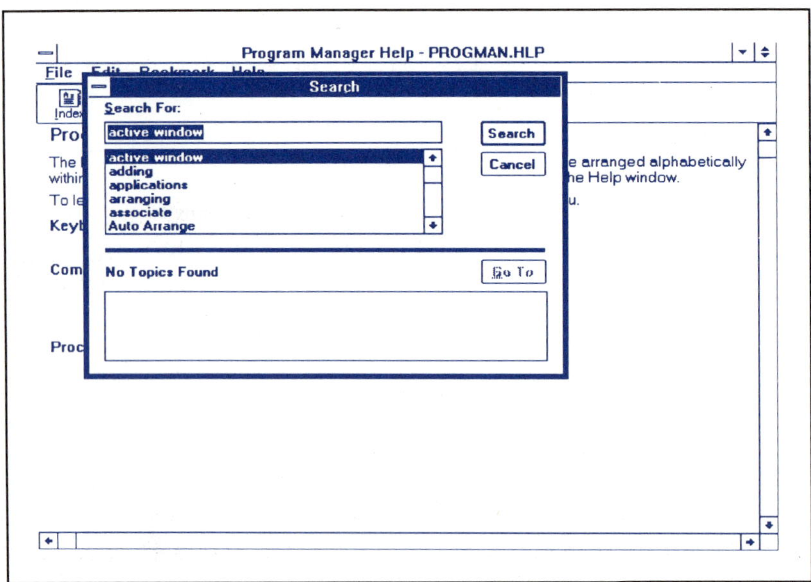

Figure 12.3: Windows' Help keyword search dialog box

Using the Search window's scroll bar, you can search quickly through the list of available topics. When your topic of interest appears, aim the mouse pointer at the topic and click.

At the top of the Search window, beneath the words Search For is a box where you can type in the topic you wish to find. As you type each letter, Search quickly moves to the topics that correspond to the letters you have typed so far. To display topics beginning with the letter *I*, for example, you simply type the letter I. When Search highlights the desired topic, press Enter.

How to Display Related Topics

When you select a topic, Search will display a list of matching topics in its bottom box. To display information about a related topic, simply select the topic using your mouse or keyboard arrow keys and press Enter.

Printing a Topic's Help Text

In some cases you may want to print the Help text on a specific topic so you have it available as a reference. To do so, select the topic of interest and invoke the Help File menu using your mouse or by pressing Alt+F. Next, select the Print Topic option.

How to End a Help Session

You can end your Help Session in one of two ways. First, using the Help window's Control menu, you can close the window. Second, using the Minimize button or Control menu Minimize option, you can reduce the window to an icon.

PART II

Using the Windows File Manager

LESSON 13

Getting Started with the Windows File Manager

Featuring

- Directories
- File Manager components
- Disk-drive icons

TO STORE INFORMATION FROM ONE COMPUTER SESSION to the next, you must save the information into files on disks. Files can contain letters, reports, spreadsheets, and programs such as Windows itself. The more programs and information you keep, the larger the number of files on your disk will become. To help you organize your files, DOS lets you group related files into *directories*. Conceptually, a directory is very much like a drawer in a filing cabinet. To select a specific file from your filing cabinet you must know which drawer it's in. Likewise, to acccss a file on your disk, you must know the correct directory.

To organize your disk, you should create directories for each group of files on the disk. You might, for example, store your word processing files in one directory, spreadsheets in another, and computer games in a third. In general, only disk space restricts the number of directories you can create. To simplify your use of files and directories, Windows provides a powerful yet easy to use program called the File Manager. Using the File Manager, you can create directories, copy and print files, and even run programs. Because the File Manager runs within a window, you can use all the concepts you learned in Part I.

How to Start the File Manager

Double-click on the File Manager icon in the Program Manager Main group. Your screen will display a window containing the File Manager, as in Figure 13.1.

Each time the File Manager begins, it displays a directory listing of the subdirectories that reside in your disk's root directory. The

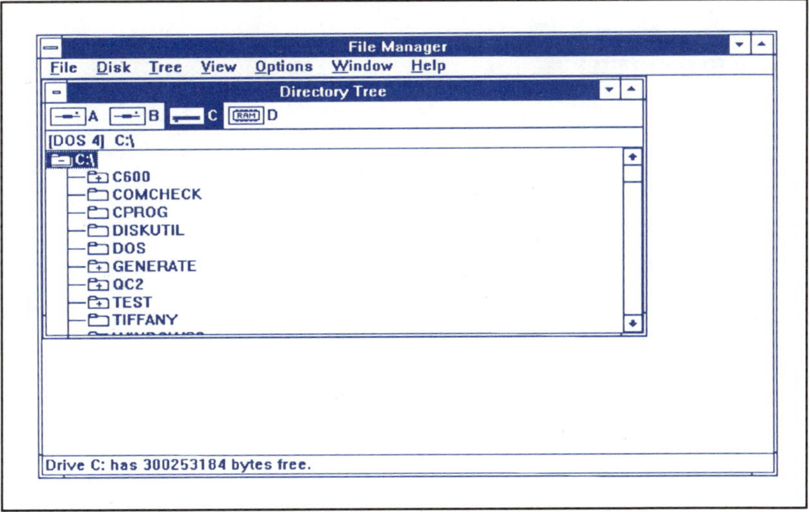

Figure 13.1: *Windows' File Manager*

File Manager displays the directories in the root directory at this point, but not any files the root directory may contain. Using the File Manager's scroll bar you can scroll through the list of directory names. The File Manager will display the current file or directory in reverse video. In addition to the list of directory names, the File Manager displays the additional information seen in Figure 13.2.

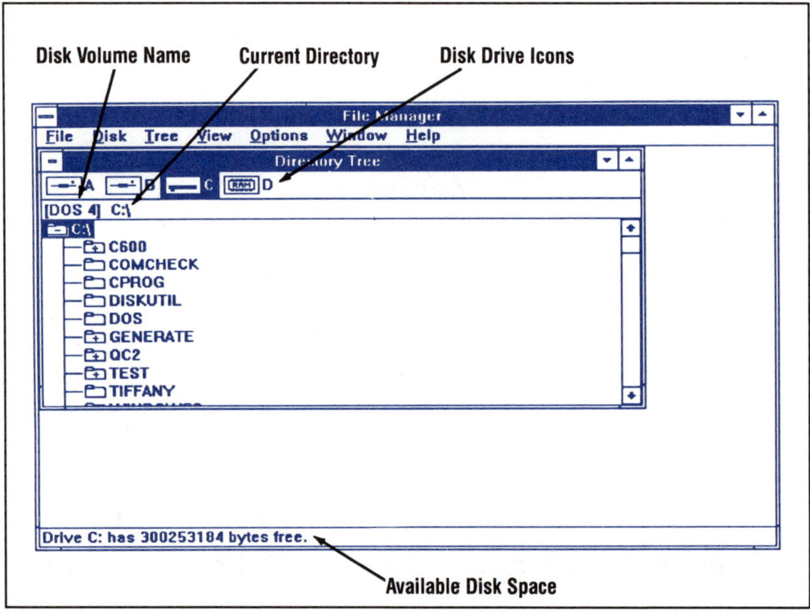

Figure 13.2: *File Manager components*

Disk-Drive Icons

Immediately below the Directory Tree Title Bar, the File Manager displays an *icon* for each disk drive connected to your computer, as well as network-drive letters if you are connected to a local area network. The File Manager also has a special icon for CD-ROM drives. The File Manager highlights the current drive in reverse video. Depending upon the disk-drive type, the File Manager will display one of the drive icons shown in Table 13.1.

Table 13.1: *Drive Icons.*

ICON	DRIVE TYPE
A	Floppy-disk drive
C	Hard-disk drive
RAM D	RAM-disk drive
NET F	Network-disk drive

Disk-Volume Label

DOS allows you to assign an optional name to each disk you format called the volume label. You can use volume labels to specify information about a disk. If the current disk does not have a volume label, the File Manager ignores this field.

Current Directory

As discussed, a directory is similar to a filing cabinet drawer. Just as you would give a different name to each drawer, you must assign a unique name to each DOS subdirectory. The Current Directory field tells you the name of the directory the File Manager is highlighting in the directory list. As you highlight different directory names in the subdirectory list, the Current Directory field will change.

Directory Icons

To the left of each directory name are icons that resemble the files you would place in a filing cabinet. As you examine the subdirectory icons, you may find an icon with a plus sign (+). The plus sign indicates that the corresponding directory contains additional levels of subdirectories.

Available Disk Space

At the bottom of the window, the File Manager displays the amount in bytes of available disk space on the current drive. As you change disk drives or create and delete files, the File Manager updates this field accordingly.

How to Close the File Manager

Like all Windows programs, the File Manager runs in its own window. So you can use its Control menu to close the window, or you can reduce the window to an icon.

LESSON 14

Changing the Current Drive

Featuring

- File Manager disk-drive icons

BY DEFAULT, THE FILE MANAGER DISPLAYS A LIST OF THE subdirectories on the current disk drive. As you work with Windows you will eventually need to access a floppy-disk or network drive. You change disk drives by selecting a *drive icon*.

How to Select a New Current Drive

The File Manager always displays the subdirectory tree for the current drive. When you change the current drive, the File Manager will automatically display the subdirectory listing for the new drive.

To select a new current drive using your mouse, aim the mouse pointer at the disk icon corresponding to the desired disk and click.

To select a disk drive using your keyboard, you have two choices. First, you can press the Tab key to move the highlight from the subdirectory list to the drive icons. Then use the Left or Right Arrow keys to highlight the desired drive and press Enter. Second, you can simply hold down the Ctrl key and press the key corresponding to the desired drive letter. To select drive A, for example, you would press Ctrl+A.

Inadvertently Selecting a Drive That Does Not Contain a Disk

Should you select a floppy-disk drive that does not contain a disk, the File Manager will display a dialog box, giving you the choice of inserting a disk and continuing, or simply canceling the operation. Should this error occur, place a floppy disk in the drive and select the Retry option, or choose the Cancel option to return to the File menu with the current disk drive unchanged.

How to Use Network Drives

If your computer is connected to a local area network and Windows has been installed to support the network, the File Manager can access the available network drives. Depending on your network configuration, the steps you must follow to access network drives will differ. For specifics, consult your network administrator.

LESSON 15

Expanding and Collapsing the Directory Tree

Featuring

- The directory tree
- Hot keys
- Window Refresh

AS DISCUSSED IN LESSON 13, DOS SUBDIRECTORIES HELP you organize your disk by grouping related files together. For example, you might name the subdirectory where you want to store your word processing files WORDPROC. If you create many letters, reports, and memos, though, the number of files in your directory will grow quite rapidly, making it difficult for you to locate specific files. As a solution, you can create additional subdirectories within the directory WORDPROC to distinguish your letters, reports, and memos. Pictorially, your directory structure might look like Figure 15.1

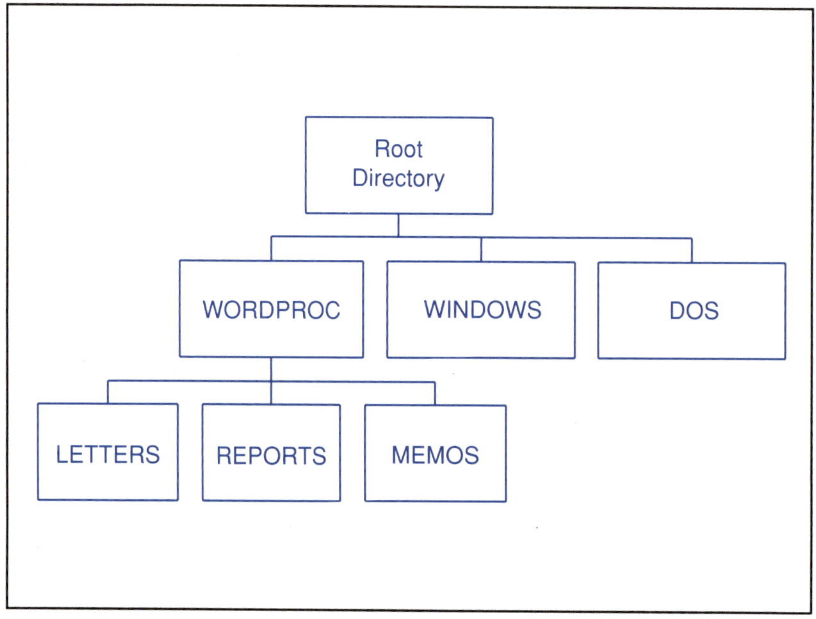

Figure 15.1: *Three-tiered directory structure*

All DOS disks have a unique directory called the root, from which all other directories grow. Because all directories grow from the root directory, much as a tree grows from a root, the directory structure is commonly referred to as the *directory tree*.

How to Expand and Collapse the Directory Tree

By default, the Windows File Manager displays only the first level of the directory tree. If you want to access subdirectories below this level quickly, you can direct the File Manager to expand its display of the directory tree to include all branches. You will find the Tree option in the File Manager Title Bar. Using your mouse or the Alt+T keyboard combination, invoke the pull-down Tree menu. Your screen will display the menu shown in Figure 15.2.

To understand each Tree menu option better, assume that your disk contains the directory structure in Figure 15.3.

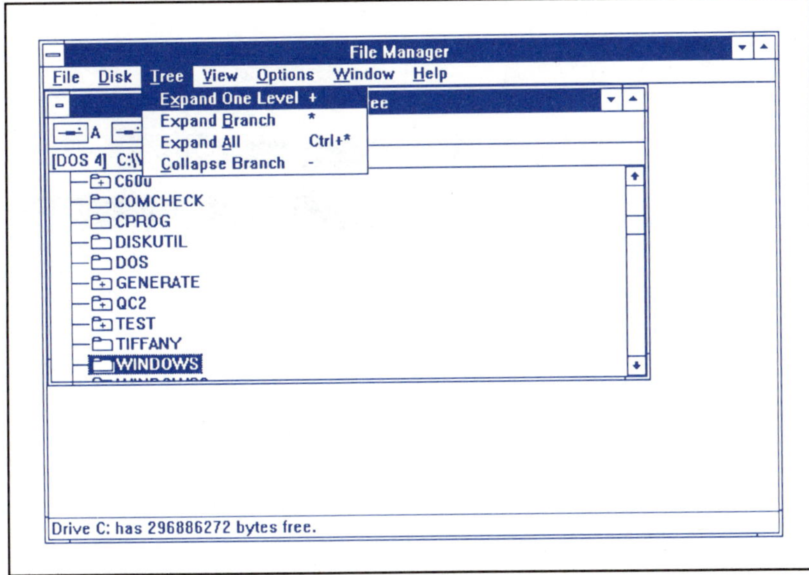

Figure 15.2: *File Manager Tree menu*

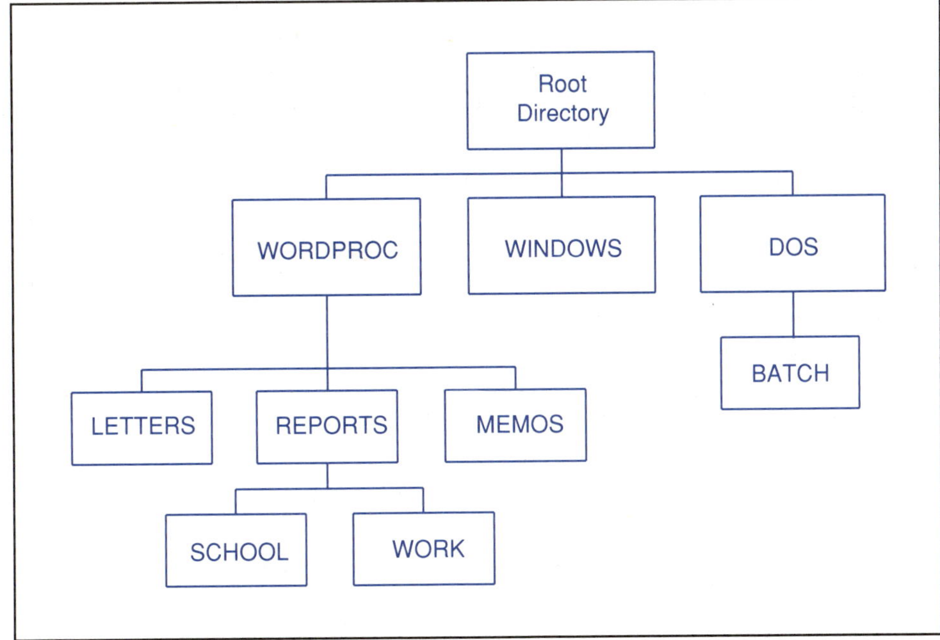

Figure 15.3: *Four-tiered directory structure*

By default, the File Manager will display only the first level of the directory tree, as in Figure 15.4.

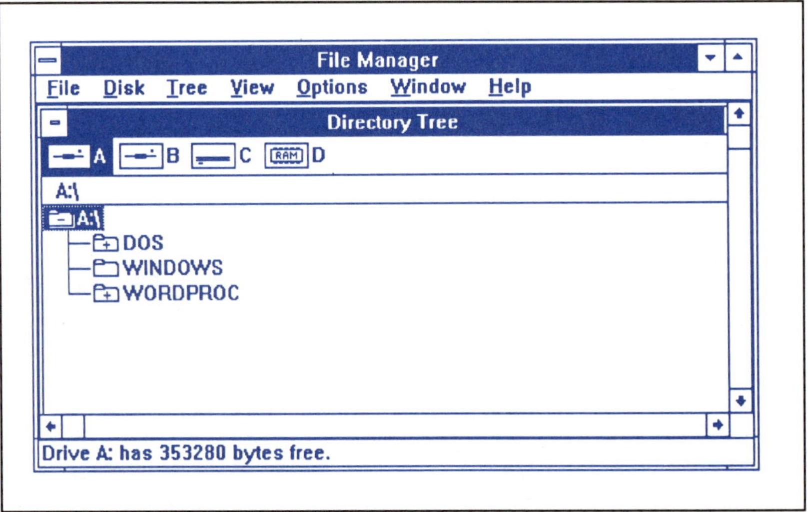

Figure 15.4: Default single-directory branch display

How to Expand the Current Branch

Continuing the tree analogy, the File Manager refers to the highlighted directory as the current branch. If you want to view directories below the current branch only, select the Expand Branch option from the File Manager Tree menu. Using the screen output from Figure 15.4, for example, selecting the directory WORDPROC as the current branch and then expanding the branch results in the output shown in Figure 15.5.

How to Collapse the Current Branch

Just as you can expand the view of a directory's branches, you can collapse or remove the branches from view when you no longer want them displayed by using the Tree menu Collapse Branch option.

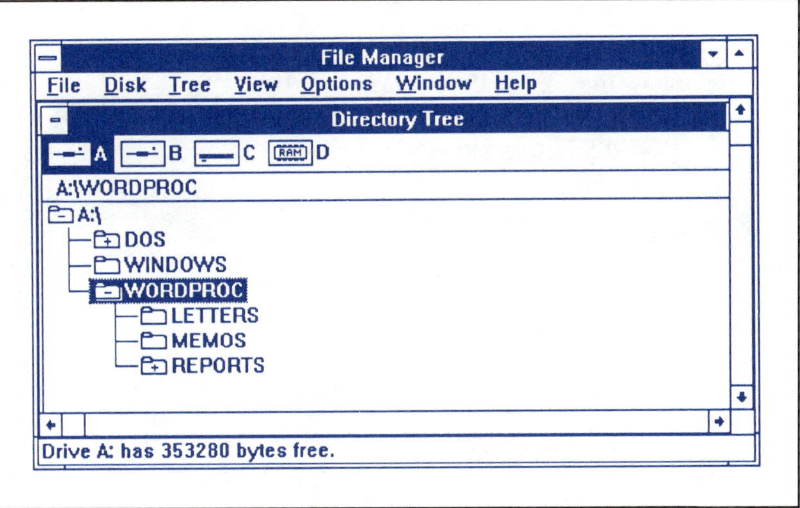

Figure 15.5: *Expanding the current directory branch*

How to Expand a Branch's First Level of Directories

If your directory tree has many levels of subdirectories, there may be times when you want to view only the next level of directories for a specific branch. The Tree menu Expand One Level option lets you do just that. When the File Manager starts, it displays only the first level of directories in the current drive's root directory.

How to Expand All Directory Branches

Most users will probably want the File Manager to display all the subdirectories in their directory so they can traverse the directory tree quickly, moving from one subdirectory to another. To do so, select the Tree menu Expand All option. Using the directory tree in Figure 15.4, for example, selecting Expand All results in the screen in Figure 15.6.

How to Use Tree Menu Keyboard Hot Keys

If you examine the Tree menu you will find that each option has a *hot key* assigned to it. Table 15.1 describes each hot key.

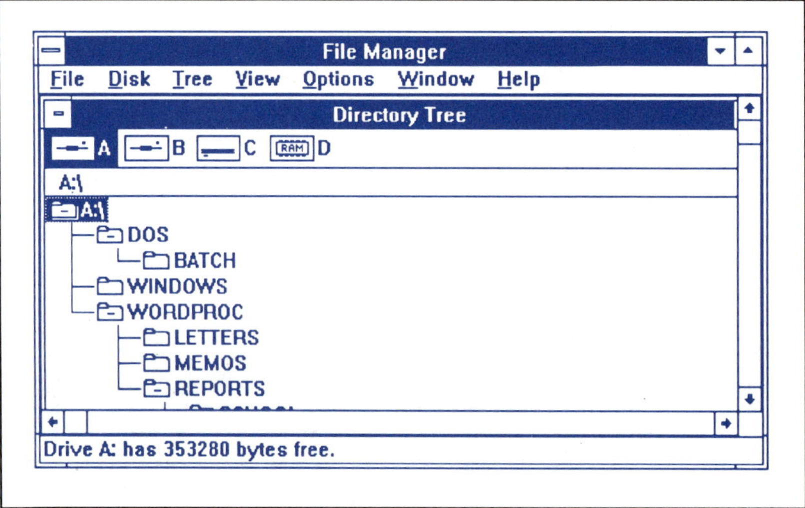

Figure 15.6: *Expanding all directory branches*

Table 15.1: *Hot Key Combinations for the Tree Menu.*

HOT KEY COMBINATION	OPTION
+	Expands the current branch to one level
−	Collapses the current branch to no levels
*	Expands all subdirectories in the current branch
Ctrl+*	Expands the entire subdirectory tree

How to Redraw the Directory Tree on the Screen

There are times when the File Manager does not immediately update the subdirectory list to reflect the expansion or collapse of the directory tree. Immediate update failure is most common when network disks are used. If the File Manager does not update the subdirectory list to reflect a change, invoke the File Manager Window menu shown in Figure 15.7 and select the Refresh option. When you select Refresh, the File Manager will immediately redraw the subdirectory list using the desired expansion.

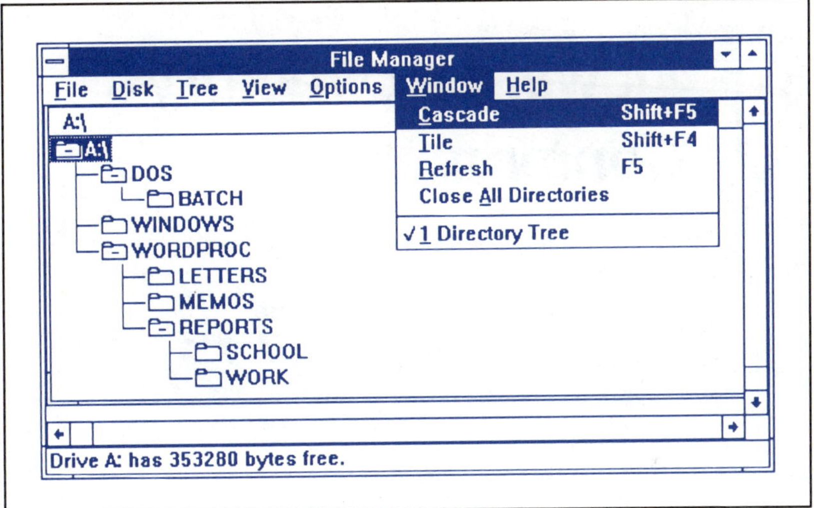

Figure 15.7: *File Manager Window menu*

LESSON 16

Viewing a Directory's Contents

Featuring

- Directory windows
- File icons

IN LESSON 15 YOU LEARNED HOW TO USE THE WINDOWS File Manager to traverse your directory tree, displaying each subdirectory in a branch. Once you determine the desired subdirectory, however, you will want to display all the files it contains.

How to Open a Directory Window

If you examine the title bars on your screen, you will find that Windows refers to the window containing your disk's subdirectory list as the directory tree. To view the list of files residing in a specific branch, you must open a *directory window* for that branch.

To open a directory window using your mouse, aim the mouse pointer at the desired directory and double-click.

To open a directory window using your keyboard, use the arrow keys to highlight the desired directory and press Enter.

How to Open a Directory Window to View the Window's Files

Using either your mouse or keyboard, open a directory window displaying the files in the subdirectory WINDOWS, as in Figure 16.1. As you can see, a directory window displays the names of each file the directory contains. Using the directory window's scroll bar, you can scroll through the list of files. In later lessons you will learn how to customize the information that the File Manager displays for each file to better suit your needs.

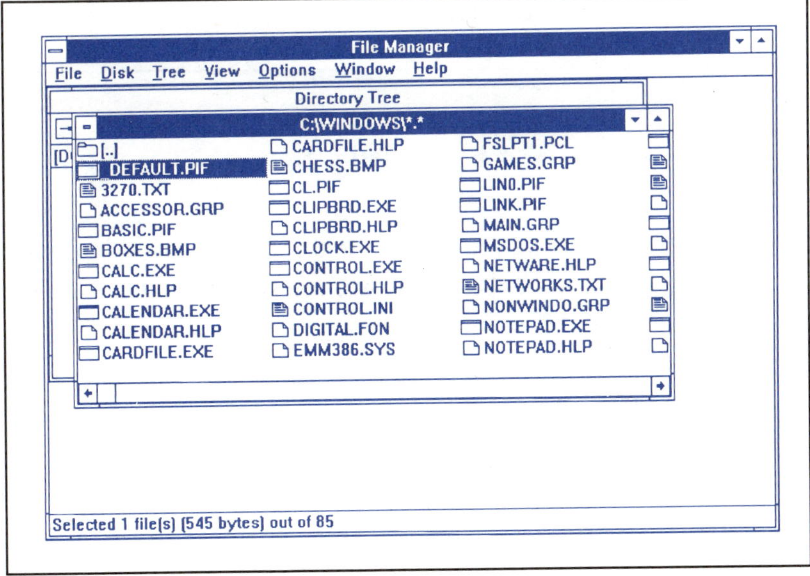

Figure 16.1: Directory window for the WINDOWS subdirectory

How to Understand File Icons

If you examine the files the File Manager displays in a directory window, you will find that the File Manager displays a different *icon* next to each file name depending on file type. Table 16.1 briefly describes each file icon.

Table 16.1: *Windows File Icons.*

ICON	FILE TYPE
	DOS subdirectory
	Program file with .EXE, .BAT, .COM, or .PIF extension
	Document files associated with a specific Windows program
	All other DOS files

How to Close a Directory Window

Like all windows, you can use a directory window's Control menu to close, move, or size a directory window, even reducing it to an icon for later use.

LESSON 17

Viewing Multiple Directory Trees at One Time

Featuring

- Side-by-side directory windows
- Tiling directory windows
- Manipulating directory windows

IN LESSON 16 YOU LEARNED HOW TO OPEN A DIRECTORY tree and view a list of the files in the directory. Since Windows displays each directory tree within a window, you can move, close, or even iconize a window containing a directory tree. As you perform file operations such as copying or moving files with Windows, you may want to view the contents of several different directory trees. For example, to copy a file from your word processing subdirectory into the subdirectory MEMOS, you might open several windows to display the contents of both directory trees *side by side*.

How to Open Multiple Directory Tree Windows

As you learned in Lesson 16, to select a directory for display or expansion, you can either aim your mouse pointer at the directory name and click, or highlight the directory name with your keyboard arrow keys. If you are using your keyboard to select a directory, Table 17.1 provides several shortcut keyboard combinations.

Using either your keyboard or mouse, open a directory window displaying the files in your DOS subdirectory. It should look similar to Figure 17.1.

As you will learn in the following lessons, you can execute programs or display text files that appear in the directory window by using point and shoot. In some cases, you may want to view files in two or more directories simultaneously.

Table 17.1: *Directory Tree Traversal Keys Supported by the File Manager.*

KEY	DIRECTORY SELECTION
Up Arrow	Directory name immediately above the highlighted directory
Down Arrow	Directory name immediately below the highlighted directory
Home	The root directory
End	The last directory in the directory list
PgUp	Scrolls to the top directory on the previous screen
PgDn	Scrolls to the bottom directory on the next screen
Ctrl+PgUp	Selects the previous directory at the same depth in the directory tree if one exists or leaves the highlight unchanged
Ctrl+PgDn	Selects the next directory at the same depth in the directory tree if one exists or leaves the highlight unchanged
Letter	Selects the first directory whose name begins with the letter typed, if matching directory exists, or leaves the highlight unchanged

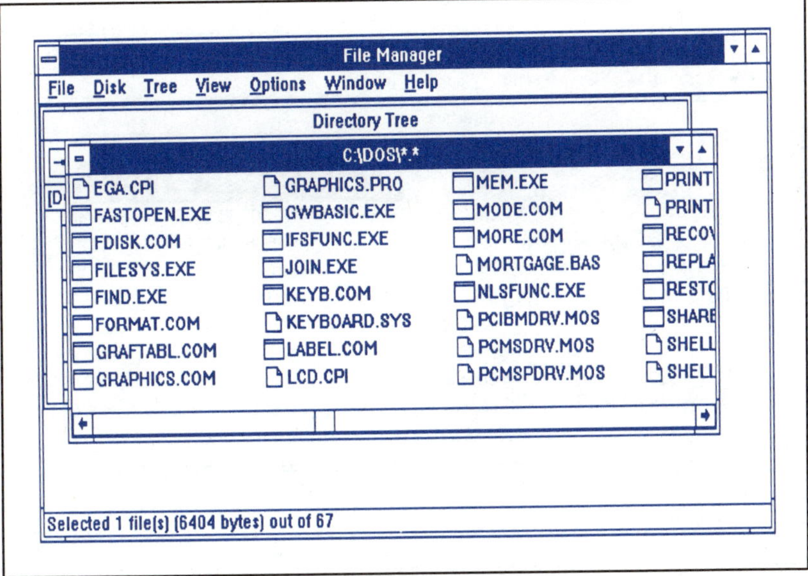

Figure 17.1: *Directory window for the DOS subdirectory*

To open additional directory windows, you need to select the File Manager window as active.

To select the File Manager window as active using a mouse, aim the mouse pointer into the File Manager window and click. If the File Manager window is not visible, invoke the visible window's Control menu and select the Next option, repeating the process until the File Manager becomes visible.

To select the File Manager window using your keyboard, press the Ctrl+Tab keyboard combination to cycle through the open windows until the File Manager is displayed. Ctrl+Tab is a hot key defined as the Control menu Next option.

After you select the File Manager as active, open a window displaying the files in the WINDOWS subdirectory. The File Manager will overlay the existing windows with the directory window, as in Figure 17.2.

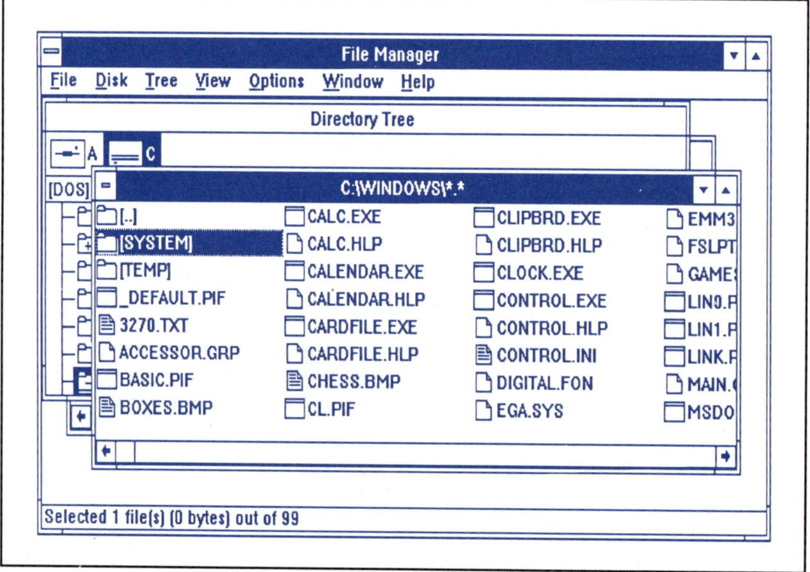

Figure 17.2: Directory window containing the WINDOWS subdirectory

Each time the File Manager opens a directory tree window, the File Manager places it over all existing windows, preventing you from viewing their contents. To view multiple directory windows better, you can tile or cascade each open window on your screen.

How to Tile Open Directory Windows

As discussed in Lesson 11, when you *tile* open windows on your screen, Windows displays a portion of each program of document in a small window. By tiling two directory trees, you can view the contents of each tree side by side.

To tile File Manager directory windows using a mouse, click on the Window option in the File Manager's menu bar. When the Window pull-down menu drops, select the Tile option.

To tile File Manager directory windows using your keyboard, press Alt+W to invoke the File Manager Window pull-down menu. Next, select the Tile option. The File Manager defines the Shift+F4 hot key as a shortcut to tiling windows.

How to Tile the WINDOWS and DOS Directory Windows

Using either your keyboard or mouse, tile the WINDOWS, DOS, and File Manager windows to obtain Figure 17.3.

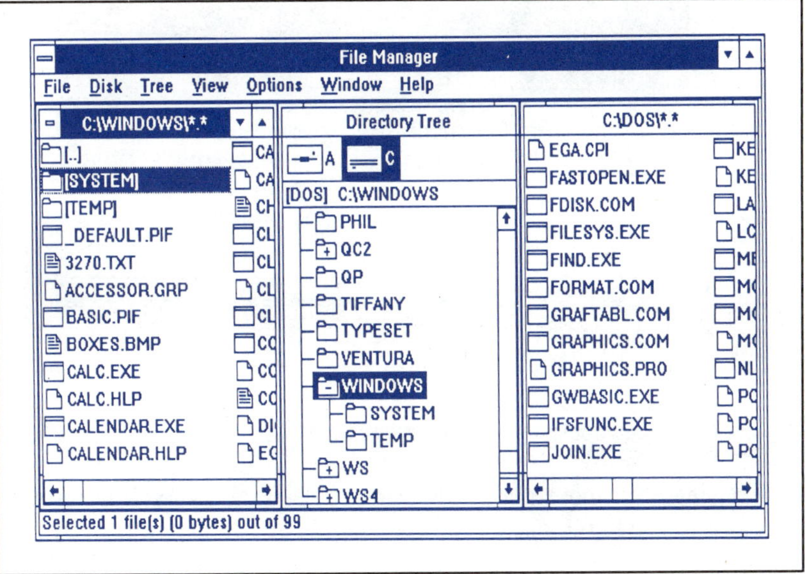

Figure 17.3: Tiling File Manager windows

Whether the directory windows are tiled or cascaded, the File Manager highlights the menu bar of the active window. To select a different window as active, simply aim your mouse pointer into the desired window and click, or press the Ctrl+Tab keyboard combination until the File Manager highlights the desired window.

How to Cascade the WINDOWS and DOS Directory Windows

After you perform your file operations, you may choose to "un-tile" your screen to view a specific directory window better. Using the File Manager Window menu Cascade option, you can display the Title Bar for each open window, as shown in Figure 17.4.

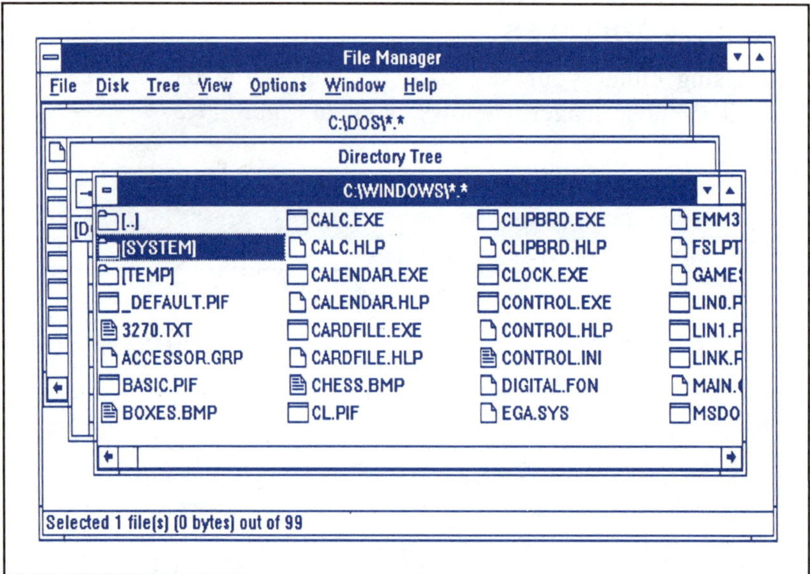

Figure 17.4: Cascading File Manager windows

Using your mouse or by pressing Ctrl+Tab, try cycling through the open windows.

How to Select a Directory Window Quickly Using the Window Menu

Throughout this lesson you have used your mouse or the Ctrl+Tab keyboard combination to select directory windows. In addition to these techniques, you can select a window using the File Manager's Window pull-down menu. Using either your mouse or Alt+W, invoke the Window menu shown in Figure 17.5.

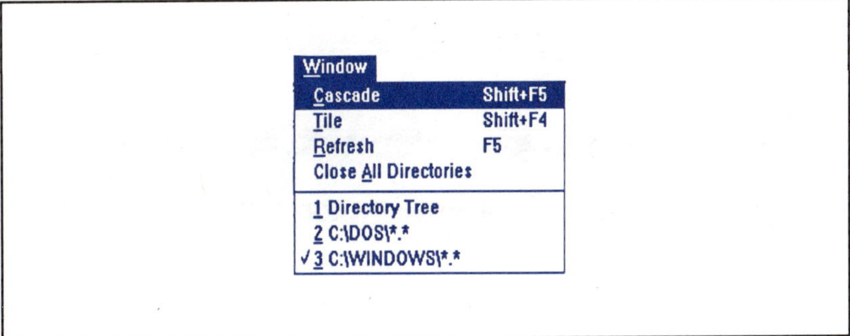

Figure 17.5: *The File Manager's Window pull-down menu*

As you can see, the File Manager displays the names of each open window at the bottom of the menu. You can then quickly select a window as active using your arrow keys or mouse, or by typing the number next to a window name.

How to Size, Move, and Close a Directory Window

Because the File Manager displays each directory tree within a window, you can size or close directory trees individually as your needs require. To see these capabilities, select the DOS subdirectory as the active window. Using the Control menu or Maximize button, expand the window to use the entire screen. Next, reduce the window to the icon in Figure 17.6.

When you need to expand the icon, simply aim at the icon and double-click your mouse, or press Ctrl+Tab until the icon is highlighted and then press Enter. Finally, use the DOS window's Control menu to close the directory tree window.

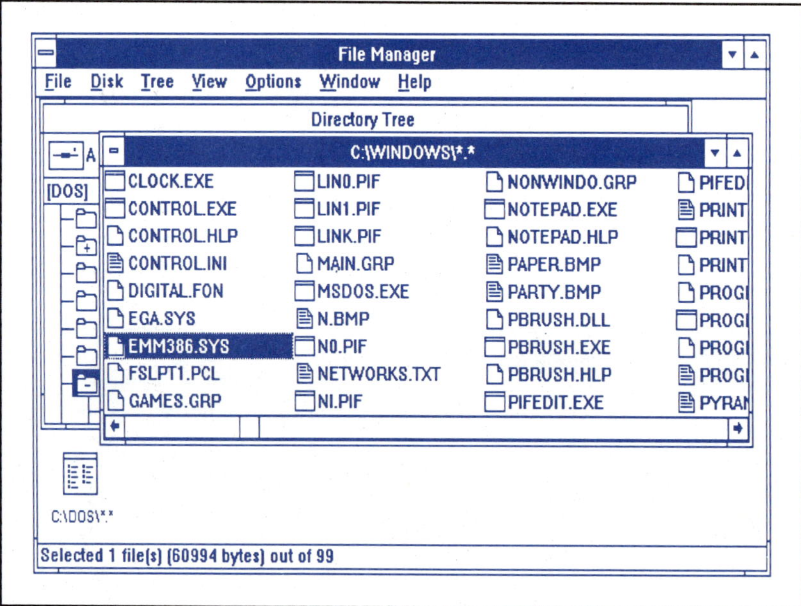

Figure 17.6: Reducing a directory window into an icon

LESSON 18

Creating Directories to Improve Your File Organization

Featuring

- Relative versus complete directory names

AS DISCUSSED, DOS LETS YOU ORGANIZE YOUR FILES BY grouping related files into DOS subdirectories. Using the Windows File Manager, you have selected several different subdirectories and displayed a list of the files each directory contains. As you create more files, you will need to create additional subdirectories to better organize your files. Creating directories is very straightforward with the File Manager.

Using your mouse or the Alt+F keyboard combination, invoke the File Manager File menu and select the Create Directory option. When you do so, the File Manager will prompt you to enter a subdirectory, as in Figure 18.1.

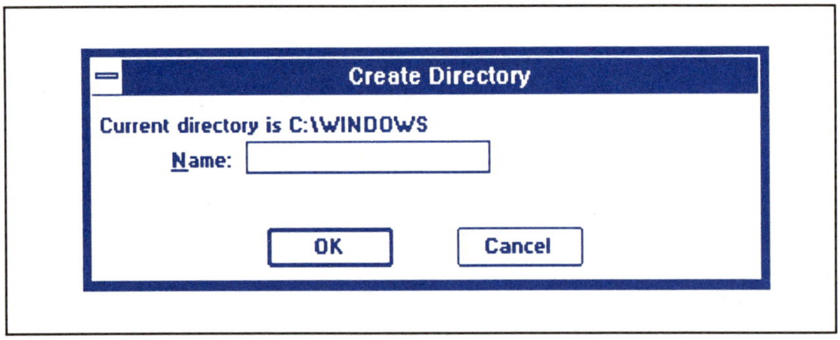

Create Directory
Current directory is C:\WINDOWS
Name:
OK Cancel

Figure 18.1: File Manager prompt for a directory name

The dialog box displays the name of the current directory. If you want to create a subdirectory within this directory, simply type the 8-character directory name and press Enter. If you want to create a subdirectory in a directory other than the default, you must specify a complete path name beginning with the root.

To avoid confusion about when to type a complete path name versus a subdirectory name only, most users select the directory where they want the new subdirectory to reside as the default. Once the target directory is selected, they can type in the subdirectory name without having to specify a complete path name.

LESSON 19

Running Programs in the File Manager

Featuring

- Point and shoot
- Command lines
- File Manager Run command
- Dangerous non-Windows applications

IN PART I YOU LEARNED HOW TO EXECUTE SEVERAL OF the Windows accessory programs, such as the Clock and Calculator, contained in the Windows Accessories group. As discussed, during its installation, Windows builds the Accessories and Games groups, assigning different programs to each group. In addition, Windows searches your disk for Windows programs, which always run in a window. If Windows locates any of these programs, it builds the Windows Applications group. By selecting this group, you can run the programs in it quickly. Lastly, as Windows searches your disk, it looks for other commonly used programs that don't run within a window (non-Windows applications). If Windows locates any of these programs, it builds the Non-Windows Applications group, placing an icon for each program in the group.

Windows groups are convenient because they let you select and run your commonly used programs quickly from within the Windows Program Manager. As you work more with Windows, you can add new programs to existing groups or even create your own groups. Periodically, however, you will need to run a program or batch file that is not in a group. To do so, you can use the Windows File Manager.

How to Execute Programs Using Point and Shoot

For you to run a program using Windows' *point-and-shoot* capabilities, the active directory window must display a directory listing containing the desired program or batch file.

To select and run a program using your mouse, aim the mouse pointer at the desired program name and double-click.

To select and run a program using your keyboard, highlight the desired program name and press Enter.

How to Respond to a Command Line Dialog Box

In Lesson 43 you will learn how to inform DOS about non-Windows programs using the PIF Editor, provided with Windows. PIF stands for Program Information File. Using the PIF Editor, you can create files with the PIF extension that tell Windows how to execute all non-Windows programs on your disk. A program information file contains a program's memory and other hardware requirements. In addition, the PIF can direct Windows to prompt you to enter a *command line* each time a program runs.

If you use the point-and-shoot technique to run a program whose PIF requires a command line, Windows will display a dialog box that asks you to enter a command line, as in Figure 19.1. Depending on the program, you may need to type in a file name or simply press Enter to run the program without a command line.

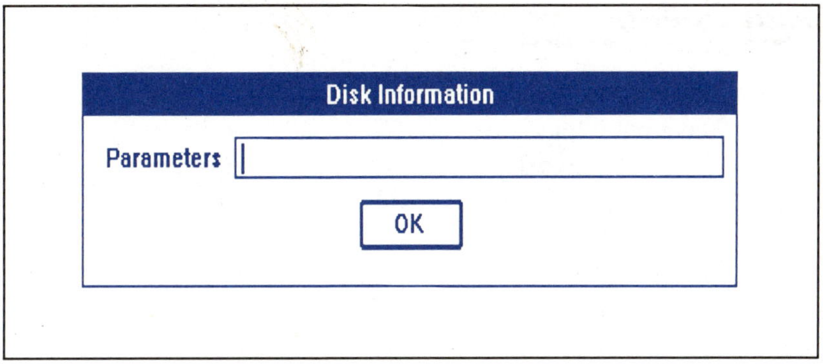

Disk Information

Parameters

OK

Figure 19.1: Dialog box prompting for a command line

If you run a program that does not have a corresponding PIF, Windows uses a default PIF that does not prompt for a command line.

How to Run Non-Windows Programs

As discussed, a Windows program is a program that runs within a window, whereas a non-Windows program uses the entire screen, preventing the display of other windows. By default, when you run a non-Windows program, Windows clears the screen, displays the program's output, and then immediately returns to the File Manager. For applications such as word processors or spreadsheet programs, immediately returning to the File Manager is acceptable. For other programs, however, the return to the File Manager may occur too quickly for you to view their output. For such applications, create a PIF file as discussed in Lesson 43 and disable the Close Window on Exit option. When you do so, Windows will prompt you to press a key to continue before it returns you to the File Manager.

Note that if you are running Windows in 386 Enhanced mode, Windows tries to display most programs within a window. In some cases, Windows can even run non-Windows programs within a window. For Real and Standard mode, however, Windows will display non-Windows programs on their own screen.

How to Run Programs Using the File Manager Run Option

To simplify the execution of programs that require a command line but have no defined PIF, the File Manager's File menu provides the *Run* option. To invoke the File menu, click on the menu with your mouse or press the Alt+F keyboard combination. When you select the Run option, the File Manager will display a dialog box prompting you to enter the command name and command line parameters, as in Figure 19.2.

The dialog box displays the name of the current directory. If the program you want to run resides in that directory, simply type the command's name. If the command resides in a different directory, you must specify a complete subdirectory path name to the file containing the command. In either case, you must include the file's extension.

If you are running Windows in the 386 Enhanced mode discussed in Lesson 2, you can run several non-Windows applications at the same time. The Run Minimized box lets you direct Windows to run a program as an icon, instead of displaying its output to the

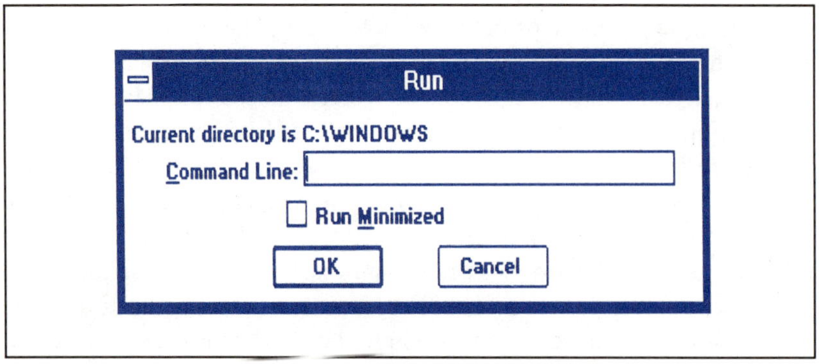

Figure 19.2: *File Manager Run dialog box*

screen. Running a program this way is convenient for programs that don't require user input and don't display essential output to the screen.

Running the DOS TREE Command

Using the File Manager, open a directory window for the DOS subdirectory. Next, invoke the Run option from the File menu. When the File Manager displays its dialog box, type in **TREE.COM C:** as shown in Figure 19.3.

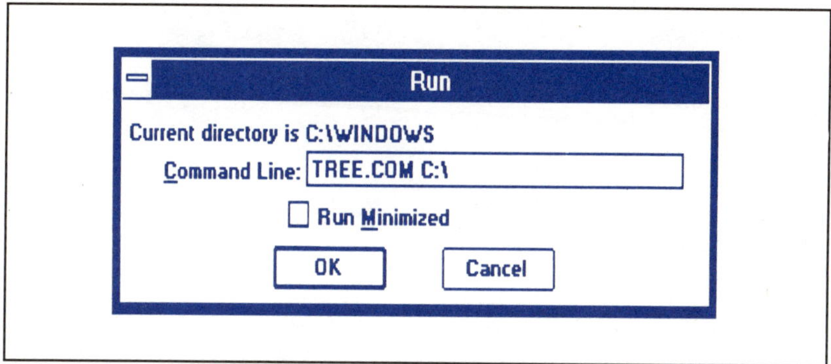

Figure 19.3: Invoking the DOS TREE command

When you press Enter or select OK using your mouse, Windows will invoke the command. As discussed, as soon as the command is completed, Windows will redisplay the File Manager. To direct Windows to wait for you to press a key before returning to the File Manager, you must create a PIF for TREE.COM or edit the Windows default PIF.

A Word of Warning

Some non-Windows applications are *dangerous* to run from within Windows. The applications of primary concern are hard-disk utility programs that perform low-level disk operations, such as undeleting files. Such programs modify your disk's file allocation table and SHOULD NOT be run from within Windows. For the same reason, you should not execute the DOS CHKDSK /F command while running Windows.

Always exit Windows before you run these kinds of programs. If you don't, you may damage your disk and very likely lose the information it contains.

LESSON 20

Customizing the Directory Window Display

Featuring

- Using the View pull-down menu
  Changing a directory window's sort order
- Restricting file names in a directory window to a specific type
- Reusing a directory window

EACH TIME YOU INVOKE THE FILE MANAGER'S ICON, THE screen displays your disk's directory tree. From the directory tree you can open a directory window displaying the names of files in specific directories. By default, each directory window displays only file names, sorted alphabetically. Using the File Manager *View pull-down menu*, however, you can direct the File Manager to display a file's size, modification dates and times, or attributes. In addition, you can change the order in which each file appears in the directory window, sorting by extension, size, or date the file was last changed. By displaying file names only, the File Manager can display more files in a window at one time.

How to Display More Information about Each File

To understand the different View options better, open a directory window for the WINDOWS subdirectory. By default, the File Manager displays file names only. Using either your mouse or the Alt+V keyboard combination, invoke the View pull-down menu shown in Figure 20.1.

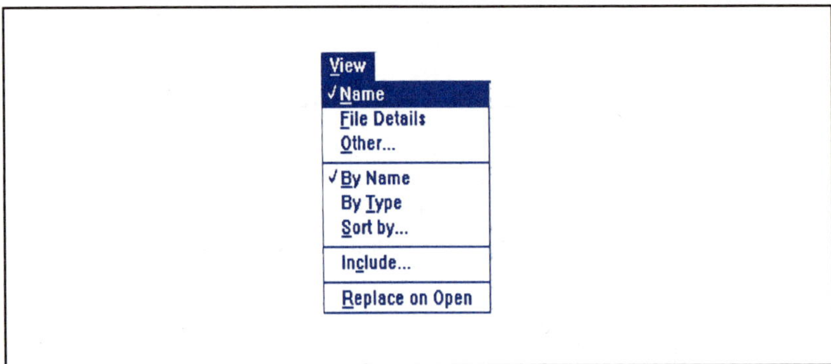

Figure 20.1: *The File Manager View menu*

The menu options that have check marks next to them are the current settings. The Name option directs the File Manager to display only file names in the directory window. The File Details option directs the File Manager to display each file's size, modification date and time, and attributes. If you select this option, the directory window display will change to resemble Figure 20.2.

The three periods after the Other option indicate that the menu option will generate a dialog box. If you select the Other menu option, your screen will display the dialog box in Figure 20.3, which lets you select different file information fields individually for display. To select a dialog option you must X the box to the left of the option.

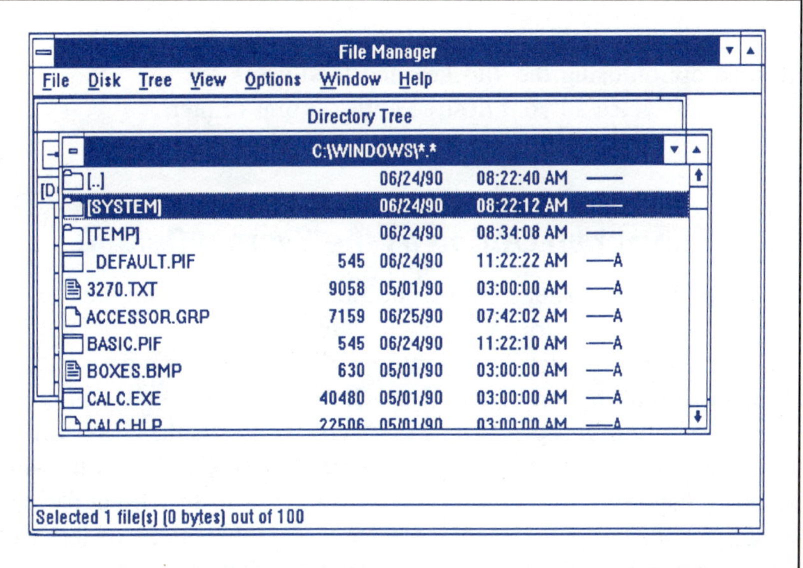

Figure 20.2: Viewing each file's name, size, date stamp, and attributes

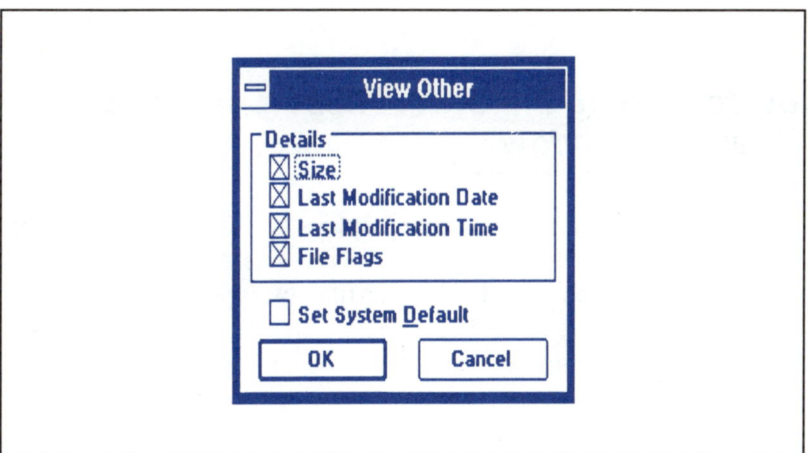

Figure 20.3: View menu Other option dialog box

To select a dialog box option using a mouse, aim the mouse pointer at the option and click. When you have finished selecting your options, aim the mouse pointer at the OK option and click.

To select a dialog box option using your keyboard, highlight the desired option using the Tab key and then press the spacebar. When you have selected all your desired options, press Enter.

How to Select an Option as the System Default

The File Manager lets you choose the file information to be displayed for each directory window individually or define a default format for every directory window the File Manager opens. The Set System Default option of the View Other dialog box lets you define the information you want the File Manager to display each time it opens a directory window. For example, if you want the File Manager to display the name and size of each file in the directory window, you select the Size and Set System Default options of the View Other dialog box. If you want additional information displayed, simply select additional options.

How to Change the Order Files Appear in a Directory Window

By default, the File Manager displays the files sorted alphabetically by name in a directory window. The File Manager View pull-down menu lets you also display the files by type (extension), size, or modification date. The Type option directs the File Manager to display the files in alphabetical order by extension. When you select the Sort option, your screen displays the dialog box shown in Figure 20.4.

This dialog box lets you select the ordering method you want the File Manager to use when it displays the files in a directory window. By selecting the Set System Default option, you can specify the *sort order* for all windows the File Manager opens.

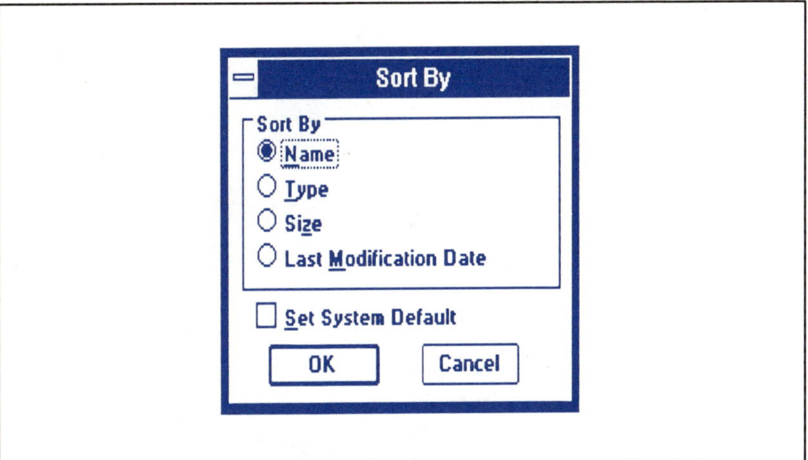

Figure 20.4: View menu Sort option dialog box

How to Restrict File Name Display to Files of a Specific Type

By default, the File Manager displays every file in a subdirectory in its directory window. The View menu Include option lets you control which file *types* the File Manager displays. When you select the Include option, your screen displays the dialog box shown in Figure 20.5.

The asterisks following the Name option tell you the File Manager is displaying all of the files that match the attributes that follow. If you want to reduce the directory listing to only executable program files, change ***.*** to ***.EXE**. The File Type options let you select files by type. Table 20.1 briefly describes each option.

As the number of files in your directory increases, you may have difficulty locating a specific file. By displaying only a specific file type, you can reduce the number of files on your screen, which makes locating an individual file much easier. As before, the Set System Default option lets you define the file types you want the File Manager to display for all windows it opens. Most users don't change the file types the File Manager displays.

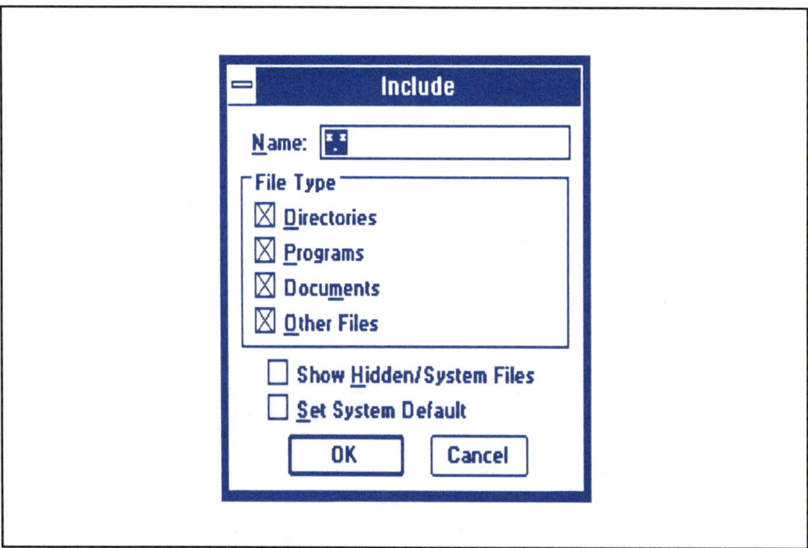

Figure 20.5: *View menu Include option dialog box*

Table 20.1: *File Types Distinguished by the File Manager.*

FILE TYPE	CORRESPONDING FILES
Directories	All subdirectories within the current directory
Programs	All files with the extension EXE, COM, BAT or PIF
Documents	All text and graphics files associated with an application
Other Files	All remaining files not classified by an option listed above
Show Hidden/ System Files	Files with either the system or hidden attribute set—normally essential DOS files in the root

How to Reuse a Directory Window

By default, each time you select a directory, the File Manager opens a new directory window. So even if you just want to quickly examine a directory's contents, you might end up with several open directory windows that you then must close. The Replace On Open option in the the File Manager View menu directs the File Manager to replace the contents of the active directory window with a new list of files each time you select a directory (*reusing* the Window). By using Replace On Open, you can traverse through directories quickly without the clutter of many directory windows.

LESSON 21

Searching Your Disk for Specific Files

Featuring

- Disk and directory search operations

ALTHOUGH DOS SUBDIRECTORIES CAN GREATLY IMPROVE your disk organization, you may eventually misplace a file. One method of looking for the file is simply traversing each subdirectory on your disk using the File Manager. Fortunately, though, the File Manager File menu provides a much easier and faster technique via the *Search option*. Using the Search option, you can direct the File Manager to search a directory or your entire disk for a specific file or group of files.

How to Locate a File or Group of Files

To search your disk for files, you must first select the File Manager File menu using your mouse or the Alt+F keyboard combination. Next, select the Search option. The File Manager will display the dialog box shown in Figure 21.1, prompting you to enter the file name or wildcard combination you want to search for. The Search For option lets you type in the name of the desired file. If you are searching for a group of files, you can use the DOS wildcard characters.

The Search Entire Disk option lets you direct the File Manager to search either the entire disk or just the current directory. If you X the box to the left of the option, the File Manager will search the entire disk. If you remove the X, the File Manager will search only the current directory.

Right now, type in the file name **WIN.COM** and press Enter. The File Manager will search your disk for the specified file. If successful, the File Manager will open a directory window containing the path name to each matching file or group, as in Figure 21.2. If the File Manager cannot find a matching file, it will display a dialog box indicating a matching file was not found, as in Figure 21.3.

This command will search only the current disk drive. If you have a hard disk partitioned into a number of drives, which is common, you will have to do a separate search for each drive.

You can treat the window containing the Search results as you would any other directory window. If the window contains programs,

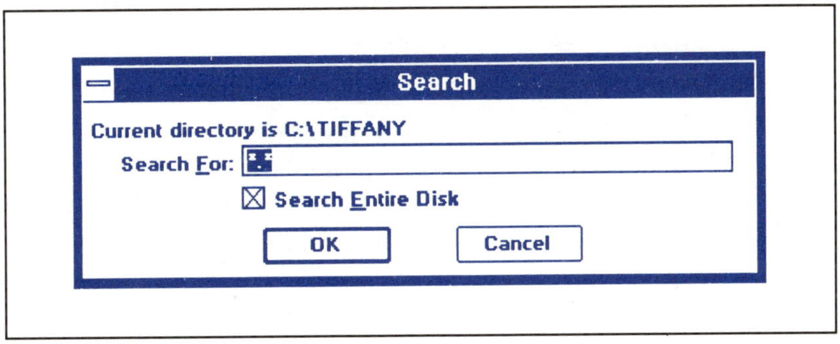

Figure 21.1: Search option dialog box

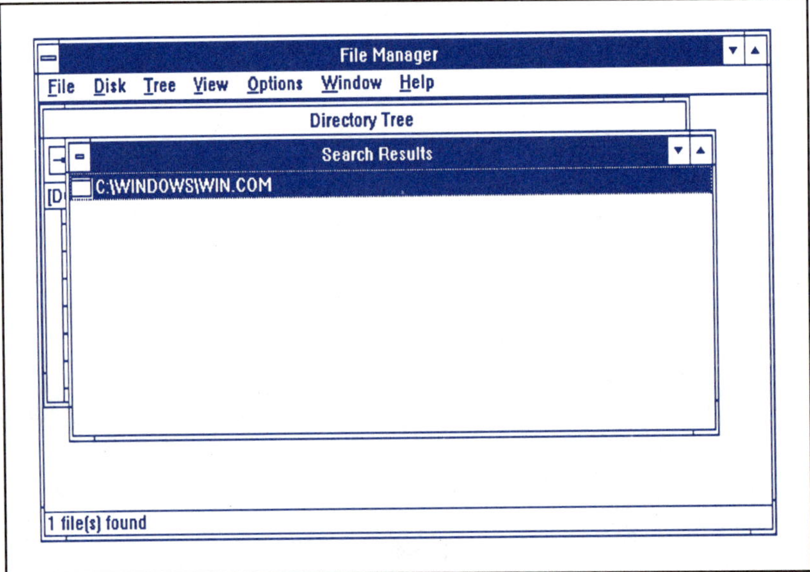

Figure 21.2: A directory window containing the path names for each file matching the search specifications

Figure 21.3: The File Search Error dialog box

you can execute them using point and shoot. If the window contains a directory, you can select and display it within its own directory window. Unlike a regular directory window, however, you can't change the order or format in which the File Manager displays file names in the search window. When you no longer need the Search Window, use its Control menu to close it.

As the number of files and directories on your disk increase, the ability to search quickly for specific files becomes very convenient.

LESSON 22

Selecting Groups of Files to Speed File Operations

Featuring

- Selection of successive files
- Selection of non-successive files
- Select All and Deselect All operations

LESSON 23 THROUGH 27 TEACH YOU HOW TO PERFORM common file operations such as copying, moving, printing, and deleting files. Using point and shoot, you can perform these operations quickly on a highlighted file. Many times, though, you will want to perform the same file operation on several files. In this lesson you will learn how to select multiple files for file operations.

How to Select a Group of Successive Files

Files whose names appear in the directory window in sequence, one immediately after the other, are called *successive* files. The screen in Figure 22.1 illustrates the selection of several successive files within the WINDOWS subdirectory.

To select a group of successive files using your mouse, aim the mouse pointer at the first file in the group and click. Next, aim the mouse pointer at the last file in the group, hold down the Shift key, and click.

To select a group of successive files using your keyboard, highlight the first file in the group. Then, holding down the Shift key, use the arrow keys to highlight the remaining files in the group.

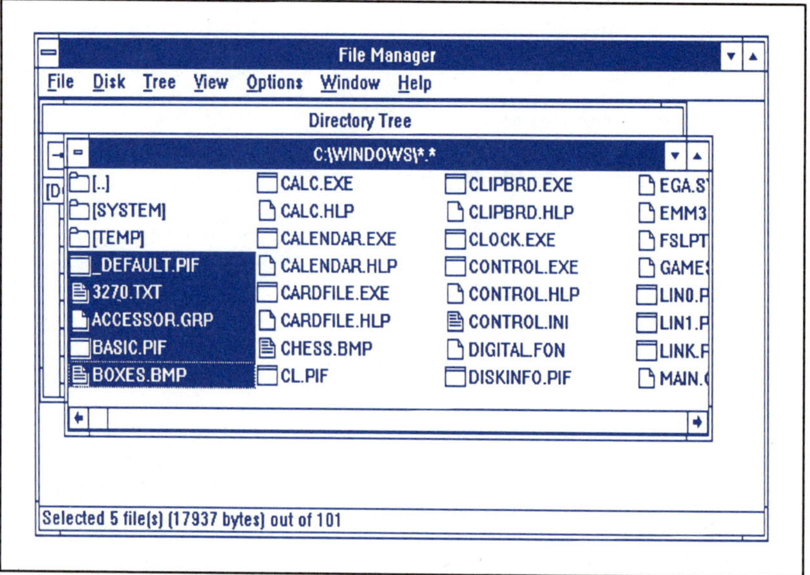

Figure 22.1: Selection of successive files

How to Select a Group of Non-Successive Files

In many cases, the files you want to work with will not appear successively within the directory tree. The screen in Figure 22.2

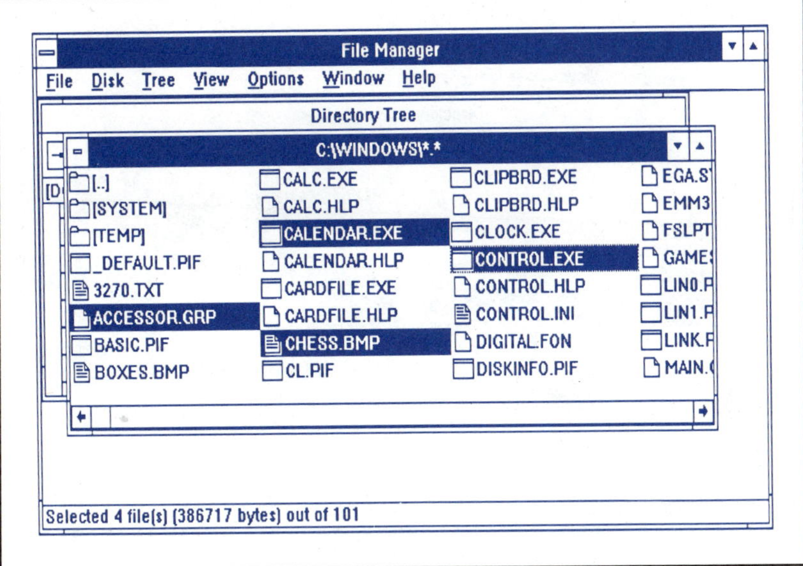

Figure 22.2: Selection of non-successive files

illustrates the selection of several *non-successive files* within the WINDOWS directory.

To select a group of non-successive files using your mouse, aim the mouse pointer at a desired file, hold down the Ctrl key and click. Repeat this step for each file in the group.

To select a group of non-successive files using your keyboard, press Shift+F8. The file highlight selector will begin to blink. Use the arrow keys to highlight the desired files, pressing the spacebar to select them.

How to Select Non-Successive Groups of Successive Files

Depending on the directory, there may be times when the desired files fall into several non-successive groups that contain successive files, as in Figure 22.3.

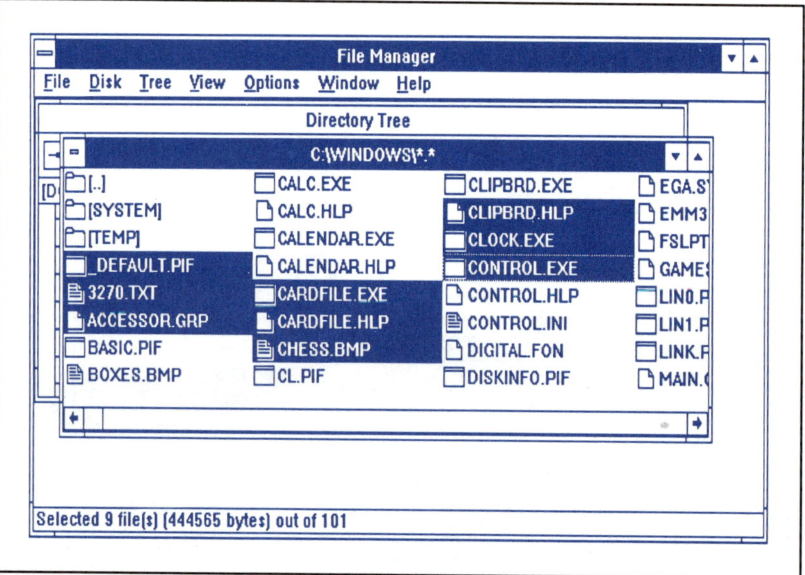

Figure 22.3: Non-successive groups of successive files

Select the first group by clicking on the first file, holding down the Shift key, and clicking on the last file. For the remaining groups, hold down the Ctrl key when you click on the first file and the Ctrl+Shift keys when you click on the last file.

Select the first group by highlighting the first file and then hold down the Shift key while using the arrow keys to highlight the remaining files. To select additional groups, press Shift+F8. With the selection cursor blinking, move the cursor to the first file in the next group and press the spacebar. Then, hold down the Shift key while you use the arrow keys to select additional files. After you have selected the last group of files, press Shift+F8 once again.

How to Select All the Files in a Directory Window

Depending on your application, there may be times when you want a file operation to apply to every file in a directory window. To do this, choose the File menu *Select All* option or press the keyboard combination Ctrl+Slash (/).

How to Cancel a File Selection

If you inadvertently select a file you don't want to include, you can cancel its file selection leaving the other selected files unchanged.

To cancel a selection with your mouse, aim the mouse pointer at the file to be removed, hold down the Ctrl key, and click.

To cancel a file selection using your keyboard, press Shift+F8, which will cause the selector cursor to blink. Using the arrow keys, select the file you want to remove from the list. Press the spacebar to cancel the file selection. After you have canceled all files you want to remove, press Shift+F8 again.

How to Cancel All File Selections

If you want to cancel all of the file selections you have made, choose the File menu *Deselect All* option or press the Ctrl+Backslash (\) keyboard combination.

LESSON 23

Printing One or More Files with the File Manager

Featuring

- The Windows Print Manager
- Multiple file print operations

AS DISCUSSED, FILES LET YOU STORE INFORMATION from one computer session to the next. Files can contain letters, reports, spreadsheet information, or programs such as Windows itself. As you work with your computer you will create files that you will want to print. If you are creating the files with a Windows application program, such as Write or Paintbrush, you should use the application itself to print the file to ensure that correct formatting is used. Almost all Windows applications provide a Print option in the File menu. If you want to print a regular text file such as a DOS batch or other ASCII file, you can use the File Manager.

Understanding ASCII Files

Many of the files on your disk, such as programs with the EXE or COM extension, contain information that is meaningless if you print it. Likewise, many word processing files contain special characters required for paragraph or line formatting. If you attempt to print such files, your printed output (or hardcopy) will contain many meaningless characters.

When you store information in your computer or on disk, your computer represents each character and number using a unique value called an ASCII value. So when you create a DOS batch file or a simple memo, the computer doesn't actually store the letters such as A, B, or C. Files that don't contain programs or other unique embedded word processing or spreadsheet values are called ASCII or text files. Using the File Manager Print option you can print ASCII files.

How to Print One File at a Time

In most cases you will print only one file at a time. Begin by highlighting the desired file. Using either your mouse or Alt+F, invoke the File menu. Select the Print option and the File Manager will display a dialog box displaying the current directory's name and the selected file, as in Figure 23.1. If the information displayed is correct, select the OK option. If you want to print a different file, press the backspace key and type the desired file name. When you select the OK option to print the file, Windows will run the Print Manager.

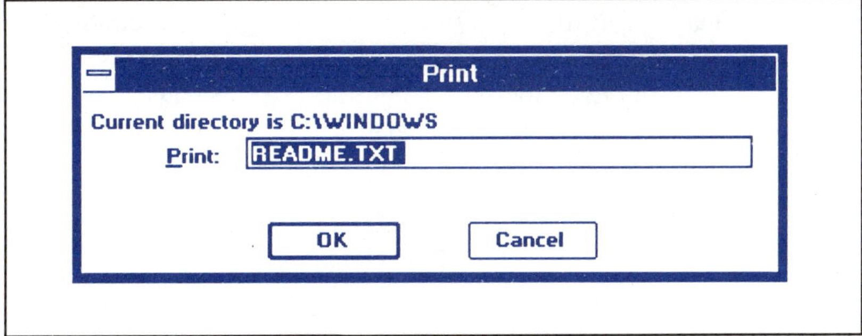

Figure 23.1: The Print option dialog box

Understanding the Print Manager

As you have learned, the Windows Program Manager helps you run programs that reside in a program group. Likewise, the Windows File Manager helps you organize and work with your files and directories. When you print files from within Windows, the *Print Manager* runs to oversee printer operations.

When you use DOS, you can run only one program at a time. As such, only one program can attempt to use the printer at any given time. Windows, though, lets you run and print several programs simultaneously.

If two or more programs wrote to the printer at the same time, your printer output would contain a mixture of both programs' output. Therefore, the Windows Print Manager controls printer access, ensuring that one program's printer output does not interfere with another's. If two or more programs try to print at the same time, the Print Manager determines which program will print first. In Lesson 57 you will examine the Print Manager in detail. For now, simply think of the Print Manager as a traffic cop who oversees printer operations. When Windows runs the Print Manager, your screen will contain the Print Manager icon near the bottom of the screen, as shown in Figure 23.2.

How to Print Multiple Files at One Time

In Lesson 22 you learned to select several files for use in file operations. To print several files at one time, select the files as discussed in Lesson 22 and then invoke the File menu Print option. As before, the File Manager will display a dialog box asking you to continue or cancel the operation. The File Manager will display as many file names as it can in the dialog box. Then the Print Manager will print the files in the order they appear in the directory window.

How to Solve Printer Problems

If you select a file for printing and nothing prints, you may have to use the Windows Control Panel as discussed in Lesson 52 to

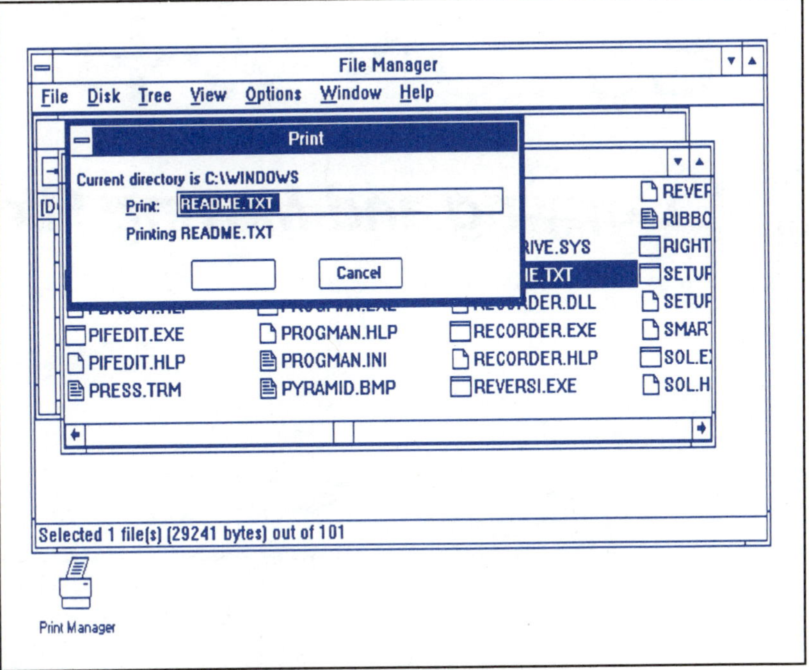

Figure 23.2: Print Manager icon

change your printer configuration. In most cases, the Print Manager will display an error message dialog box informing you of the printer problem.

LESSON 24

Copying and Moving Files

Featuring

- File and directory copying
- File and directory relocation

JUST AS THERE ARE TIMES WHEN YOU MUST COPY THE files in a filing cabinet or move them from one drawer to another, the same is true for files stored on your disk. Using the File Manager you can quickly move or copy a file, a group of files, or even an entire directory tree.

How to Copy a File or Group of Files

The Windows File Manager lets you *copy* a file from one directory to another or to a different disk drive.

When using your mouse, you must follow the same steps, whether you are copying files to another disk or to another directory. To begin, make sure you can see both the window containing the files you want to copy and the window containing either the target directory or the target disk-drive icon. You may need to tile your windows or move a window to make both visible. Next, select the file or group of files you want to copy. If you select a directory, the File Manager will copy all of its subdirectories. While holding down the Ctrl key, aim the mouse pointer into the target directory or at the target disk-drive icon. (You need to hold down the Ctrl key only if you are copying onto the same disk. For copying to a different drive, you do not need to hold down the Ctrl key.) As you move the mouse pointer out of the directory window, the pointer will change into either a subdirectory icon or one of several file icons, depending on your file copy operation. When you release the mouse select button, the File Manager will display the dialog box shown in Figure 24.1, asking you to confirm the file copy operation. To copy the file or files, select the Yes option.

To copy files from one directory to another disk or directory, first select the desired files or directory. If you are copying a directory, the File Manager will copy the entire directory tree. Next, use Alt+F to invoke the File menu and choose the Copy option. The File Manager will display the dialog box in Figure 24.2, listing the names of the file or files to copy and prompting you to enter the target drive or directory.

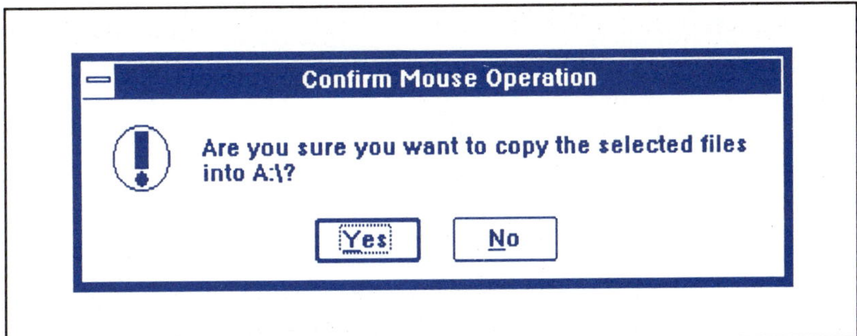

Figure 24.1: *File copy confirmation dialog box*

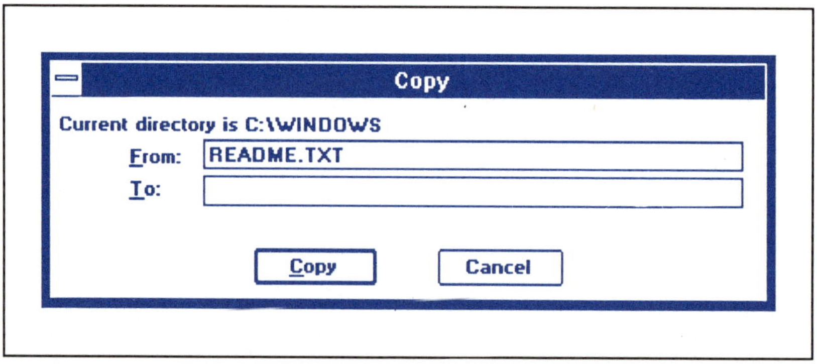

Copy
Current directory is C:\WINDOWS
From: README.TXT
To:
Copy Cancel

Figure 24.2: Copy option dialog box

Type in the name of the target subdirectory or the drive letter and a colon (for example, **A:**) and press Enter to select the Copy option.

How to Move a File or Group of Files

The steps to *moving* a file or subdirectory from one directory to another directory or drive are very similar to those used to copy a file. If you are using a mouse, simply hold down the Alt key instead of the Ctrl key, which you used to copy files. If using the keyboard, select the File menu Move option instead of Copy.

Overwriting Existing Files

By default, the File Manager prompts you before overwriting the contents of an existing file during a move or copy operation by displaying the dialog box in Figure 24.3.

If you want to overwrite the existing file's contents, select the Yes option. To leave the existing file unchanged and continue with the copy operation, select the No option. To abort the file copy operation, select Cancel.

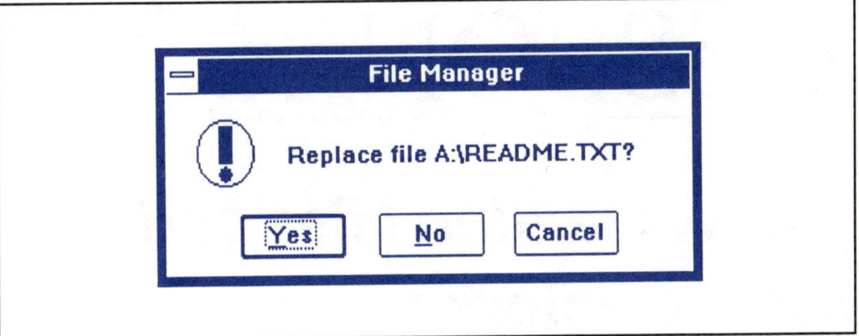

Figure 24.3: Existing file dialog box

How to Resolve Disk Full Errors

Should your target disk run out of space during a file copy or move operation, the File Manager will display a dialog box like the one in Figure 24.4, informing you the target disk is full. Select the OK option to continue. Note that if the target disk runs out of space during a move operation, the File Manager may move only some of your files to the target directory, leaving portions of files in two directories. If this error message occurs, copy the remaining files to a second disk to ensure your copy or move operation is complete.

Figure 24.4: Disk full dialog box

LESSON 25

Renaming Files and Directories

Featuring

- Renaming an existing subdirectory

AS YOU KNOW, FILES LET YOU STORE INFORMATION FROM one computer session to another. You can treat DOS files the way you would treat files in a filing cabinet. For example, you can create files, copy their contents, move them to new locations, delete them when they are no longer needed, and rename them as needed. The Windows File Manager lets you perform all of these operations with a single file or a group of files. In this lesson, you will examine the File Manager's file *renaming* capabilities. Unlike the DOS RENAME command, which lets you rename only files, the Windows File Manager lets you rename even subdirectories.

How to Rename a File or Subdirectory

Using your keyboard or mouse, select the file or subdirectory that you want to rename. Next, invoke the File menu and choose the Rename option. The File Manager will display a dialog box prompting you to enter the new file name, as in Figure 25.1.

Type in the new file name and press Enter. When you rename a file, you cannot specify a disk-drive letter or subdirectory path before the new file name. If you do, the File Manager will display the dialog box in Figure 25.2, telling you that you can't rename a file from one disk or directory to another.

Also, if you attempt to rename a file with the name of an existing file in the target directory, the File Manager will display a dialog box telling you a file with the name specified already exists. This dialog box, shown in Figure 25.3, gives you the option of overwriting

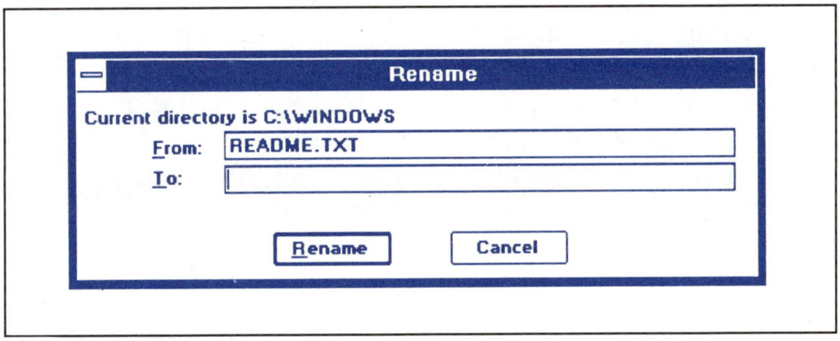

Rename
Current directory is C:\WINDOWS
From: README.TXT
To:
Rename Cancel

Figure 25.1: Rename option dialog box

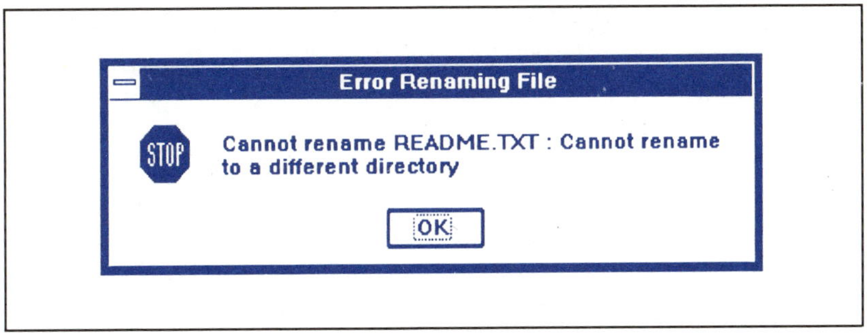

Error Renaming File
STOP
Cannot rename README.TXT : Cannot rename to a different directory
OK

Figure 25.2: Illegal rename target file dialog box

Figure 25.3: Renaming a file to overwrite an existing file

the existing file. If this dialog box appears, select the No or Cancel option. A File Rename operation cannot overwrite an existing file. The File Manager File Move operation performs that task. If you select the Yes option to overwrite the existing file, the File Manager will display a dialog box containing an Access Denied error message. Expect this dialog box to disappear in future versions of Windows.

Renaming a subdirectory requires the same steps as a File Rename operation. Simply select the desired directory name and choose the File menu Rename option. When the File Manager displays its dialog box prompting you to enter the new subdirectory name, type in the directory name with a drive letter or subdirectory path.

LESSON 26

Deleting Files and Directories

Featuring

- Deleting one or more files
- Deleting a directory tree
- Deleting a read-only file

JUST AS THE FILE MANAGER LETS YOU CREATE FILES AND subdirectories when you need them, it also lets you delete them when they are no longer needed. If you have used the DOS DEL command to delete files in the past, you will find that the File Manager gives you much greater file selection capabilities when you want to delete a group of files. In addition, the File Manager lets you delete not only files in a subdirectory, but also subdirectories below a directory. Using the File Manager, you can quickly delete an entire directory tree. Be very careful when you use the File Manager to delete files, though, because once you delete a file, the File Manager does not provide a way to get it back.

How to Delete One or More Files

To begin, select the file or files you want to delete. Using your mouse or Alt+F, invoke the File Manager File menu and choose the Delete option. The File Manager will display the dialog box in Figure 26.1, listing the current directory and the files you have selected for deletion.

To complete the file deletion, select the Delete option. To return to the File Manager without deleting the files, select Cancel. If you choose the File menu Delete option without preselecting files, you can type in the name of each file you want to delete.

By default, the File Manager will prompt you for each individual file you have selected to ensure you want to delete the file. To delete the file, select the Yes option, to leave the file on disk, select No, and to end the delete operation, select Cancel. The File Manager refers to the dialog box in Figure 26.2 as a confirmation box. Using

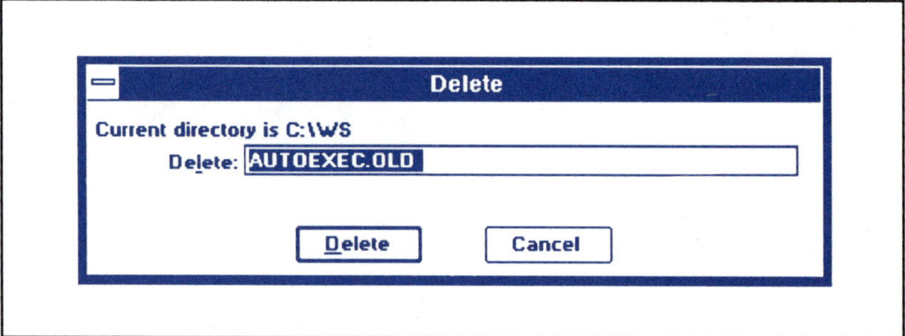

Figure 26.1: Delete option dialog box

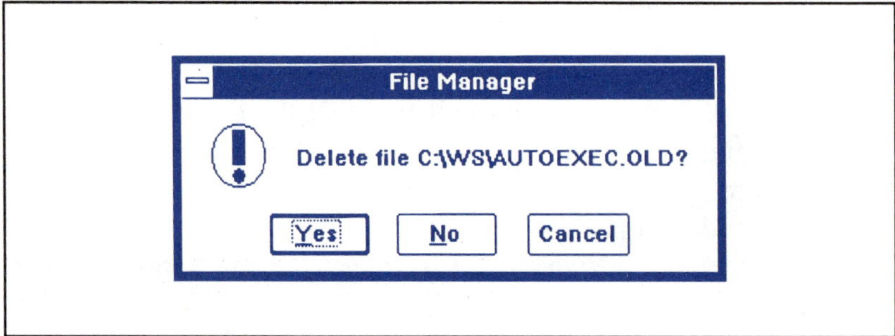

Figure 26.2: Delete file confirmation dialog box

confirmation boxes, the File Manager can ensure (or confirm) you really want to perform a specific operation. In Lesson 29 you will learn how to enable and disable the display of various confirmation boxes. This can increase the speed of your operations as you become more conversant with Windows.

How to Delete a Subdirectory

To delete a subdirectory using the File Manager, you perform the same steps as for a file deletion, selecting instead the name of a subdirectory. As before, select the File menu Delete option. When you use the File Manager to delete a subdirectory, the File Manager will delete all of the branches below the subdirectory. For example, assume your directory contains the branches shown in Figure 26.3. If you delete the directory WORDPROC, the File Manager will also delete the directories below WORDPROC, resulting in the directory structure shown in Figure 26.4.

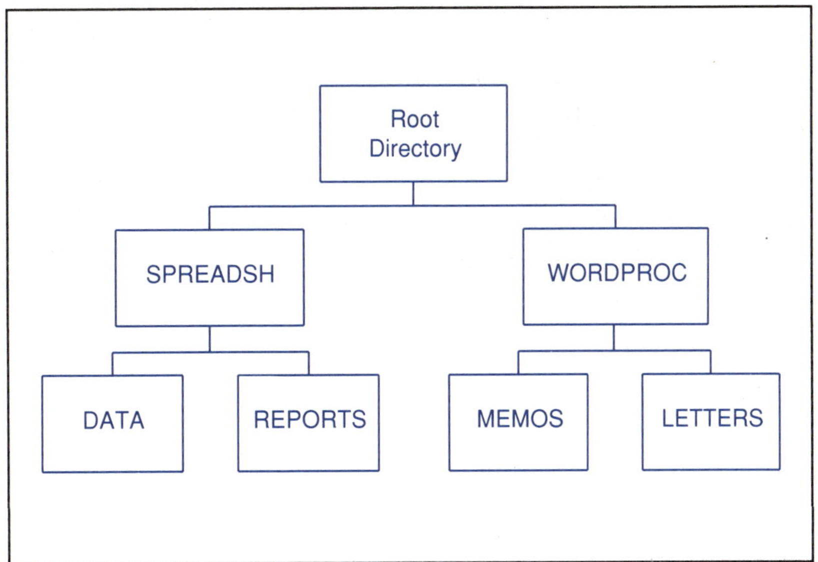

Figure 26.3: Directory tree prior to a subdirectory delete operation

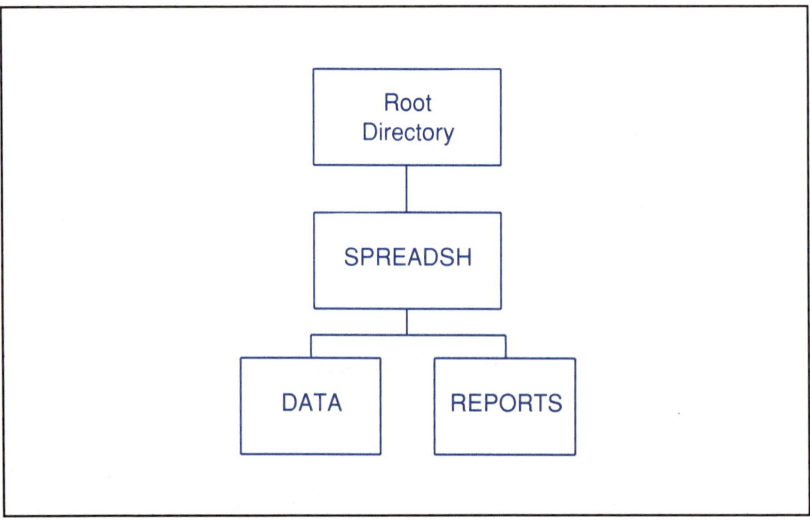

Figure 26.4: *Directory structure following a subdirectory delete operation*

How to Delete Read-Only Files

In Lesson 27 you will examine DOS file attributes and learn how to set a file's Read-Only attribute, thereby preventing it from being deleted inadvertently. If you attempt to delete a file set as read-only, the File Manager displays the confirmation box shown in Figure 26.5, warning you that the file has been set to read-only, but providing you with a means of overriding the setting to delete the file. To delete the read-only file, select Yes. To leave the read-only file on disk, select No.

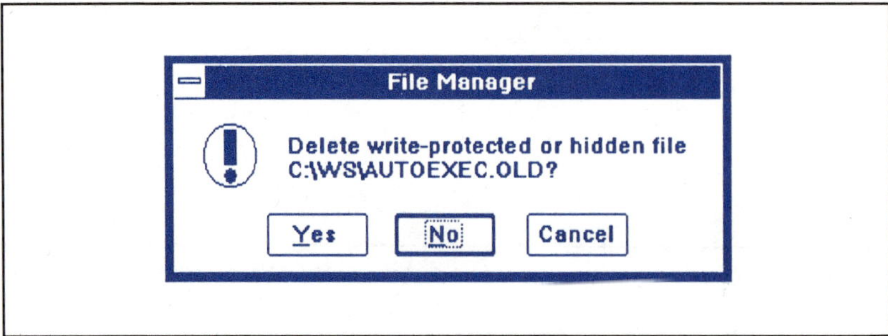

Figure 26.5: *Delete read-only file confirmation dialog box*

Warning! Don't Run Undelete Utilities in Windows

Once you delete a file with the File Manager, the File Manager does not provide you with a way to get the file back. There are, however, third-party software packages available that can undelete files. If you have such software, do not use it in Windows. Always close Windows first and exit to the DOS prompt before you use a disk utility program. Running such programs from within Windows may damage data structures on your disk, resulting in a loss of information.

LESSON 27

Understanding and Setting DOS File Attributes

Featuring

- Defining the DOS file attributes
- When to assign file attributes
- Assigning one or more attributes

TO PROTECT YOUR FILES FROM BEING OVERWRITTEN OR deleted inadvertently, and to assist in file backup operations, DOS lets you assign attribute values to each file on your disk. In Lesson 20 you learned how to display a file's attributes in a directory window by selecting the File Details option from File Manager View menu. In this lesson you will learn both how to set file attributes and when you would want to do so.

How to Understand DOS File Attributes

DOS uses six *file attributes* to manage your files. Table 27.1 briefly describes each attribute.

Table 27.1: *Description of the DOS File Attributes*

ATTRIBUTE	MEANING
Read-Only	DOS can display or print the file's contents, but DOS cannot overwrite or delete the file.
Archive	The file has been created or changed since the last backup operation.
Hidden	Although the file resides in a directory, the file will not appear in the directory listing. This option is normally reserved for DOS system files.
System	The file is a DOS system file, used to start your system. The file will not appear in a directory listing.
Subdirectory	The name specified is a subdirectory containing a list of DOS files.
Volume	The name specified corresponds to the disk's volume label or name.

Although DOS uses these six file attribute types, the File Manager does not let you access the Volume-Label and Subdirectory attributes. These two attributes are strictly for DOS file management. Most DOS users use only the DOS Read-Only, Archive, and periodically, the Hidden File attributes. Although the File Manager also lets users set a file's System attribute, use of the System attribute should be restricted to DOS.

When to Use the Read-Only Attribute

As you work with your computer, you will create, change, and delete files on a regular basis. By default, DOS lets you delete or overwrite the files that appear in your directory. Unfortunately, an errant DOS command can overwrite or delete critical files. The DOS Read-Only attribute lets you protect files against overwriting or deletion. When you set a file as Read-Only, DOS can print or display the file's contents or even execute the file if it contains a program, but DOS cannot change or delete the file's contents. By setting those files whose contents don't change to Read-Only, you reduce the risk of losing them through an inadvertent command. When you do need to change the file's contents, you can remove the Read-Only attribute, modify the file, and then reset it to Read-Only, once again protecting against file loss.

When to Use the Archive Attribute

When you perform disk backup operations, using either the DOS BACKUP command or a third-party backup utility, you can reduce the amount of time the backup requires by backing up only those files that have been created or changed since the previous backup. DOS uses file Archive attributes to determine which files to back up. Each time you create or change a file's contents, DOS sets its Archive attribute to indicate the file needs backing up. Later, when the file is successfully backed up, DOS removes the Archive attribute. The Archive attribute gives DOS better control of your file backup, letting you back up your entire disk or only those files whose contents have changed since your last backup. By setting or clearing a file's Archive attribute, you can instruct DOS to include or exclude it from the next backup operation.

When to Use the Hidden Attribute

A hidden file is a file that exists on your disk but does not appear in a directory listing and is unaffected by DOS commands. The programs that start your computer are critical to proper system operation. Therefore, DOS hides these files to prevent users from deleting, renaming, or moving them. In some instances, users hide files to prevent other users from knowing the files exist. As you'll recall from Lesson 20, the File Manager does not display hidden or system files in a directory window unless you tell it to. However, to reduce the possibility of losing a file that you have forgotton is hidden, you should minimize your use of hidden files.

How to Set File Attributes

To set file attributes for one or more files, select the file or files and choose the Change Attributes option from the File Manager File menu. The File Manager will display the dialog box shown in Figure 27.1, letting you select the desired attributes.

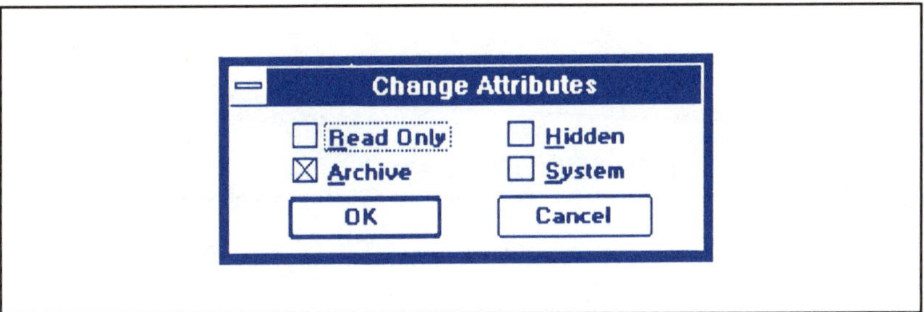

Figure 27.1: File attributes dialog box

Note that any changes you make in the dialog box will affect all selected files.

To select a file attribute using the mouse, aim the mouse pointer at the desired file attribute and click. Repeat this step for each desired attribute. Select the OK option to assign the attributes.

To select a file attribute using your keyboard, press the Tab key to highlight the attribute desired. Next, press the spacebar to select the attribute. (Note that you can also deselect with the spacebar; it acts as a toggle.) Repeat these steps for each desired attribute. Press Enter to assign the attributes.

LESSON 28

Performing Common Disk Operations

Featuring

- Disk-copy operations
- Formatting bootable and non-system floppy disks
- Assigning disk-volume labels
- Transferring DOS system files to a floppy disk

ALTHOUGH MOST OF YOUR WINDOWS DISK OPERATIONS—such as creating and deleting files—occur on your hard disk, you will periodically need to copy and format floppy disks to make backup copies of your files. The File Manager lets you quickly perform these common disk operations from its Disk menu, shown in Figure 28.1.

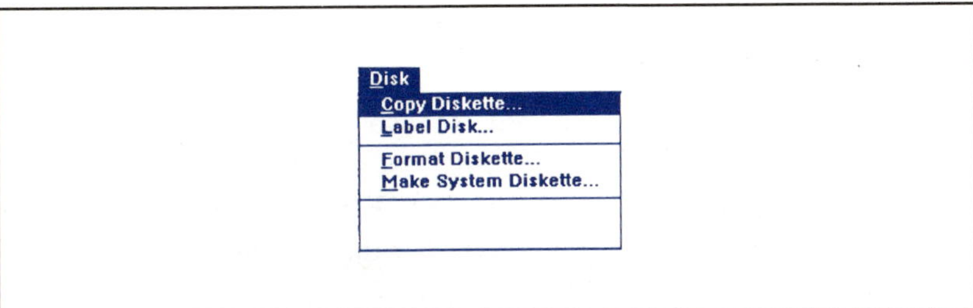

Figure 28.1: File Manager Disk menu

How to Copy a Disk

The Disk menu Copy Diskette option lets you copy the contents of one floppy disk to another. The option behaves much like the DOS DISKCOPY command in that the copy operation will make an exact duplicate of the source disk, overwriting the destination disk's existing contents. Also like DISKCOPY, the disk you are copying to must be the same size as the disk you are copying from.

To copy a disk, you must first select the floppy-disk drive containing the source disk as the default drive. Next, invoke the Copy Diskette option. If your computer has two floppy-disk drives, the File Manager will prompt you to select the drive containing the destination disk. If your computer has only one disk drive, you will have to swap the source and destination disks in the drive throughout the disk-copy operation. The File Manager will display a dialog box prompting you to insert either the source or destination disk at the correct times.

As discussed, the Copy Diskette option overwrites the destination disk's contents. As such, the File Manager will display a dialog box warning you that the copy operation will overwrite the destination disk. To continue the disk-copy operation, select the Copy option. If you don't want to continue the operation, select Cancel.

If you continue the operation, the File Manager will display a dialog box that continually displays the status of the operation (percentage completed). You can end the operation at any time by selecting the dialog box's Cancel option. However, if you end the operation before it is completed, the information contained on the destination disk will be incomplete and unusable.

How to Assign a Disk Label

DOS lets you assign a name to every disk you create, called a disk volume label. Most hard-disk users simply assign the name DOS to their disk or leave it unnamed. However, assigning volume names to your disks helps you remember the files you have placed on them. For example, if you store budget files on a floppy, you might name the disk BUDGET91.

As discussed in Lesson 13, if your disk has a volume name assigned to it, the File Manager displays the volume name in brackets below the disk-drive icons. The Disk menu Label Disk option lets you assign or change a disk's volume name.

Place a formatted floppy disk in drive A and select drive A as the default drive. Next, select the Label Disk option. The File Manager will display a dialog box prompting you to enter a disk-volume label, as shown in Figure 28.2. A disk-volume label can contain up to 11 characters. Depending on your DOS version, the name may include blank characters. In this case, type the name **WINDOWS** and press Enter. The File Manager will assign the volume name to your disk, displaying the volume name below the disk-drive icons that appear in the File Manager window.

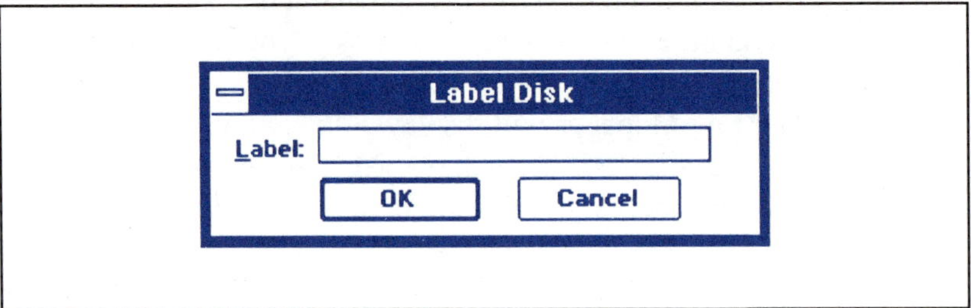

Figure 28.2: Disk-volume label dialog box

How to Format a Floppy Disk for Use by DOS

Before DOS can store information on disk, the disk must be formatted for use by DOS. The File Manager lets you quickly format disks of all sizes, optionally creating a system disk you can use later to start your computer. Best of all, unlike the DOS FORMAT command, you don't have to remember difficult command lines.

To format a disk using the File Manager, place an unused disk into the floppy-disk drive. Next, select the Disk menu Format Diskette option. If your computer has more than one floppy drive, the File Manager will display a dialog box prompting you to select the drive containing the disk you want to format.

When you format a disk, all information on the disk is erased. If you inadvertently format a floppy disk containing valuable information, you cannot get the information back. To reduce the possibility of an inadvertent disk format, the File Manager will display a dialog box prompting you to verify that you want to continue the operation.

If you choose to continue the disk format, the File Manager will display a dialog box prompting you to specify the format options (Figure 28.3).

The High Capacity option lets you format a 1.2Mb or 1.44Mb disk. If you need to format a 360K or 720K disk, do not select the High Capacity option. The Make System Disk option lets you direct the File Manager to include the DOS system files on the disk after the format operation completes.

A DOS system disk is one containing several hidden files that DOS needs to start your system. If you are not planning to use a floppy disk to start DOS, don't place these hidden files on your disk, since they consume valuable disk space.

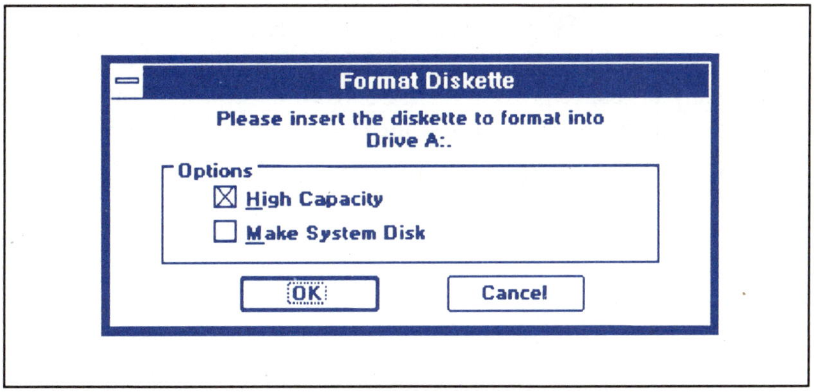

Figure 28.3: Disk format options dialog box

A non-system disk is a disk formatted for use by DOS, but that does not contain the hidden startup files. To create a non-system disk, remove this option from the dialog box. When you select OK to continue formatting, the File Manager will display a message box showing the progress of the operation (percentage completed). When the operation is finished, the File Manager will display a dialog box that asks you if you want to format additional disks. If you select Yes, the File Manager will prompt you to insert a new floppy disk, and the operation will repeat. If you select No, you will return to the File Manager window.

How to Add DOS System Files to a Previously Formatted Disk

As we discussed, a system disk is one containing the hidden system files that DOS needs to start your computer. If you have a formatted disk that does not contain other files, the Make System Disk option on the Disk menu lets you transfer the hidden files to the disk.

When you select this option, the File Manager will ask you to select the disk drive containing the target disk. Next, the File Manager will display a dialog box asking you to verify that you want to copy the hidden system files to the disk. If you select Yes to continue, the File Manager will attempt to transfer the files.

The difficulty in transferring system files to a disk already containing files is that DOS requires system files to reside in the disk's first two directory entries. If your disk contains other files, these two entries may be used, preventing DOS from accessing them. In such cases, the File Manager cannot transfer the hidden files and will display the dialog box shown in Figure 28.4. Should this dialog box appear, format an unused disk as a system disk and then copy the files from the original disk to the newly formatted system disk.

Network Operations

If your computer is connected to a local area network (LAN), the File Manager will display disk-drive icons for available network

Figure 28.4: *Dialog box displayed when a Make System Disk operation fails*

drives. Using the Disk menu, you can inform the File Manager about additional network drives (connect) or remove a network drive from your list of drive icons (disconnect). Depending on your network software, the steps you must follow to access your network disks will differ. For specifics, see your network administrator.

LESSON 29

Eliminating Confirmation Dialog Boxes

Featuring

- Speeding up file deletion and copying

IN LESSON 26 YOU USED THE FILE MANAGER TO DELETE single files, groups of files, and even directory trees. Each time you attempted to delete a file, the File Manager displayed a dialog box to confirm that you really wanted to delete the file. If you use the File Manager regularly to delete groups of files, continually responding to confirmation dialog boxes can become quite time consuming.

After you are comfortable performing file operations such as moving, copying, or deleting files, you can direct the File Manager to *suppress* the display of several confirmation dialog boxes.

How to Suppress Confirmation Dialog Boxes

Using your mouse or Alt+O, invoke the Options menu, as in Figure 29.1. Next, select the Confirmation option and the File Manager will display a dialog box containing four confirmation options, as in Figure 29.2. Table 29.1 briefly describes these options.

To prevent inadvertent file deletions or overwrites, most users should leave the confirmation boxes enabled. If you are intentionally deleting many files from a directory or an entire directory branch, you can temporarily disable confirmation box display during the operation, later re-enabling the boxes after the operation is complete.

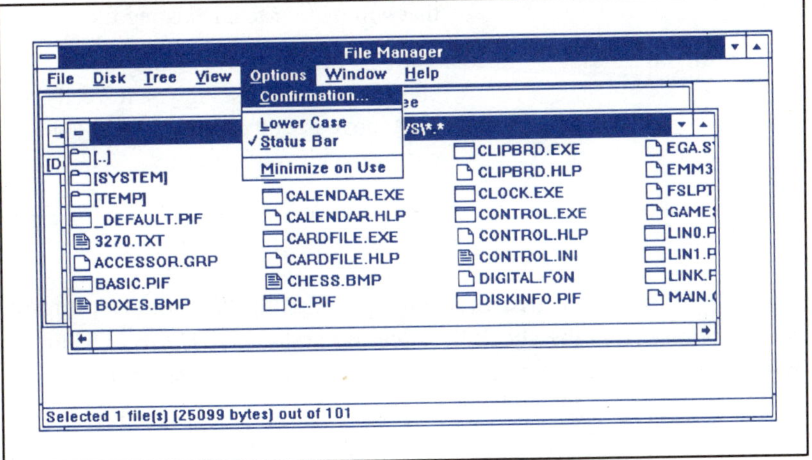

Figure 29.1: File Manager Options menu

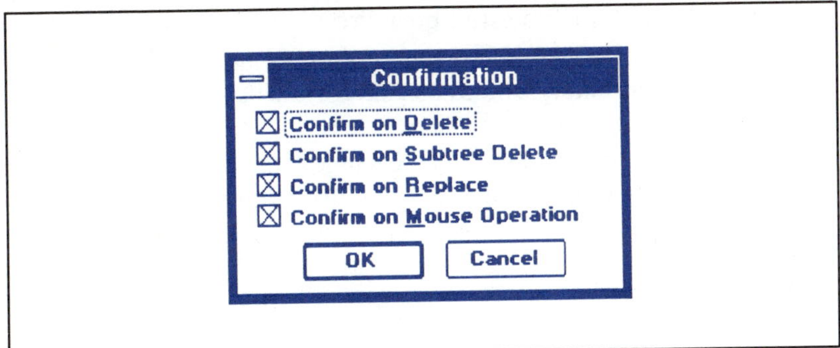

Figure 29.2: File Manager Confirmation dialog box

Table 29.1: *Summary of Confirmation Options.*

OPTION	CONFIRMATION RESULT
Confirm on Delete	The File Manager will display a confirmation dialog box asking you to verify every file you attempt to delete.
Confirm on Subtree Delete	The File Manager will display a confirmation dialog box asking you to verify each subdirectory deletion.
Confirm on Replace	The File Manager will display a confirmation dialog box asking you to verify each move or copy operation that will overwrite an existing file.
Confirm on Mouse	The File Manager will display a confirmation box asking you to verify each move or copy operation that you perform with your mouse.

To disable a confirmation box option using your mouse, aim the mouse pointer into the check box desired and click. The File Manager will remove the X. To enable a confirmation box, perform the same step with an empty check box and the File Manager will add the X.

To disable a confirmation box using your keyboard, press the Tab key to highlight the desired box. Press the spacebar and the File Manager will remove the X. To enable a confirmation box, repeat the same steps to an empty check box and the File Manager will add the X.

Note that if you select Save Changes when you exit the File Manager, any changes you made to confirmation boxes will become permanent.

LESSON 30

Other File Manager Options

Featuring

- Customizing the File Manager window
- Minimizing screen clutter by reducing the File Manager to an icon

IN LESSON 29 YOU USED THE FILE MANAGER OPTIONS menu to enable and disable confirmation dialog boxes. In this lesson you will use the Options menu's remaining options to display file and directory names in lowercase, to remove the available disk space status line, and to direct the File Manager to become an icon automatically each time you invoke a program.

How to Display File and Directory Names in Lowercase

By default, the File Manager displays file and subdirectory names in uppercase letters. Using the File Manager, open a directory window containing the files in the WINDOWS subdirectory. Next, using your mouse or Alt+O, invoke the Options menu and choose the Lowercase option. The File Manager will immediately redisplay the file names using lowercase letters as shown in Figure 30.1. Whether you choose to display file and subdirectory names in upper- or lowercase is simply your preference.

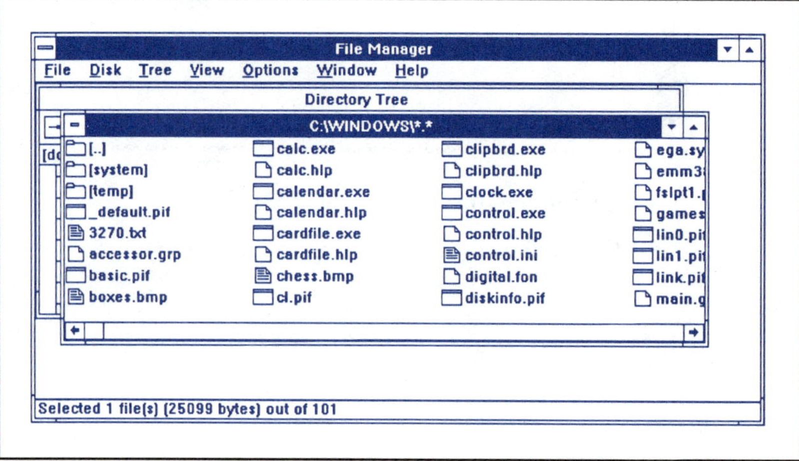

Figure 30.1: Displaying file and directory names in lowercase

How to Remove the Available Disk Space Status Bar

By default, at the bottom of the File Manager window, there is a status bar showing the amount of available disk space (in bytes) for the current disk. As you change drives, the File Manager automatically updates the status bar to reflect the current disk's available space.

The Options menu Status Bar option lets you remove and display this status bar. The check mark to the left of the Status Bar menu option tells you the File Manager will display the status bar. If you select this option, the File Manager will remove the check mark and the status bar. The option works as a toggle. The first time you select the option, the File Manager removes the status bar. The next time you select the option, the File Manager redisplays the status bar.

How to Automatically Reduce the File Manager to an Icon

You can run programs you have not yet assigned to an applications group by selecting the program's name from a directory window. Depending on the application you want to run, you may wish to iconize the File Manager to move its window out of the way.

The Options menu Minimize On Use option directs the File Manager to become an icon each time a program is run. If you need to access the File Manager later on, you can expand its icon as discussed in Lesson 9.

Other Ways to Run Programs

There are four ways to run programs in Windows. If you have a mouse, just double-click on the program's name. If you want to use your keyboard, select the file, then choose the File menu Open option. Note that you can use either your keyboard or mouse to run a program through the File menu Open dialog box. Finally, a program will open automatically if you use either of the first two methods listed above to open a document associated with that program.

LESSON 31

Associating a File or Group of Files with a Specific Program

Featuring

- Simplifying program execution

THE FILE MANAGER LETS YOU EXECUTE PROGRAMS WITH EXE or COM extensions or DOS batch files with the BAT extension simply by selecting them. To select a file, double-click on its icon, or highlight it and use the File Open command. In addition, the File Manager lets you invoke specific programs, such as the Windows Notepad or your own word processor, when you select files created with that or similar programs.

For example, the File Manager associates TXT extension files with the Windows Notepad. If you select a file with the TXT extension, the File Manager automatically invokes the Notepad, allowing you to edit or view the file's contents. By associating different file types with your commonly used application programs, you can greatly simplify executing programs.

How to Associate a File Type with a Specific Program

The File Manager associates file types with programs using file extensions, which you can manipulate as needed. For example, you may want to associate TXT files with the Windows Write word processor rather than the Windows Notepad. To do so, select a file with the TXT extension. Next, select the File menu and choose the Associate option. The File Manager will then display a dialog box showing you the current association, if one exists, letting you type in the name of the program you want associated with the file type, as in Figure 31.1.

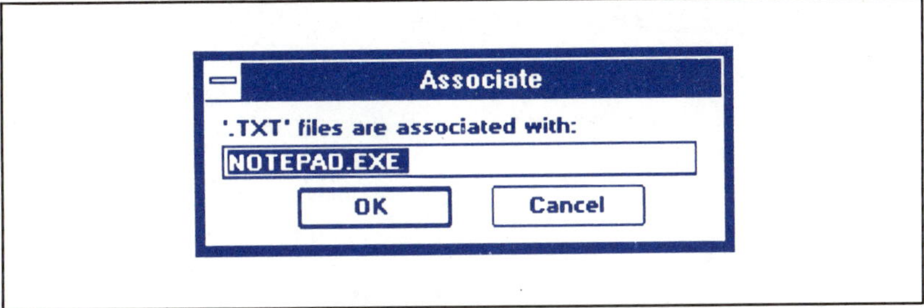

Figure 31.1: File association dialog box

To associate files with the TXT extension to the Write word processor, type in WRITE.EXE and press Enter. If you later select a file with the TXT extension, such as SYSINI.TXT in the WINDOWS subdirectory, the File Manager will invoke Write with the file as shown in Figure 31.2.

Lesson 40 examines the Write word processor in detail. For now, use the window's Control menu to close the window, ending the Write program. Do not save changes to the file.

Before you continue to Lesson 32, use the File menu Associate option to re-associate TXT files with the Windows Notepad (NOTEPAD.EXE) if you have changed the association.

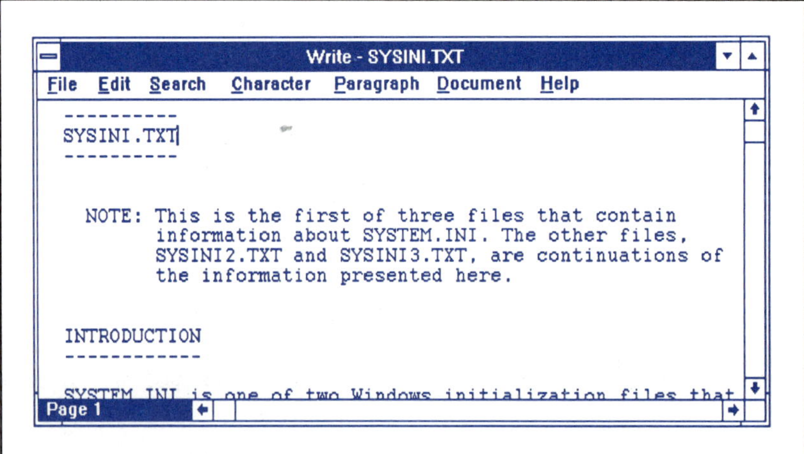

Figure 31.2: Write word processor with the file SYSINI.TXT

LESSON 32

Using the File Manager's On-line Help

Featuring

- Quick access to File Manager commands and topics

LESSONS 13 THROUGH 31 HAVE EXAMINED DIFFERENT File Manager capabilities in detail. As you work with the File Manager, remember that help is always at your fingertips. Like the Windows Program Manager, the File Manager has extensive on-line help.

To invoke the File Manager's help facility, select the Help menu option with your mouse or by pressing Alt+H. The File Manager will drop a pull-down menu with the options explained in Table 32.1.

Table 32.1: *File Manager Help Menu Options.*

MENU OPTION	DISCUSSION
Index	Displays an alphabetical listing of each available topic, letting you display help on your topic of interest.
Keyboard	Displays a listing of the keyboard hot keys defined for the current application.
Commands	Displays a listing of each option available in the pull-down menus for the current program and lets you display specific help text for each.
Procedures	Displays a detailed description of the steps you must follow to perform each feature of the current program, such as printing a file or selecting a specific option.
Using Help	Displays a description of the Windows Help program and Help's user interface.
About File Manager	Displays copyright information for the Windows File Manager.

Select the Index option, and the File Manager will create a Help window. Using the Help window's Control menu or Maximize button, expand the window to use the entire screen, as shown in Figure 32.1.

As you will recall, you can get additional help on each underlined topic. Using your mouse or the Tab key, choose the Associating Documents with an Application topic from the Procedures section. The File Manager will display a screen full of text, describing the steps you must follow to associate a file type with an application, as in Figure 32.2.

When you are done with the File Manager's on-line help, close the Help window to return to the File Manager.

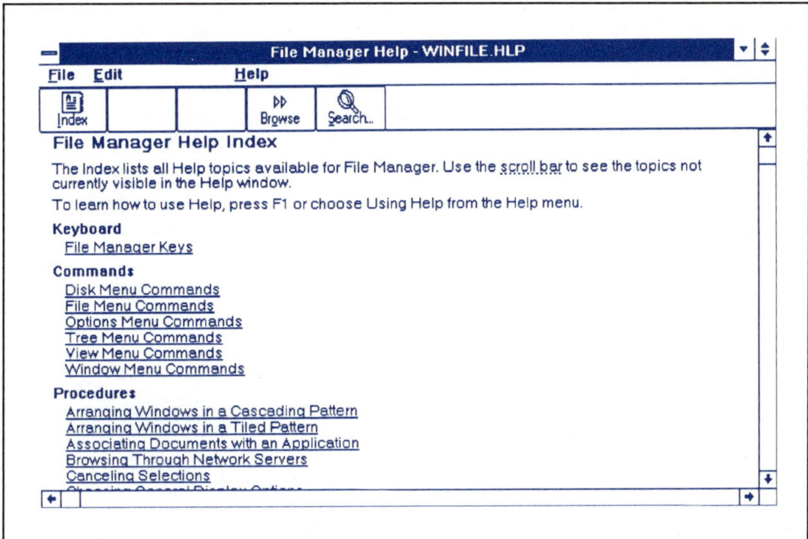

Figure 32.1: File Manager on-line Help Index

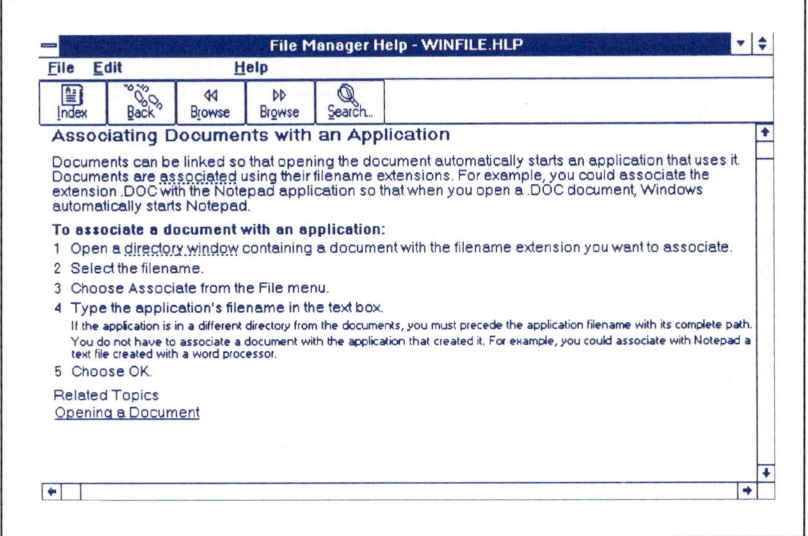

Figure 32.2: Help text on associating a file type to a program

PART III

Running Windows Accessory Programs

LESSON 33

Automating Your Desktop

Featuring

- Windows' Accessories group

ONE WAY THAT WINDOWS MAKES YOU MORE PRODUCTIVE is by making your computer seem a natural extension of your desk. Lesson 4 called the screen background behind your active windows the *desktop*. To help you use your computer more productively, Windows provides several software programs that correspond to items normally found on an office desk, such as a calculator or notepad. Windows calls these programs accessory programs. The lessons in Part III examine each accessory program.

How to Access the Windows Accessory Programs

Each time you invoke Windows, the Program Manager displays the screen in Figure 33.1 containing the primary Windows applications and several icons that correspond to available program groups.

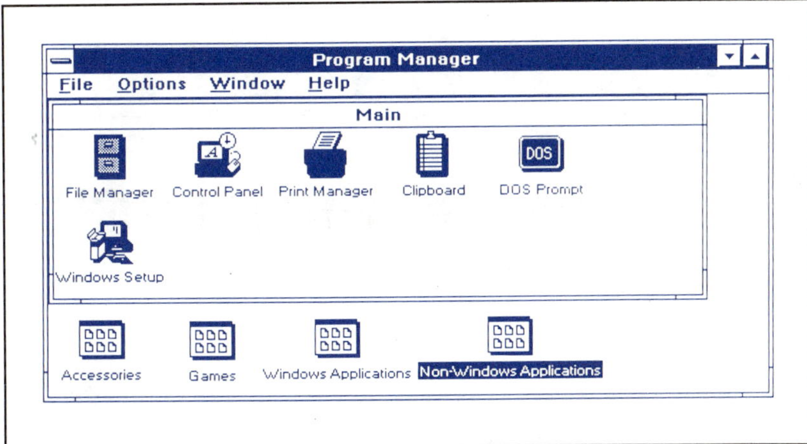

Figure 33.1: The Windows Program Manager and available program groups

The Windows accessory programs reside in the *Accessories group*. Using your mouse or Ctrl+Tab, select the Accessories group icon. The Program Manager will open a window containing the icons that correspond to available desktop programs, as in Figure 33.2. Using your mouse or the keyboard arrow keys, you can select program icons for execution.

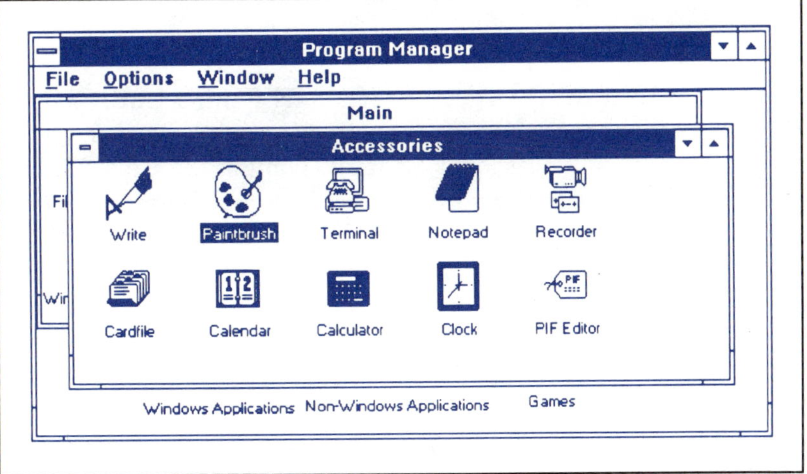

Figure 33.2: Icons corresponding to the Windows accessory programs

LESSON 34

Using the Windows Clock

Featuring

- Running the Clock as an icon

SEVERAL OF THE LESSONS IN PART I USED THE WINDOWS Clock program to teach you how to move, expand, and close a window. So you should be fairly familiar with the Clock and how it works. In this lesson, however, you will learn a very convenient use of the clock: running it *as an icon*. Unlike most icons, which never change, the Clock icon continually changes to reflect the current time. By placing the Clock icon at the bottom of your screen, you can display the current time when you are using the File Manager or other Windows programs.

How to Run the Windows Clock

When you select the Clock program, Windows will create a small window for the Analog Clock as in Figure 34.1.

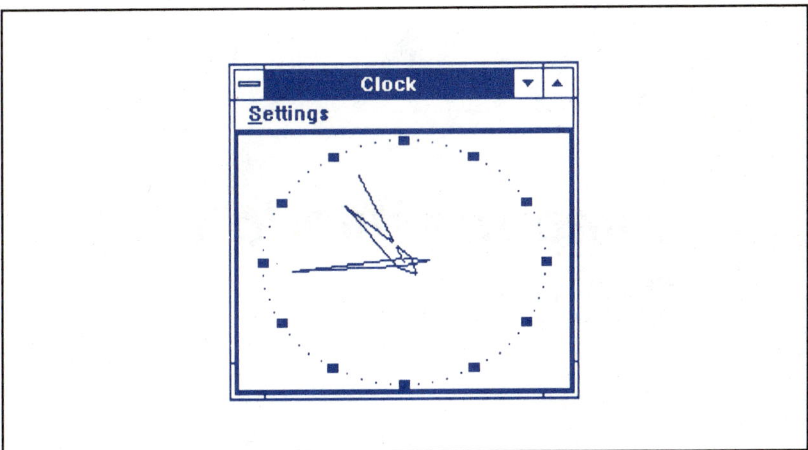

Figure 34.1: Windows' Analog Clock

If you prefer a digital clock, use your mouse or press Alt+S to invoke the Clock's Settings menu and then choose the Digital option. The Clock will change from an analog to a digital display, as shown in Figure 34.2.

Using the Clock window's Control menu or Minimize button, you then can reduce the Clock to an *icon*, leaving the current time displayed in the lower-left corner of your screen.

Figure 34.2: Windows' Digital Clock

LESSON 35

Using the Windows Calculator

Featuring

- The Standard Calculator
- Using the Scientific Calculator
- Performing statistical operations

SEVERAL OF THE LESSONS IN PART I OF THIS BOOK HAD you start the Windows Calculator. In this lesson you will learn how to use the Calculator's features to perform basic, scientific, and even statistical calculations.

How to Use the Standard Calculator

Invoke the Windows Calculator from the Program Manager's Accessories group. Windows will open a window displaying the Calculator. Figure 35.1 lists the keyboard equivalents to the buttons found on the *Standard Calculator*.

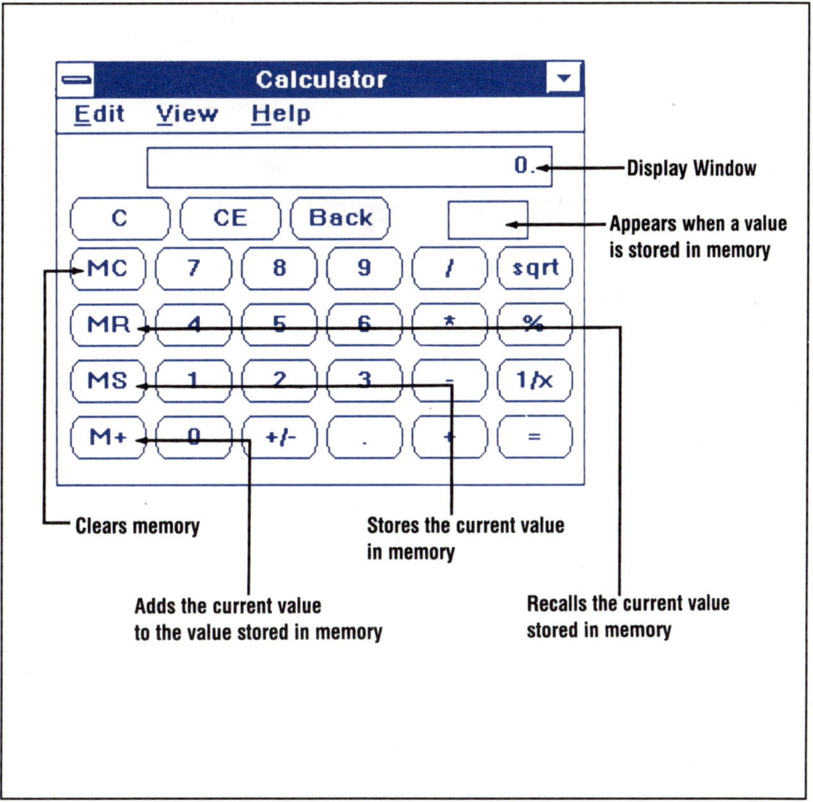

Figure 35.1: *Calculator key definitions for the Windows Standard Calculator*

To access a specific Calculator button with your mouse, aim the mouse pointer at the key desired and click.

To enter numeric values using your keyboard, you can use either the number keys that appear across the top of your keyboard, or the numeric keypad to the right of your keyboard. If you use the numeric keypad, make sure the NumLock key is active. Table 35.1 shows which keyboard keys correspond to which of the Calculator's non-numeric buttons.

Table 35.1: *Keyboard Equivalents to Non-Numeric Buttons.*

KEYBOARD KEY	CALCULATOR BUTTON
/	/
*	*
–	–
+	+
@	Sqrt
%	%
r	1/x
= or Enter	=
F9	±
. or ,	.
Esc	C
Delete	CE
Backspace or Left Arrow	BACK
Ctrl+C	MC
Ctrl+R	MR
Ctrl+S	MS
Ctrl+P	M+

How to Calculate a Simple Result

Using either your keyboard or mouse, enter the value **33** the Calculator. As you enter the value, it will appear on the Calculator's display. Next press the Calculator's plus button and enter the value **67**. When you press the equals button, the Calculator will display the result **100** on its screen. The Standard Calculator can perform most basic arithmetic operations. If you need to perform complex options, though, you will need to use the Scientific Calculator.

How to Use the Scientific Calculator

To select the Windows *Scientific Calculator*, select the Calculator's View menu and choose the Scientific option. The Program Manager will increase the size of the Calculator window displaying the Scientific Calculator shown in Figure 35.2.

The Scientific Calculator is very powerful. At first glance, its many buttons can be quite intimidating. If you examine the buttons by grouping, however, they will be less intimidating. The buttons in the middle of the Scientific Calculator are the ones you just examined for the Standard Calculator. The buttons to the left and right of the standard buttons perform additional arithmetic functions. Table 35.2 describes the functions of these buttons, also listing the keyboard keys you must use to access them.

How to Convert a Value from One Numeric Base to Another

By default, the Calculator displays values in decimal (base 10). Depending on your application, you may need to display a value in binary (base 2), octal (base 8), or hexadecimal (base 16). The four buttons labeled Hex, Dec, Oct, and Bin let you select the desired base.

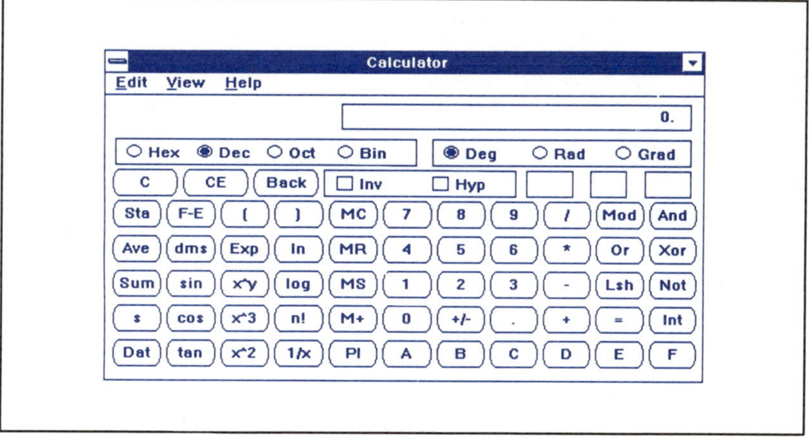

Figure 35.2: *Windows' Scientific Calculator*

Table 35.2: *Advanced Calculator Functions.*

<table>
<tr><th>BUTTON</th><th>KEY</th><th>FUNCTION</th></tr>
<tr><td>Mod</td><td>%</td><td>Performs modulo division.</td></tr>
<tr><td>AND</td><td>&</td><td>Performs a bitwise AND.</td></tr>
<tr><td>Or</td><td>|</td><td>Performs a bitwise OR.</td></tr>
<tr><td>Xor</td><td>^</td><td>Performs a bitwise exclusive or.</td></tr>
<tr><td>Lsh</td><td><</td><td>Performs a bitwise left shift.</td></tr>
<tr><td>Not</td><td>^t</td><td>Performs a bitwise NOT (inverse).</td></tr>
<tr><td>Int</td><td>;</td><td>Truncates the value to the right of the decimal point, creating a whole number.</td></tr>
<tr><td>Inv</td><td>i</td><td>Selects the inverse function for the following operators: sin, cos, tan, PI, x^y, x^2, x^3, log, Ave, Sum, and s for one operation.</td></tr>
<tr><td>Hyp</td><td>h</td><td>Selects the hyperbolic sine, cosine, or tangent.</td></tr>
<tr><td>F-E</td><td>v</td><td>Toggles the display between scientific and standard notation.</td></tr>
<tr><td>dms</td><td>m</td><td>Displays the current value in degrees-minutes-seconds format.</td></tr>
<tr><td>sin</td><td>s</td><td>Calculates an angle's sine.</td></tr>
<tr><td>cos</td><td>o</td><td>Calculates an angle's cosine.</td></tr>
<tr><td>tan</td><td>t</td><td>Calculates an angle's tangent.</td></tr>
<tr><td>(</td><td>(</td><td>Opens a precedence grouping.</td></tr>
<tr><td>)</td><td>)</td><td>Closes a precedence grouping.</td></tr>
<tr><td>Exp</td><td>x</td><td>Allows the input of exponential numbers.</td></tr>
<tr><td>x^y</td><td>y</td><td>Computes x to the y power.</td></tr>
<tr><td>x^3</td><td>#</td><td>Computes x cubed.</td></tr>
<tr><td>x^2</td><td>@</td><td>Computes x squared.</td></tr>
<tr><td>Ln</td><td>n</td><td>Computes the natural logarithm.</td></tr>
</table>

Table 35.2: *Advanced Calculator Functions. (cont.)*

BUTTON	KEY	FUNCTION
log	l	Computes the base 10 log.
n!	!	Computes the factorial.
1/x	r	Computes a value's multiplicative inverse.
Deg	F2	Selects degrees as the unit of measure.
Rad	F3	Selects radians as the unit of measure.
Grad	F4	Selects gradients as the unit of measure.
PI	p	Computes Pi.

How to Change an Angle's Unit of Measure

By default, the Calculator displays angles in units of degrees. The buttons Deg, Rad, and Grad let you select degrees, radians, or gradients as the unit of measure. If you select a base other than decimal, the Calculator changes these options to Dword, Word, and Byte, letting you control the number of bits in the displayed result.

How to Use the Statistical Calculator

To do *statistics*, such as calculating averages, you must manipulate groups of numbers in complicated ways. To simplify this, the Scientific Calculator provides a row of statistical buttons (Str, Ave, Sum, S, and DAT). Table 35.3 contains the keystrokes you must enter to access these buttons.

Assume, for example, you need to compute the average of the following values: 10, 20, 30, 40, and 50. To begin, select the Sta button, and the Calculator will open a window for you to store the values, as shown in Figure 35.3.

Using your mouse or the window's Control menu, move the window to a visible location. Next, enter the value **10** and press the Calculator's Dat button. The Calculator will display the value in the statistical box. Repeat this process for the values 20, 30, 40, and 50.

Table 35.3: *The Calculator's Statistical Functions.*

KEYSTROKE	BUTTON
Ctrl+S	Sta
Ctrl+A	Ave
Ctrl+T	Sum
Ctrl+D	s
Ins	Dat

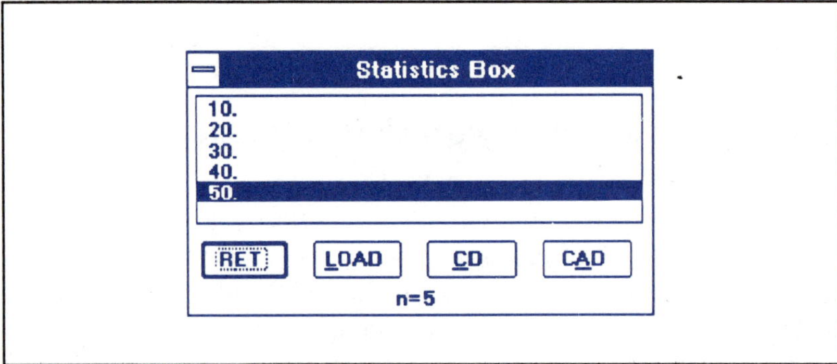

Figure 35.3: The Calculator's statistical value window

Next, select the Calculator's Sum button. The Calculator will display the sum of all the values in the box (150). If you press the Calculator's Ave button, the Calculator will display the average of the values in the box (30). Likewise, the s button displays the value's standard deviation.

How to Learn More about the Calculator

The Windows Calculator is a powerful program with many useful features. To help you make the best use of these features, the Calculator provides an extensive on-line help. Spend a few moments now traversing the Help to increase your understanding of the Calculator's capabilities.

LESSON 36

Keeping Track of Appointments Using the Windows Calendar

Featuring

- Tracking your daily appointments
- Scheduling appointments by month
- Printing your appointments

IN ADDITION TO ITS POWERFUL DESKTOP CALCULATOR, Windows also gives you an on-line appointment calendar. Using the Windows Calendar, you can *track your daily appointments* through the year 2099. In addition, if you are connected to a local area network, the Calendar program lets you access other users' calendars to resolve scheduling conflicts.

How to Use the Daily Calendar

Invoke the Calendar program from the Program Manager Accessories group. Windows will open a window containing a calendar of the current day's events, as in Figure 36.1.

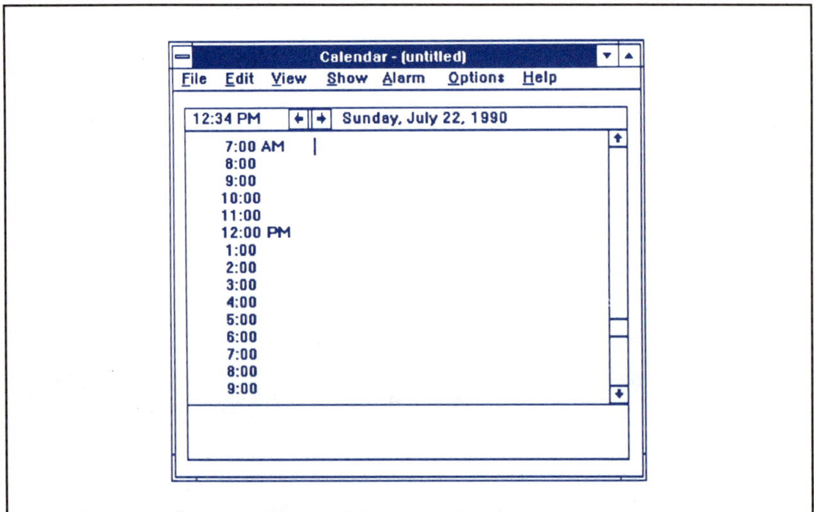

Figure 36.1: *Windows' Calendar for a specific day*

The Calendar lets you schedule appointments in 24-hour blocks at one-hour intervals. The default is to show only the hour, but appointments can be made for any time. To enter an appointment, use your mouse or arrow keys to select the desired time, and type in your appointment. The Calendar program lets you enter up to 80 characters describing the appointment, and at the bottom of each daily calendar is a three-line scratch pad where you can enter additional reminders. To access the scratch pad, aim your mouse into the pad and click, or press the Tab key. Figure 36.2 displays a sample daily calendar containing several appointments and a reminder in the scratch pad.

Displaying Appointments for a Different Day

By default, the Calendar program displays the appointments for the current day. To display the schedule for a different day, you have several alternatives. If you are using a mouse, you can view the previous or following day by clicking on the left- or right-scroll arrows in the date bar. The second way of selecting a different date for display is to use the Show menu in Figure 36.3.

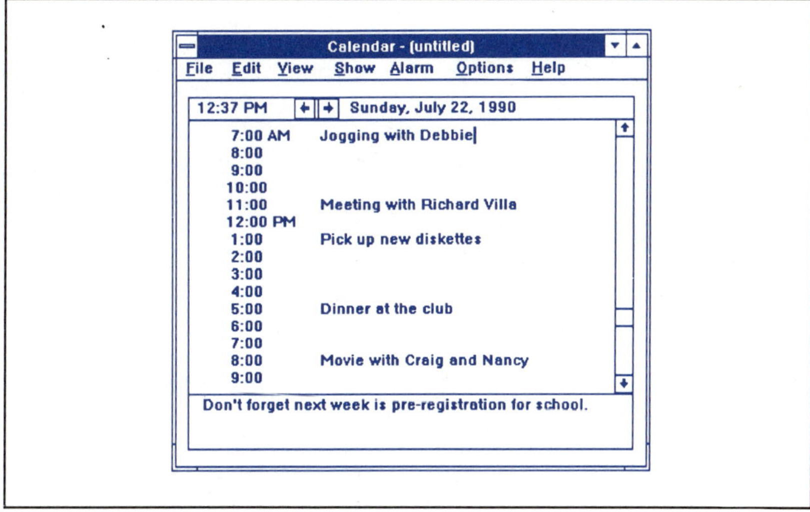

Figure 36.2: *Daily calendar in use*

Figure 36.3: *Calendar Show menu for date selection*

The Show menu Today option displays the current day. Likewise, the Previous and Next options display the preceding or following day. If you select the Date option, the Calendar will display a dialog box prompting you to enter the date desired. This must be entered in the form MM/DD/YY.

How to Use the Monthly Calendar

The Calendar program also lets you examine *appointments by month*. Using The Calendar's View menu, select the Month option. The Calendar program will display the calendar in Figure 36.4, which contains the days in the current month.

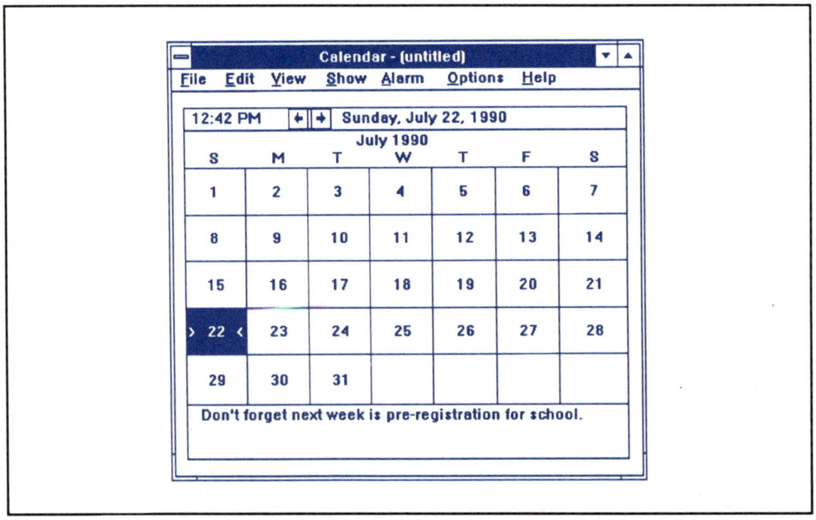

Figure 36.4: Monthly calendar

The Calendar uses the greater than (>) and less than (<) symbols to highlight the current day's date. Viewing previous or future months is similar to viewing previous or future days. First, you can use your mouse to select the left- or right-scroll arrow. Second, you can use the Show menu, discussed previously. In this case, the menu selects previous and future months as opposed to days.

When you display a month calendar on the screen, you can view a specific day by double-clicking on the day with your mouse, or by highlighting the day with your keyboard arrow keys and pressing Enter. As you highlight different days, the Calendar program will display each day's scratch pad information in the box at the bottom of the monthly calendar.

How to Save Your Appointment Calendar

After you enter appointments into your calendar, you need to save the calendar to a file. To do so, select the File menu and choose the Save As option. The Calendar program will display a dialog box prompting you to enter the file name, as in Figure 36.5.

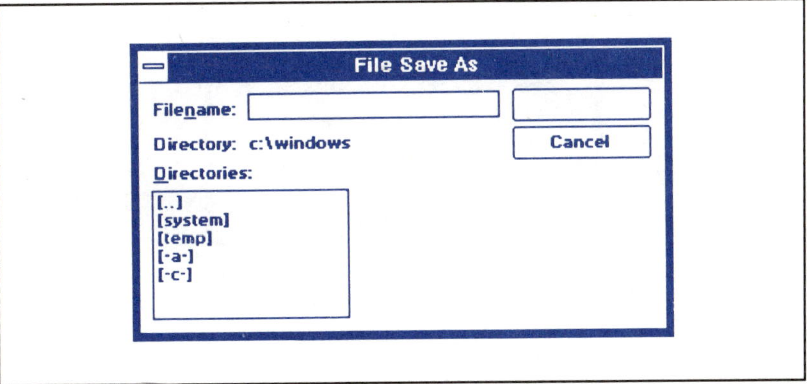

Figure 36.5: Calendar file-name dialog box

Calendar files have the extension CAL. Assign a meaningful file name to your calendar file. Many users use their last name, followed by the CAL extension.

When you next invoke the Calendar program, you will need to open your calendar file using the File menu Open option. Likewise, each time you exit the Calendar program, Calendar will display a dialog box asking you if you want to save your changes to the calendar file.

How to Print a Copy of Your Appointments

In addition to displaying your appointments on screen, there will be times when you want to *print a hard copy* of one or more days' appointments. To do so, invoke the Calendar File menu and choose the Print option. When you do, the Calendar program will display a dialog box prompting you to enter the range of dates for which you want to print appointments, as in Figure 36.6. As before, type the dates in the form MM/DD/YY.

How to Learn More about the Calendar

Like most of the Windows accessory programs, Calendar's features and capabilities are many. Using Calendar's on-line help facility,

Figure 36.6: Dialog box used to determine the range of appointment dates you want to print

you can learn how to set alarms to remind you of key appointments, to move appointments from one time or day to another, and even to change the daily appointment Calendar to display appointments on 15-minute intervals as opposed to hourly. Spend some time traversing Calendar's on-line help to increase your understanding of the Calendar.

LESSON 37

Using the Windows Cardfile

Featuring

- Storing phone numbers and addresses on-line
- Printing your card file
- Searching through your card file

THE WINDOWS CARDFILE PROGRAM LETS YOU KEEP track of information such as phone numbers or other small, related pieces of information on-line using automated 3×5 cards. Using the Cardfile, you can store information by topic, view the information on your screen, or even print hard copies of your cards.

How to Get Started with Cardfile

Select Cardfile from the Program Manager Accessories group and open the program by double-clicking on its icon or by selecting it and choosing the File Open option. Cardfile will open a window displaying your first 3×5 card, as in Figure 37.1.

Microsoft Windows Technical Support

Windows interface: (206) 637-7098
Windows applications: (206) 637-7099

Microsoft Corporation
1 Microsoft Way
Redmond, Washington 98052-6399

Next, using your mouse or the Alt+E keyboard combination, invoke the Edit menu and choose the Index option. Cardfile will display the dialog box in Figure 37.2, prompting you to enter the card's title.

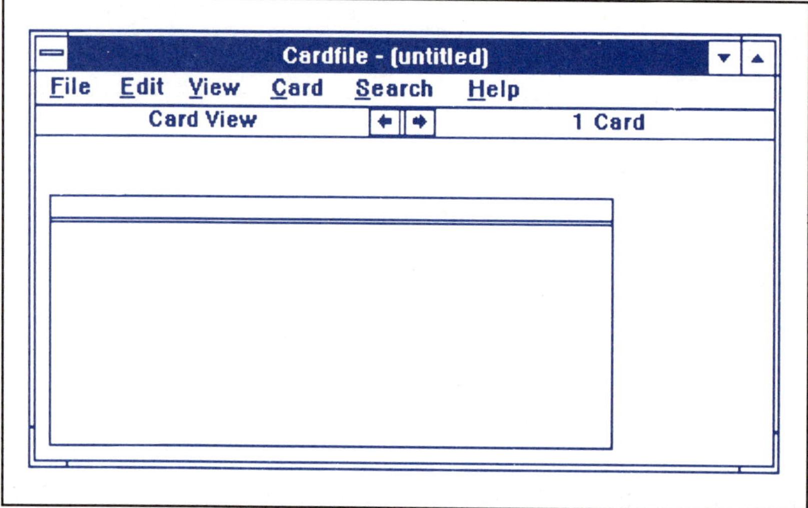

Figure 37.1: Windows' Cardfile program and an unused 3×5 index card

Index
Index Line:
OK
Cancel

Figure 37.2: Cardfile dialog box prompting for a card index

In this case, type **Windows Product Support Services**. Your index card should now contain the information shown in Figure 37.3.

Using your mouse or Alt+C, invoke the Cardfile's Card menu. Choose the Add option to create a second card. Cardfile will prompt you to enter the new card's index. In this case, type in **SYBEX Computer Books**. Next, add the information shown in Figure 37.4 to the card.

Each time you add an additional index card, Cardfile overlays the previous cards with the new blank card.

How to Save Your Index Cards to a File

You must save your index cards to a file each time you add one or more cards or make changes to existing cards. In this case, select the Cardfile File menu using your mouse or by pressing Ctrl+F. Select the Save As option. Cardfile will display a dialog box prompting you to enter the new file name. Cardfile files can be stored with any extension, but the default is CRD. In this case, store the cards in the file PHONE.CRD. When you invoke the Cardfile during later computer sessions, you can access these cards by opening this file with the File menu Open option.

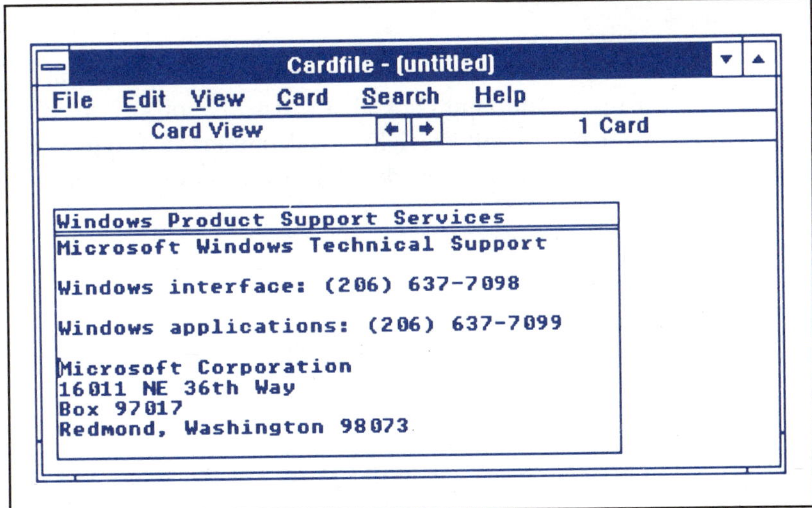

Figure 37.3: Completed index card

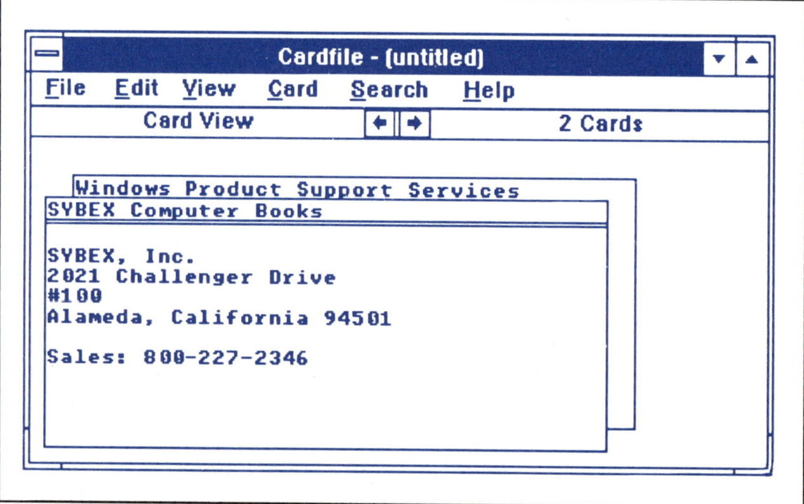

Figure 37.4: Additional index cards

How to Print Your Card File

Using the Cardfile File menu you can *print* either the top card on your stack or all of the cards. To print a single card, place the desired card on top of the stack and choose the File menu Print option.

To select a card using your mouse, aim the mouse pointer at the card, if the card is visible, and click. If the card is not visible, click the mouse pointer on the left or right scroll buttons that appear below the Cardfile menu bar until the desired card comes into view.

To select a card using your keyboard, press the PgUp or PgDn keys until the card comes into view.

To print all of the cards in your card file, invoke the File menu and choose the Print All option.

How to Search Your Cards for Specific Text

As the size of your card file increases, browsing through the entire stack to find a specific card can be quite time-consuming. To locate a specific card quickly, you can use Cardfile's *Search* menu. Using your mouse or Alt+S, invoke the Search menu, which lets you locate a card by its index or by the text written on the card itself. Select the GOTO option. The Cardfile will display a dialog box prompting you to enter index text. In this case, type **Windows** and press Enter. The Cardfile will bring the Microsoft card to the top of the deck. Next, invoke the Search menu and select the Find option. Cardfile will prompt you to enter a word or phrase from a card's text. In this case, type **Calif** and Cardfile will locate **California** from the Sybex address, bringing that card to the top of the deck.

How to View Your Cards as a List

As the number of cards in your card file increases, you might find it more convenient to view your cards as a list of indexes. To do so, select the Cardfile View menu and choose the List option. Figure 37.5 illustrates a large collection of cards displayed by index.

Using your mouse to move the list's scroll bars, or the PgUp and PgDn keys, you can scroll quickly through the list of indexes.

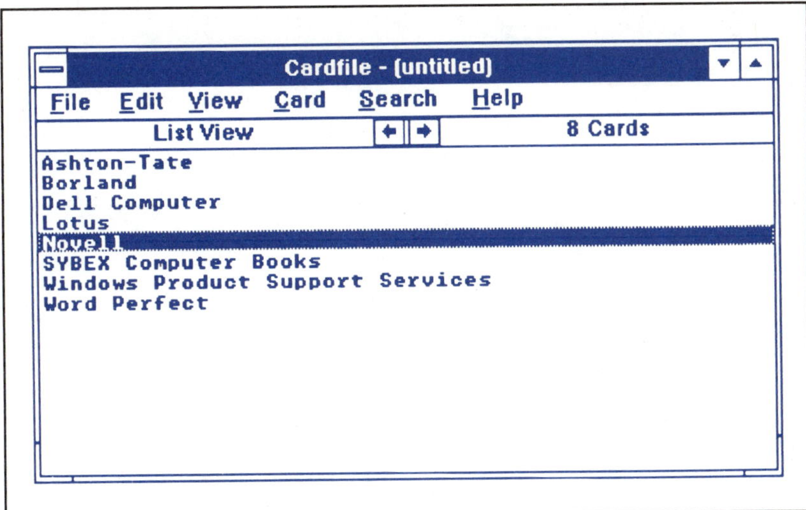

Figure 37.5: Cards displayed as a list of indexes

How to Find Out More about Cardfile

The Windows Cardfile is a very powerful program with many features we have not discussed. Using Cardfile's on-line help, you can learn how to merge several lists of cards into one list, how to edit or delete cards, and even how to dial phone numbers, using your modem to call a number on the current card.

LESSON 38

Using the Windows Notepad

Featuring

- Editing simple text files
- Printing text files
- Moving and deleting blocks of text
- Saving text files

THE WINDOWS NOTEPAD IS A SIMPLE TEXT EDITOR THAT lets you *edit text files* (often called ASCII files) such as DOS batch files, the CONFIG.SYS file, or the Windows configuration file, WIN.INI. A text editor differs from a word processor in that text editors don't provide text-formatting capabilities like flush margins or different fonts. Instead, a text editor simply lets you add, change, or delete text from a file.

How to Start Notepad

The Windows Notepad is well-suited to edit or read files that are text-only. One such is a file named README.TXT, located in your WINDOWS subdirectory. README.TXT provides additional documentation on Windows that is not printed in your Windows manual. We will use README.TXT now to learn about Notepad.

Using the File Manager, select WINDOWS as the current directory. You can start the Windows Notepad several ways. First, you can simply double-click on the file README.TXT if the File Manager is running. Since the File Manager associates TXT files with the Notepad, if you start a TXT file, Notepad will open automatically to display the file. Second, you can double-click on the NOTEPAD.EXE file in the File Manager. And third, you can invoke Notepad by clicking on the Notepad icon from the Program Manager Accessories group. If you invoke Notepad using the icon, you will need to open README.TXT from Notepad's File menu Open option.

When you select the File menu Open option, Notepad will display a dialog box prompting you to select the desired file name.

To open a file using your mouse, click on the file name if it is visible. If the file name is not visible, use the vertical scroll bars to bring it into view.

To open a file using your keyboard, you can either type the name of the desired file or press the Tab key until the file name box is selected. Next, using your keyboard arrow keys, you can scroll through the file names until the desired file is highlighted. Press the Enter key to open the file.

Using any of the above techniques, open the file README.TXT. The Notepad will display the file as shown in Figure 38.1, although the text may vary.

Using your mouse and scroll bars or your keyboard arrow, PgUp, and PgDn keys, scroll through the file's contents. Table 38.1 defines additional keys you can use to traverse your document.

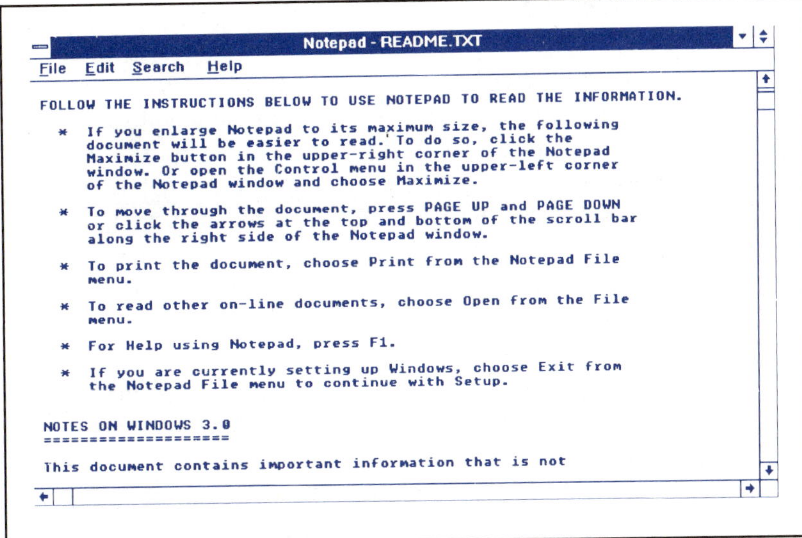

Figure 38.1: *Notepad displaying the file README.TXT*

Table 38.1: *Additional Editing Keys.*

KEY COMBINATION	FUNCTION
Home	Move to beginning of current line
End	Move to end of current line
Ctrl+Home	Move to beginning of the document
Ctrl+End	Move to end of the document

How to Print a Notepad Document

You should *print* a copy of README.TXT and read it. As discussed, the file contains the latest Windows update information. To print a Notepad file, invoke the File menu and choose the Print option. Notepad will begin printing your document. As the document prints, Windows will display the Print Manager icon in the lower-left corner of your screen.

How to Search for Specific Text within a File

When you continue a Notepad session from one day to another, there will be many times when you want to continue editing at a specific location. Rather than have to scroll through an entire document, Notepad lets you quickly search the document for a key word or phrase. To search the file README.TXT for information on the Program Manager, invoke the Notepad Search menu and choose the Find option. Notepad will display a dialog box prompting you to enter the search text. Type **Program Manager** into the dialog box shown in Figure 38.2.

By default, Notepad begins searching from the current file location and continues toward the end of the file. To search toward the beginning of the file, you must select the Backward option. Also by default, Notepad considers an uppercase string identical to a lowercase string. If you want Notepad to perform a case-sensitive search, you must select the Match Upper/Lowercase option. In this case, when you press Enter or select the OK option, Notepad will select the first line in the file containing the words **Program Manager**. If Notepad does not locate the string, it will display a dialog box stating so and remain at the current file position.

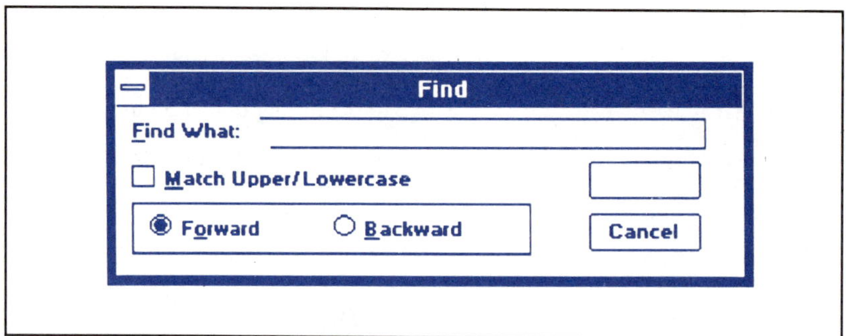

Figure 38.2: Notepad Find dialog box

How to Copy, Delete, or Move Large Blocks of Text

The Notepad's Edit menu helps you move, copy, or delete large blocks of text. Before you try this feature, use the File menu New option to start a new editing session. If you have made changes to the file README.TXT, Notepad will display a dialog box asking you if you want to save changes. If you have not made changes, Notepad will clear the edit menu placing the name **(untitled)** in the Title Bar. So you will have some text to edit, type in the information shown in Figure 38.3.

The Notepad lets you copy, move, or delete a character, a word, a sentence, or even several paragraphs. Any text you are working with is normally called a *block* of text.

To select a block of text using your mouse, aim the mouse pointer at the start of the desired text and press the mouse button down. Next, holding down the mouse button, move the mouse pointer to the end of the block. As you move the mouse pointer, Notepad will highlight the selected text.

To select a block of text using your keyboard, use your arrow keys to place the text cursor at the start of the block. Next, while

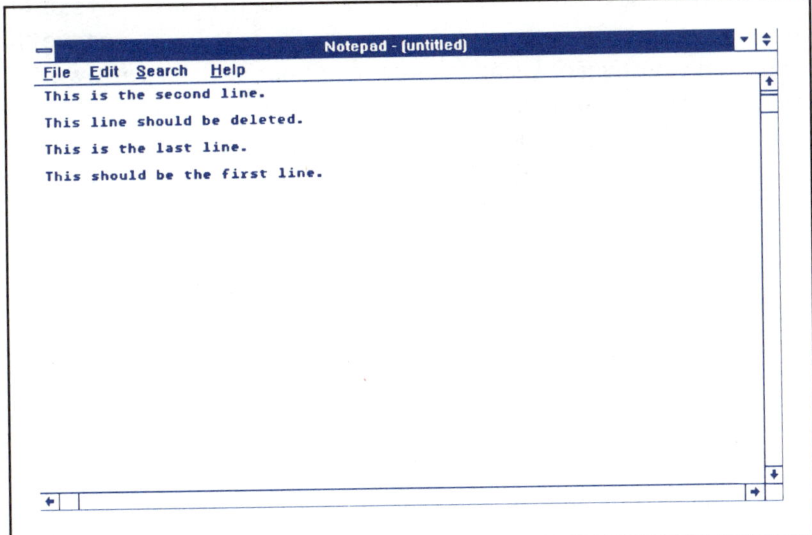

Figure 38.3: Text in an untitled Notepad document

holding down the shift key, use your arrow keys to move the text cursor to the end of the block. As you move the cursor, Notepad will highlight the selected text.

How to Delete Text

Deleting text is often called cutting text. To delete the line "This line should be deleted", select the line using your mouse or keyboard. Next, invoke the Edit menu and choose the Cut option. Note that if you inadvertently delete the wrong text, you can use the Paste option discussed next to restore the text.

How to Move Text

Moving text is often called cutting and pasting. To move the line "This should be the first line" to the top of the file, you must first select the line and cut it using the Edit menu Cut option. Next, move the text cursor to the top of the document and restore the line using the Edit menu Paste option. The order of your sentences should now be numerically correct. To move two or more lines of text, select the desired lines using your mouse or keyboard. Next, invoke the Edit menu and select the Cut option, and Notepad will remove the text from your memo. Using the mouse or your keyboard arrow keys, move the text cursor to the location where you want to place the text. Invoke the Edit menu and choose the Cut option. Notepad will move the lines to the new location as desired.

How to Save a Notepad File

Any time you create or change a file using Notepad, you need to *save* the file's new contents to disk. If the file is named, you can use the File menu Save option. If the file is untitled, use the file menu Save As option, and Notepad will display a dialog box prompting you to type in a new file name.

If you try to exit the Notepad or Windows without saving a file's contents, Notepad will display a dialog box prompting you to save the changes.

How to Learn More about Notepad

Like most Windows programs, Notepad has an extensive on-line help system. Using Notepad's Help, you can learn how to time-stamp the changes you make to files, as well as how to undo inadvertent edits.

LESSON 39

Using the Windows Paintbrush

Featuring

- Creating your own drawings
- Integrating text and graphics
- Printing your drawings

THE WINDOWS PAINTBRUSH IS A POWERFUL DRAWING tool that lets you create illustrations or charts. These drawings can be used as stand-alone images or integrated into letters or reports created with other programs. Depending on your artistic ability, Paintbrush has the sophisticated features needed to create very detailed illustrations. In this lesson you will learn how to create a simple pie chart that incorporates both text and graphics, as in Figure 39.1.

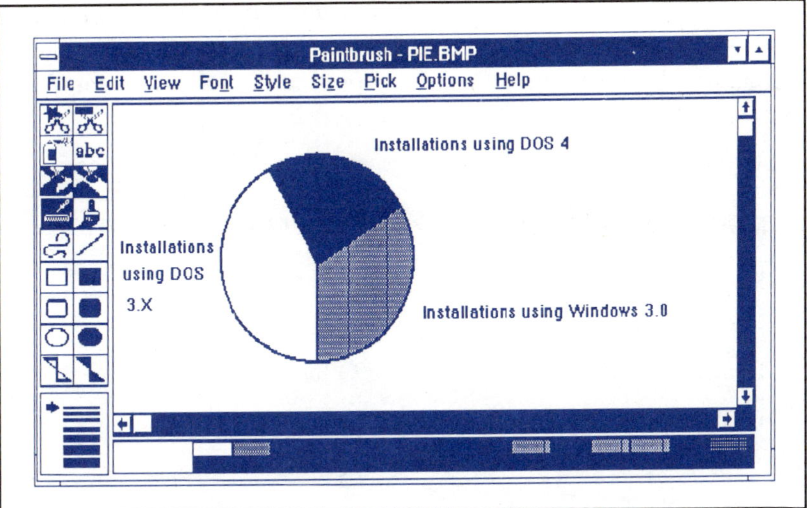

Figure 39.1: A Paintbrush drawing containing text and graphics

How To Start the Windows Paintbrush

Invoke the Paintbrush program from the Program Manager Accessories group. Paintbrush will create a window containing the items shown in Figure 39.2.

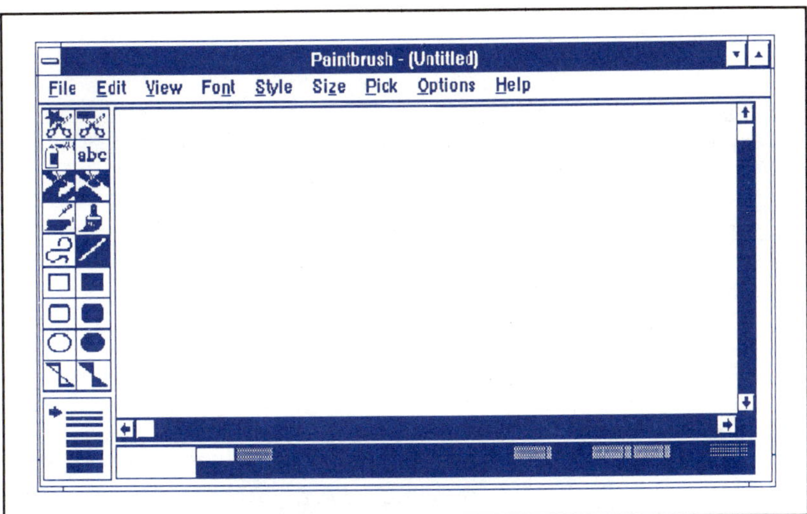

Figure 39.2: Windows' Paintbrush program

The Windows Paintbrush is best suited for use with a mouse. If you are using your keyboard to create Paintbrush images, Table 39.1 defines the keys Paintbrush uses to represent the left and right mouse buttons.

Table 39.1: *Paintbrush Keyboard Assignments for Mouse-Button Operations.*

MOUSE OPERATION	KEYBOARD COMBINATION
Click left mouse button	Ins
Click right mouse button	Del
Double-click left mouse button	F9+Ins
Double-click right mouse button	F9+Del

The Paintbrush window comprises several distinct parts. The left side of the window is bordered by two columns of Paintbrush tools, which let you quickly draw or fill common shapes, enter text in your drawing, erase unwanted lines, and even move portions of your drawing. Table 39.2 briefly describes each toolbox icon.

Table 39.2: *Paintbrush Toolbox.*

ICON	NAME	FUNCTION
	Scissors	Cuts a portion of the drawing for moving or deletion.
	Pick	Cuts a rectangular portion of the drawing for moving or deletion.
	Airbrush	Sprays the current color.
abc	Text tool	Enters text.
	Color Eraser	Erases text or graphics that use the current color.
	Eraser	Erases all text and graphics regardless of the current color.

Table 39.2: *Paintbrush Toolbox. (cont.)*

ICON	NAME	FUNCTION
	Paint Roller	Fills a shape with the current color.
	Brush	Draws with the current color.
	Curve	Creates a curved line.
	Line	Draws a straight line.
	Box	Draws an empty box.
	Filled Box	Draws a box filled with the current color.
	Rounded Box	Draws an empty box with rounded edges.
	Filled Rounded	Draws a box with rounded edges filled with the current color.
	Circle/Ellipse	Draws an empty circle or ellipse.
	Filled Circle/ Ellipse	Draws a circle or ellipse filled with the current color.
	Polygon	Draws an empty polygon.
	Filled Polygon	Draws a polygon filled with the current color.

By default, each time Paintbrush starts, the Brush tool is selected.

To select a different Paintbrush tool using your mouse, aim the mouse pointer at the desired tool and click.

To select a different Paintbrush tool using your keyboard, press the Tab key until the Paintbrush pointer moves into the toolbox area. Using the keyboard arrow keys, highlight the desired tool and press Ins.

Below the toolbox, the Paintbrush displays a box containing the available line widths that Paintbrush uses to create lines or borders around shapes.

To select a new line width using your mouse, simply aim the mouse pointer at the desired line width and click.

To select a line width using your keyboard, press the Tab key until the Paintbrush pointer moves into the line width box. Using your keyboard arrow keys, highlight the desired line width and press Ins.

At the bottom of the window, below the drawing area, the Paintbrush displays the available color palette as well as the current color selection.

To change the current color using your mouse, aim the mouse pointer at the desired color in the color palette and click.

To select a new current color using your keyboard, press the Tab key until the Paintbrush pointer moves into the color palette box. Using your keyboard arrow keys, highlight the desired color and press Ins.

How to Create a Simple Image

Select the hollow circle tool from the Paintbrush toolbox. If you are using your keyboard, press the Tab key until the Paintbrush pointer is in the drawing area. Next, using your mouse or the keyboard arrow keys, move the crosshair pointer to the top of the screen and click or press the Ins key. Next, with the mouse button or the Ins key depressed, move the crosshairs until the Paintbrush displays the size of circle you desire. Release the mouse key or Ins. Your screen should contain a circle similar to the one in Figure 39.3.

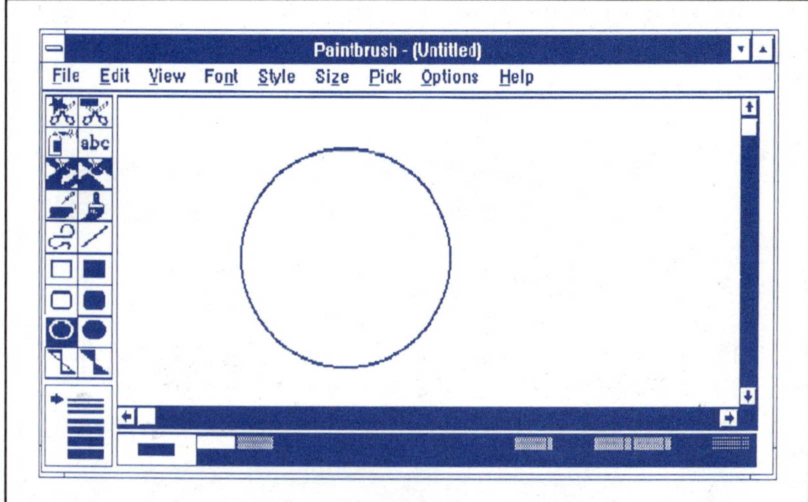

Figure 39.3: Creating a circle using Paintbrush

Next, select the Paintbrush line tool and divide the circle into a pie chart. Using the Paintbrush roller, you can fill each region of the pie chart with a different color. Using the text tool, add labels to the pie chart, as shown in Figure 39.4.

How to Print Your Image

To *print* the pie chart, invoke the Paintbrush File menu and choose the Print option. The Paintbrush will display the following dialog box, which lets you choose the desired print resolution, the percentage of the window to print, the number of copies desired, and the printed image's scale. For now, print the image using the default values by selecting the OK option or pressing Enter.

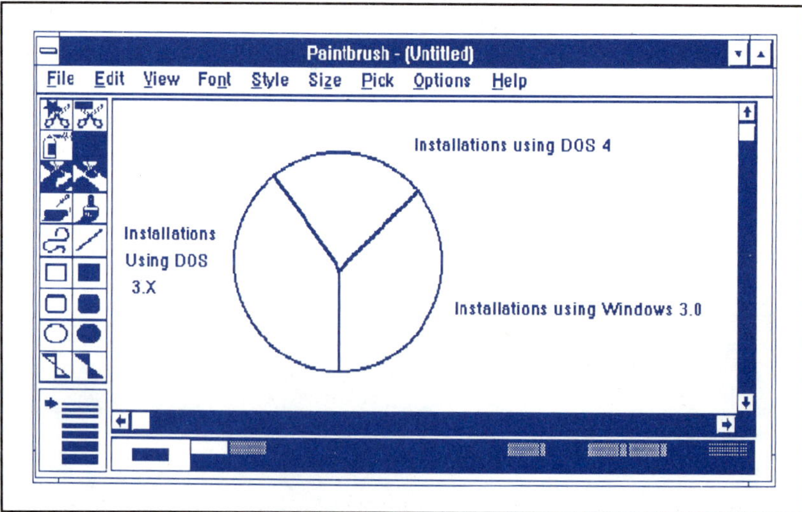

Figure 39.4: Integrating text and graphics

The Paintbrush will begin printing your document and the Print Manager icon will appear in the lower-left corner of your screen, indicating that the Print Manager is overseeing the printing of the image.

How to Save Your Image to a File

Depending on the complexity of your image, it may take you several sessions to complete your drawing. If so, you will need to save the image to disk. To do this, invoke the Paintbrush File menu and choose the Save As option. Paintbrush will display the dialog box in Figure 39.5, prompting you to enter the desired file name.

Depending on your requirements, such as your printer type or application, Paintbrush lets you save the image in one of five formats.

A PCX Paintbrush file

A Monochrome bitmap

A 16-color bitmap

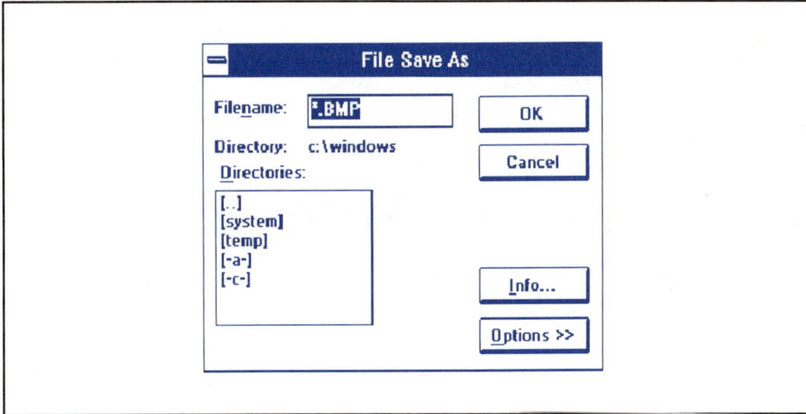

Figure 39.5: Paintbrush file save dialog box

A 256-color bitmap

A 24-bit bitmap

If you select the dialog box's option button, the Paintbrush will expand the dialog box's size, letting you choose the desired format. For PCX files, Paintbrush will save files with the extension PCX. For bitmap files, Paintbrush will save files with the extension BMP. In this case, use the default of 16-color bitmap to save the image as **PIECHART.BMP**.

How to Learn More about Paintbrush

The Paintbrush program is both sophisticated and versatile. This lesson has touched on its capabilities only briefly. Like most Windows programs, however, Paintbrush provides extensive on-line help. Using Help, you can quickly learn how to use Paintbrush to create a wide variety of graphic elements to enhance your reports and presentations.

LESSON 40

Using the Write Word Processor

Featuring

- Editing and printing a document
- Using character fonts
- Text search-and-replace operations
- Formatting text

IN LESSON 38 YOU LEARNED HOW TO USE THE WINDOWS notepad to create or edit small ASCII files. You also learned that a word processor differs from a text editor (such as Notepad) in that a word processor lets you format your documents. With a word processor, you can align margins, change fonts for emphasis, and add headers and footers to each page, giving your documents a more professional appearance. Windows provides the Write word processor, which has many sophisticated word-processing features that you can use to create professional quality reports and letters.

How to Start Write

Invoke the Write word processor from the Program Manager Accessories group. Write will open a window as shown in Figure 40.1.

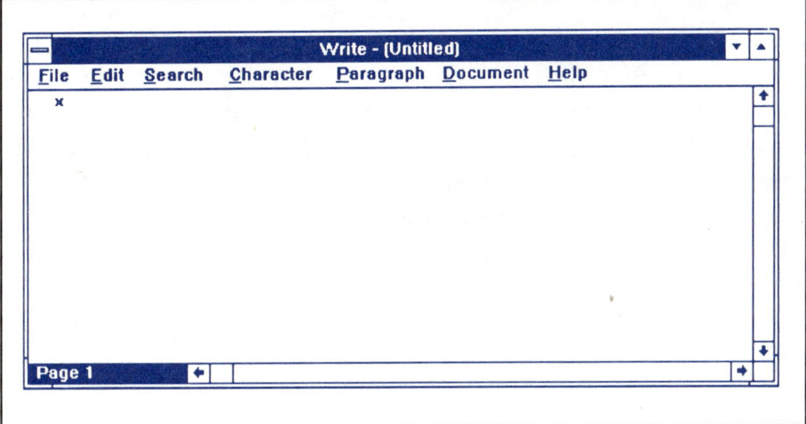

Figure 40.1: *Windows' Write word processor*

Write is now ready for you to start typing. Enter the text in Figure 40.2.

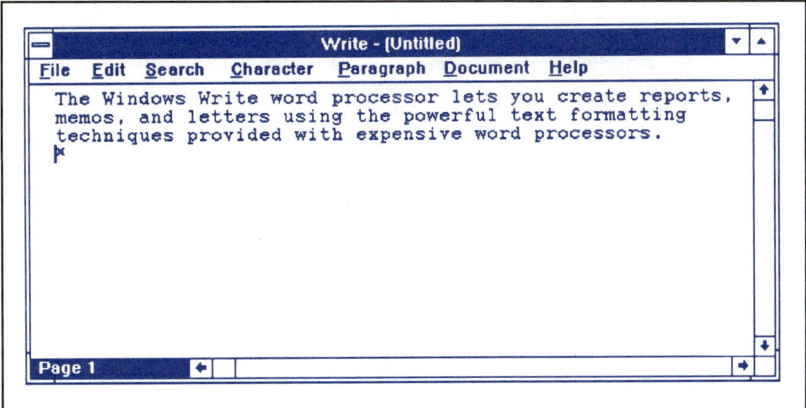

Figure 40.2: *Using Write to enter text*

Each time your text reaches the end of a line, Write automatically wraps your text to the start of the next line. You must press Enter to start a new paragraph.

How to Print Your Document

Using your mouse or Alt+F, select the Write File menu and choose Print. Write will display a dialog box that prompts you to enter the number of copies you want to print, as well as the starting and stopping page if you don't want to print the entire document. For now, select the OK option or press Enter. Write will begin printing your document. The Windows Print Manager icon will appear at the bottom of your screen as the Print Manager oversees the document's printing.

How to Save Your Document

Using the Write File menu, choose the Save As option. Write will display a dialog box prompting you to Enter a file name and to select the desired file format, as in Figure 40.3.

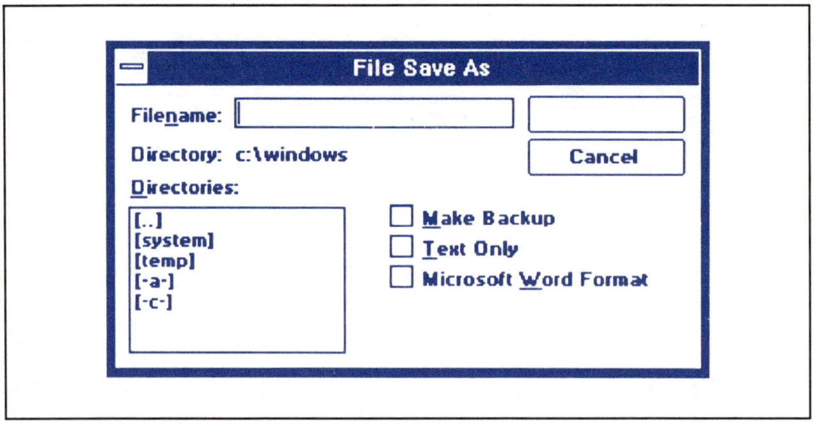

Figure 40.3: Write's File Save As dialog box

By default, Write files use the extension WRI. In this case, use the file name **EXAMPLE.WRI**.

By default, each time you use Write to make changes to a file and then save the changes, Write overwrites the file's previous contents. The Make Backup option directs Write to save the file's previous contents in a file with the BKP extension (for backup) or BAK if you are saving the file's contents in Microsoft Word format. By saving a backup copy of the file's previous contents, you can recover information inadvertently edited or discard changes you don't actually want. Select the Make Backup option by clicking on the option with your mouse, or by pressing Tab until the option is selected and then pressing the spacebar.

As discussed, a word processor lets you align text, and assign different fonts throughout your document. To do so, the word processor must embed special characters in your files that code a paragraph's alignment or a character's font. Normally, you don't see these characters when you view your document in the word processor. There will be times, though, when you don't want the word processor to place these characters in your file. For example, in Lesson 41 you will learn how to use the Windows Terminal program to send a file over phone lines by modem. If the person you are sending the file to doesn't have the same word processor you have, the embedded word-processing characters will make the file very difficult to read. The Text Only option directs Write to store files without the embedded word processing characters. Finally, if you have Microsoft Word, or are sharing the file with someone who does, Write lets you save the file in Microsoft Word format.

How to Move Around Quickly in a Large Document

If you are using a mouse, the Write window's horizontal and vertical scroll bars let you quickly scroll through your document. If you are using your keyboard to traverse your documents, Table 40.1 contains several keyboard shortcuts.

Table 40.1: *Keyboard Combinations for Traversing a Write Document*

KEYBOARD COMBINATION	DESTINATION
Home	Beginning of current line
End	End of current line
Ctrl+Right Arrow	Next word
Ctrl+Left Arrow	Previous word
Numeric keypad 5+Right Arrow	Next sentence
Numeric keypad 5+Left Arrow	Previous sentence
Numeric keypad 5+Down Arrow	Next paragraph
Numeric keypad 5+Up Arrow	Previous paragraph
Ctrl+PgDn	Bottom line in window
Ctrl+PgUp	Top line in window
Numeric keypad 5+PgDn	Next page
Numeric keypad 5+PgUp	Previous page
Ctrl+Home	Start of document
Ctrl+End	End of document

Note that you can use the page movement features, such as Next Page, only after you print your document or divide it into pages with the File menu Repaginate option.

How to Select a Specific Section of Text

Write lets you move (cut and paste), delete, or copy selected text using the Edit menu. In addition, using the Character menu, you can assign a unique font to a selected block of text.

To select text using your mouse, aim the mouse pointer at the start of the desired text and click. Write will move its text cursor to the starting position. Next, with the mouse select button depressed, move the mouse to highlight the desired text. When you have selected all of the text you wish to use, release the mouse select button.

To select text using your keyboard, use your keyboard arrow keys to position the Write text cursor at the start of the desired text. Then, hold down the Shift key and use your keyboard arrow keys to highlight the desired text.

To cancel a selection, press an arrow key without Shift depressed, or click the mouse.

How to Choose a Different Font

A *font* is essentially a graphic design used to represent letters or numbers. Many books, for example, use the *italic* font to make key words stand out. Write provides a collection of fonts you can use in your documents. Your printer type determines which fonts will actually print, though.

Using your mouse or keyboard, select the desired text. Next, invoke the Character menu, shown in Figure 40.4.

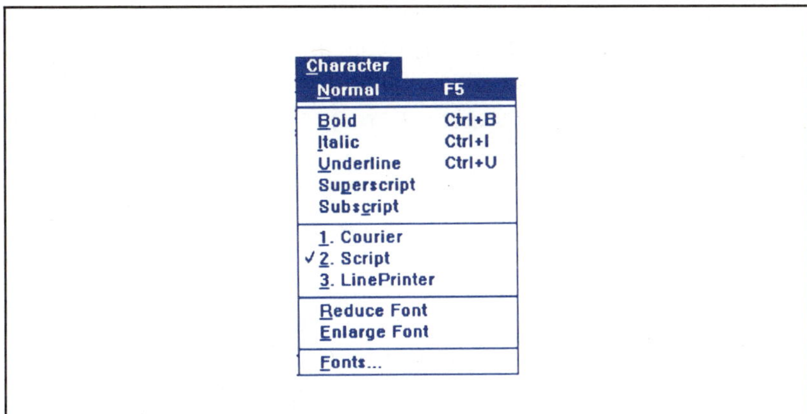

Figure 40.4: *Write's Character menu*

Using the Character menu options, you can quickly underline, bold, italicize, or change the font or font size of the selected text. Experiment a little now with different fonts and font sizes. Figure 40.5 illustrates how different fonts can improve a document's appeal.

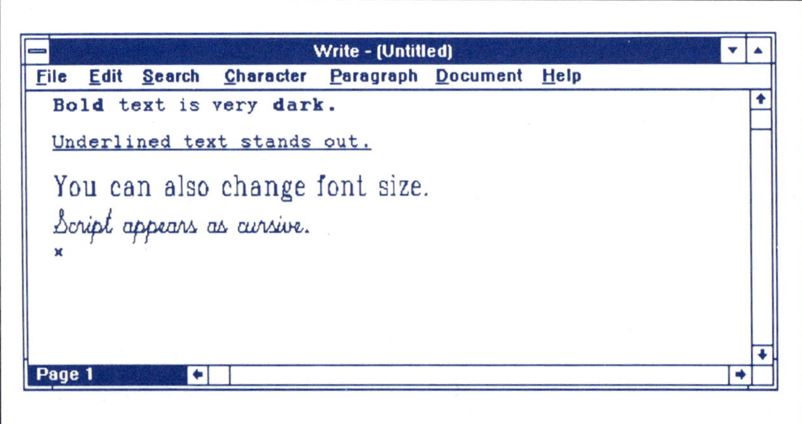

Figure 40.5: Using multiple fonts with a Write document

How to Find or Replace Text

When your documents become large, there will be times when you need to *search* for a specific word or phrase or *replace* a word or phrase with another. To do so, use your mouse or Alt+S to invoke the Search menu. If you select the Find option, Write will display the dialog box shown in Figure 40.6, prompting you to enter the desired text.

Simply type in the word or phrase you are trying to locate. The Whole Word option directs Write to locate only those places in the text where complete words appear. For example, if you are searching for the word "book," the whole-word search will not consider the words "booking" or "bookstore" to be matches. The Match Upper/ Lowercase option directs Write to perform case-sensitive searches, considering a lowercase word different from its uppercase counterpart. "WINDOWS" and "Windows" are obvious examples in this book of the uppercase/lowercase distinction.

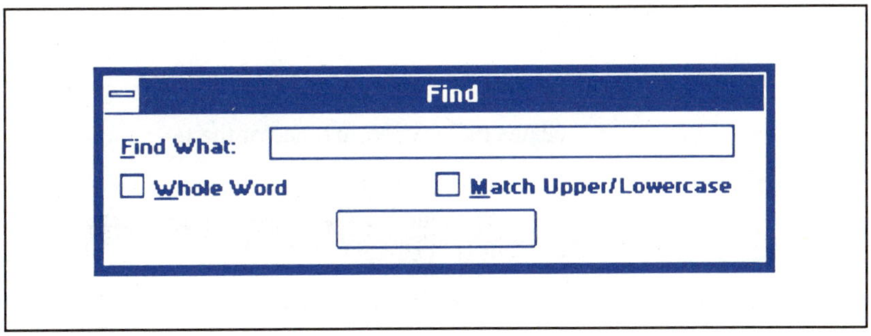

Figure 40.6: *Write's find text dialog box*

The Find Next option lets you quickly locate the next occurrence of the word or phrase in the document. When you are done with the find operation, use the dialog box's Control menu to close the box, removing it from your screen.

The Search menu Change option lets you locate and replace one word or phrase with another. When you choose the Change option, Write will display a dialog box prompting you to enter the word or phrase you want to replace, as well as the replacement string, as in Figure 40.7.

Table 40.2 defines the Change buttons.

Write's text replacement capabilities become more convenient as the size of your document grows. When you are done with the text change operation, use the Change dialog box's Control menu to close the box, removing it from your screen.

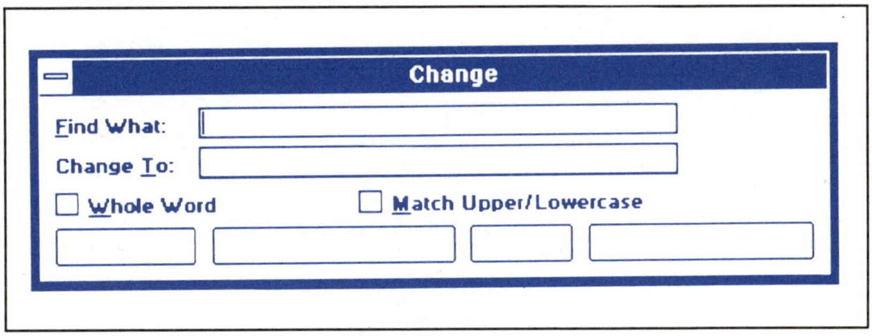

Figure 40.7: *Write's Change text dialog box*

Table 40.2: *Description of Change Dialog Box Buttons*

BUTTON	RESULT
Find Next	Locates the next occurrence of the target text.
Change, then Find	Changes the currently selected occurrence of the target and then searches the document for the next occurrence.
Change	Changes the currently selected target text.
Change All	Changes every occurrence of the target text throughout the document, automatically.
Change Selection	Changes every occurrence of the target text within a selected section of the document.

How to Format Paragraphs

By default, Write left-justifies your document, creating a smooth edge along the left margin and a jagged edge along the right margin. The Write Paragraph menu, shown in Figure 40.8, lets you select right, left, center, or right and left margin justification.

From the Paragraph menu you can also change a paragraph's spacing and indentation. To use the paragraph options, place the text pointer in the paragraph you want to format and choose the desired option.

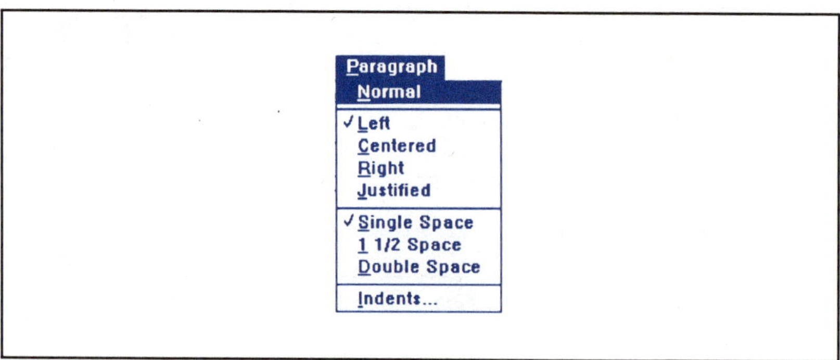

Figure 40.8: *The Write Paragraph menu*

How to Open an Existing File

The Write File menu Open option lets you open an existing file for editing. If you attempt to open a text file you have created using an application other than Write, a dialog box will appear asking you if you want to convert the file to Write format. Unless the file is a standard ASCII text file, you will need to convert it.

How to Learn More about Write

The Write word processor provides an extensive on-line help system. Using Write's Help, you can learn how to add headers and footers to your documents, set tab positions, and even how to make your documents visually interesting by incorporating graphics.

LESSON 41

Using the Windows Terminal

Featuring

- Accessing remote computers with your modem
- Data communication settings
- Dialing a remote computer

A COMPUTER *MODEM* IS A HARDWARE DEVICE THAT LETS a computer exchange information with another computer over telephone lines. If your computer has a modem you can use it to access on-line information systems, such as CompuServe, or locally-run computer bulletin boards. In addition to a modem, you must have software that lets your computer access the modem. Because such software lets your computer use telephone lines, it is called telecommunications software. If your computer has a modem, you can use the Windows Terminal telecommunications program to access these services right from Windows. Because Terminal is a Windows application, it runs within a window, using pull-down menus and dialog boxes similar to those you are already familiar with.

How to Start Terminal

Because different types of computers store information differently and communicate at different speeds, two computers wishing to exchange information must agree on several basic communications settings and speeds (baud rates). Data communication settings include the number of start bits, stop bits, and data bits. Although you don't need to understand the actual functions these settings perform, you will need to know the setting values for the computer you wish to access. As you use the Terminal program to access different computers, you can save each computer's settings in a file with the extension TRM.

Invoke the Terminal program from the Program Manager Accessories group. The Program Manager will open a window for Terminal as shown in Figure 41.1.

The Windows Terminal program has an extensive list of features, providing many advanced terminal-emulation and file-transfer capabilities. If you have used telecommunications software in the

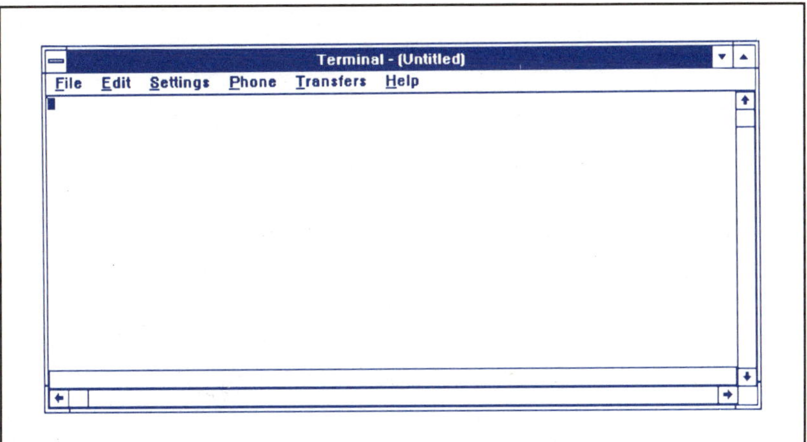

Figure 41.1: Windows' Terminal program

past, you may already be familiar with uploading and downloading files (transferring them) to and from remote computers. If you are not familiar with telecommunications, refer to the Sybex book *Mastering Pro Comm Plus* by Bob Campbell. In this lesson you will learn only the essential steps you need to access a remote computer. To fully exploit Terminal's capabilities, refer to its on-line help.

How to Specify Data Communication Settings

As discussed, you must know the target computer's *data communication settings* before you can access it. These settings include:

Baud rate from 110 to 19200

Number of data bits from 5 to 8

Number of stop bits at 1, 1.5, or 2

Type of parity: None, Odd, Even, Mark, Space

The port the modem is hooked up to

Once you know these settings, invoke the Terminal Settings menu and choose the Communications option. Terminal will display the dialog box in Figure 41.2, prompting you to enter the desired settings.

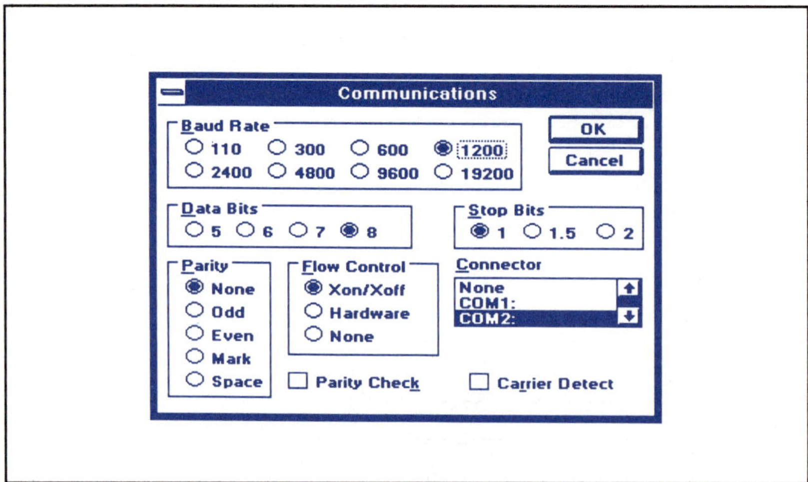

Figure 41.2: The Communications settings dialog box

To select a communication setting using your mouse, aim the mouse pointer at the desired setting and click. When you have selected all of the desired options, click on the OK option.

To select a communication setting using your keyboard, press the Tab key until Terminal highlights the setting's group. Next, using your keyboard arrow keys, select the specific option. When you have selected all of the appropriate options, press Enter.

After you have entered the communication settings, invoke the Terminal File menu and choose the Save As option. Type the name of the file in which you want to store the settings. Be sure to give your file a meaningful file name, such as DOWJONES.TRM.

How to Specify Modem Command Settings

Depending on your modem and phone type (pulse or tone dialing) you may need to change the default modem settings. To do so, select the Settings menu and choose the Modem Commands option. Terminal will display the dialog box in Figure 41.3, prompting you to enter commands specific to your modem.

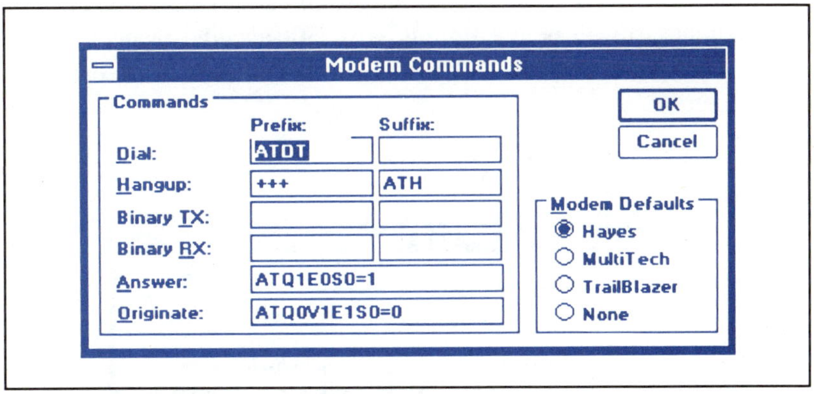

Figure 41.3: Terminal's Modem Commands dialog box

Most modems support the Hayes command set. If your modem does not, refer to your modem documentation for the correct commands. If your phone uses pulse (rotary) instead of tone dial, change the dial prefix from ATDT to ATDP. When the commands are correct, press Enter or click on the OK option.

How to Dial the Desired Number

From the Settings menu, invoke the Phone Number option. Terminal will display a dialog box prompting you to enter the phone number, as in Figure 41.4.

Type in the desired phone number, including a 1 before the area code if the call is long distance. You can use dashes and parenthesis to separate the digits of the number, but Terminal does not require them. Remember to precede the phone number with 9 if your modem is connected to a phone system that requires you to. Also, if your phone system requires a slight pause before you dial a number, you can insert commas in the phone number to achieve two-second delays.

When one modem calls another, the two exchange a series of high-pitched tones before they begin transmitting. By default, Terminal waits 30 seconds for the tone after the phone is answered. Normally, the tone exchange occurs in a matter of seconds. If the tone exchange does not occur within the number of seconds specified, Terminal will end the call. The minimum amount of time you can direct Terminal to wait before timing out is 30 seconds. Depending on the system you are trying to access, you may need to increase the timeout period.

Figure 41.4: *Terminal's Phone Number dialog box*

After you have entered the desired number, invoke Terminal's Phone menu and choose the Dial option. Terminal should dial the desired number. Should Terminal time out without successfully connecting, you may need to set the port characters for the serial port your modem is using. To do so, use the Windows Control Panel as discussed in Lesson 49.

The Redial After Timing Out option directs Terminal to repeat the phone call if the line is busy or a timeout occurs. If you are attempting to access a popular bulletin board that has only a limited number of lines, it may take several attempts for you to get through. By selecting the Redial option, you can have Terminal automatically redial these calls for you.

The Signal When Connected option directs Terminal to sound an alarm when your computer eventually connects with the target computer. This option ensures that you will be notified of the connection by the alarm, even if you are working on another project or are out of the room.

When you connect with the target computer, you can upload or download files using Terminal's Transfers menu. To end your connection, invoke the Phone menu and choose the Hangup option.

How to Learn More about Terminal

As discussed, Terminal provides extensive on-line help. Using Help you can learn to customize your Terminal characteristics, define function keys for commonly used commands, and select commonly used file-transfer protocols, such as XMODEM or Kermit.

LESSON 42

Using the Windows Recorder

Featuring

- Saving time and keystrokes by using macros

MOST USERS WILL FIND THAT THERE ARE WINDOWS features they use on a regular basis. Although Windows' point-and-shoot capabilities give you easy access to many programs and directories, you can use the Windows Recorder to further reduce the number of keystrokes or mouse operations needed to perform common Windows operations. In general, the Windows Recorder records the series of keystrokes or mouse operations used to perform a specific task. Using the Recorder, you can save the keystrokes into a file with the REC extension. Later, you can use the recorder to play back the keystrokes, thus performing the desired operation automatically. If you are familiar with DOS batch files or Lotus macros, consider the Windows Recorder as a special macro file generator for Windows keystrokes and mouse operations.

How to Start the Windows Recorder

Invoke the Windows Recorder from the Program Manager Accessories group. The Recorder will open a window as shown in Figure 42.1.

In this case, you will record the keystrokes you must perform to select the File Manager and display a directory window for the WINDOWS subdirectory. To begin, invoke the Macro menu and select the Record option. The Recorder will display a dialog box prompting you to enter specifics about the macro you are going to record.

The Record Macro Name option lets you type in a 40-character descriptive name for the macro, such as **Open a Directory Window for WINDOWS**. The Shortcut Key lets you select a hot-key combination you can enter to invoke the macro when the Recorder is an active window or icon. The Shortcut key is not mandatory, it simply makes it easier for you to invoke the macro using your keyboard. In this case, assign Ctrl+F1 as the hot key.

The Record Mouse option lets you select mouse operations you want to record. By default, the Recorder records all mouse click-and-drag operations. By clicking on the scroll button to the right of the option you can select either the Ignore Mouse option, which directs the Recorder to record only keystrokes, or the Everything option,

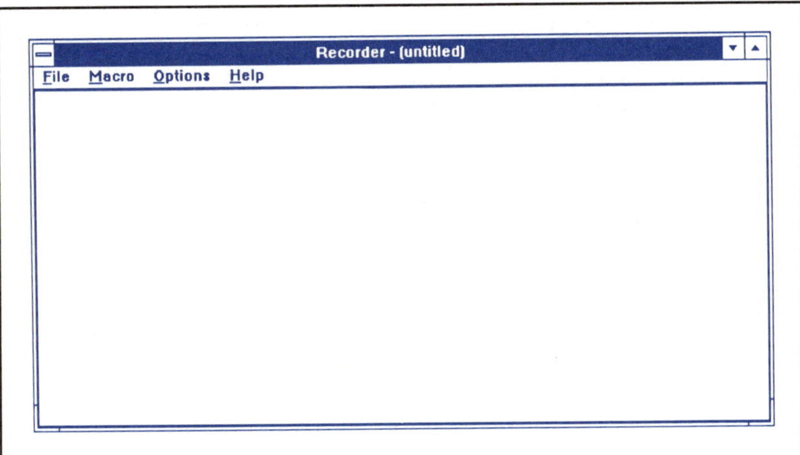

Figure 42.1: Windows' Recorder

which directs the Recorder to record both mouse operations and keystrokes.

The Description box lets you type in several lines of descriptive text that explain the macro's purpose and possible limitations. You should always include the date you created the macro. Your description will help you remember specific weeks or months after you create the macro, so be as detailed as possible. For your macro to open a directory window for the WINDOWS subdirectory, your dialog box should contain contents similar to Figure 42.2.

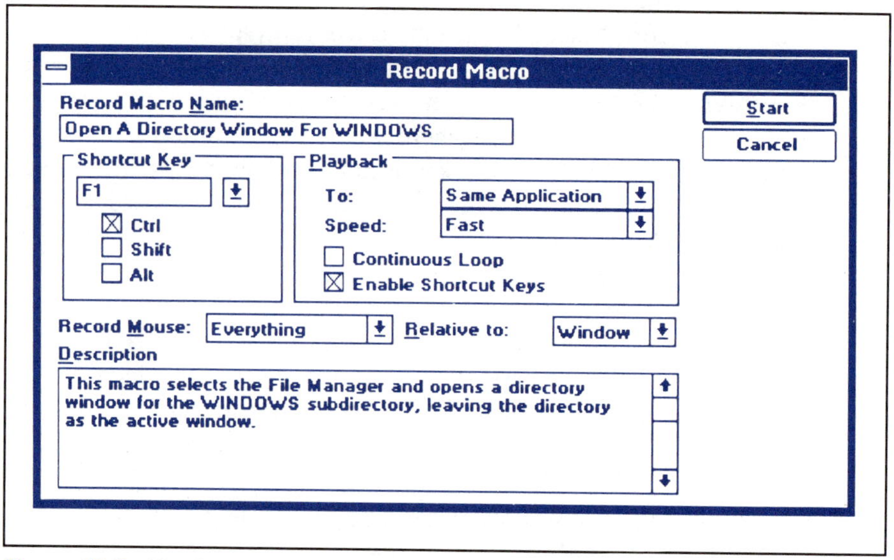

Figure 42.2: The Recorder dialog box

For now, leave the other macro settings unchanged. You are ready to record your first macro. Select the Start option. The Recorder will shrink into a flashing icon, which tells you it is recording your mouse and/or keystroke operations. Perform the following steps:

Select the Program Manager's window

Select the Main group

Invoke the File Manager

Expand the WINDOWS directory into a directory window

To end the recording session, click on the Record icon or press Ctrl+Break. The Recorder will display the dialog box in Figure 42.3, prompting you to save, resume, or cancel the current recording session.

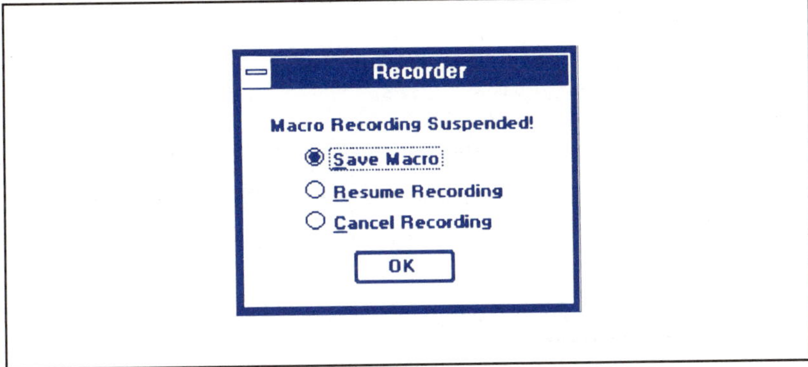

Figure 42.3: Recorder's end recording dialog box

Select the Save option by clicking on Save Macro with your mouse or by typing the letter **S** and pressing Enter. Next, close the File Manager and expand the Recorder icon. Using the Recorder File menu, save your macro as WINDIR.REC. Close the Recorder window.

How to Use Existing Macros

To use an existing macro, run the Recorder and invoke the File menu choosing the Open option. When the Recorder prompts you for a file name, type in **WINDIR.REC**. The Recorder will display the macro's descriptive name and shortcut key, as in Figure 42.4.

Invoke the macro by double-clicking on the macro name or pressing Ctrl+F1. The Recorder will perform the macro, opening the subdirectory window as desired.

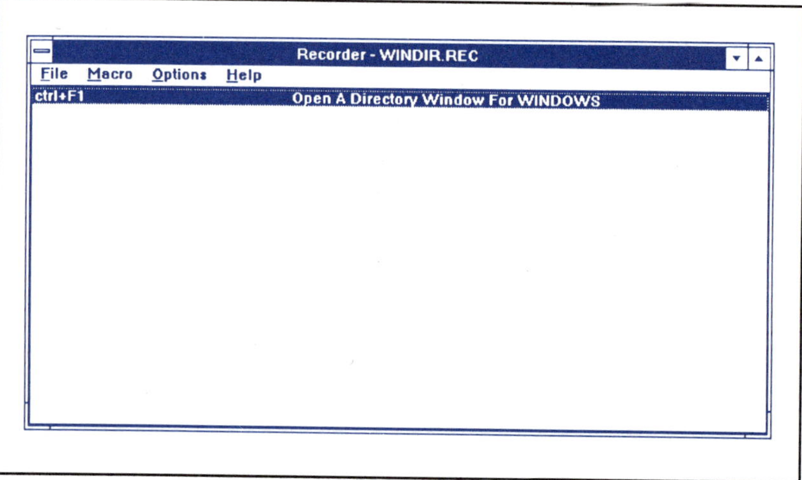

Figure 42.4: *A Recorder macro*

How to Learn More about Recorder

Like all of the Windows accessory programs, the Recorder provides an extensive on-line help. Using Help you can learn how to change a macro's execution speed, merge multiple macros into a single file, and how to continuously repeat a macro that performs training or an on-line demonstration.

LESSON 43

Creating Program Information Files (PIFs)

Featuring

- Using the PIF editor
- Controlling non-Windows applications

AS DISCUSSED EARLIER, A NON-WINDOWS PROGRAM IS A program written for DOS that Windows cannot run within a window, except in 386 Enhanced Mode. Each time you run a non-Windows application, Windows searches for a file whose name is the same as the program's, but that has a PIF extension. A PIF is a special file that tells Windows about a program's specific characteristics—such as the amount of memory required or the program's directory. PIF is an acronym for Program Information File. If Windows does not find a PIF specific to an application, it uses the file _DEFAULT.PIF.

Most non-Windows programs and batch files will run with the default PIF. Depending on your requirements, you may need to change one or two of the fields in thc default PIF, as we will discuss in this lesson.

How to Create a PIF

Invoke the PIF editor from the Windows Program Manager Accessories group. The PIF Editor lets you create new PIFs or modify existing ones. Figure 43.1 shows the Windows Standard mode PIF editor dialog box. If you are running in 386 Enhanced mode, the dialog box will look slightly different. For more information on 386 Enhanced mode PIFs, see Lesson 63.

In this case, you will create a PIF file for the DOS TREE command. As discussed, if Windows cannot find a file's PIF, it uses the default. Unfortunately, unless you change the default PIF using the PIF Editor, your program's output will display for only an instant before Windows redisplays the active windows. By creating a PIF for TREE.COM named TREE.PIF, you can direct Windows to display the program's output until you press a continuation key.

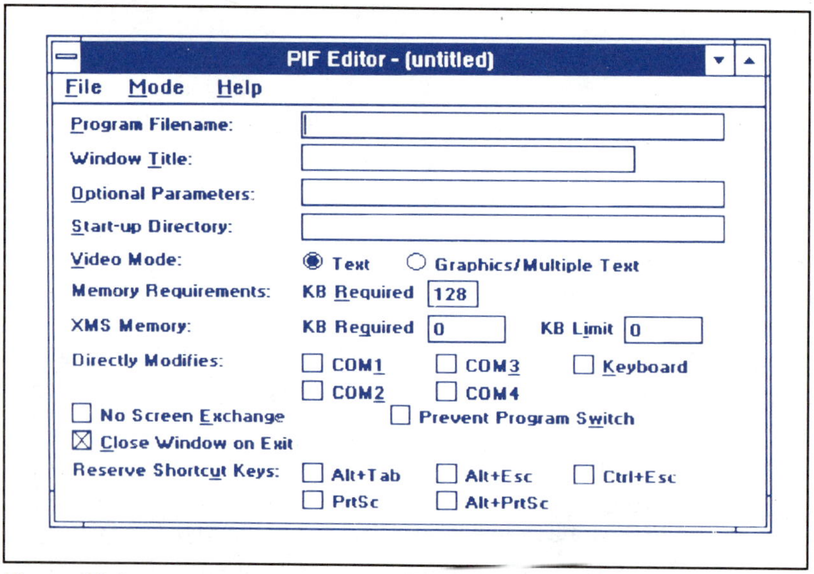

Figure 43.1: Windows' Standard mode PIF Editor

The Program Filename dialog-box entry lets you type in the program's complete path name. In this case, type **C:\DOS\TREE.COM**. Press the Tab key to advance to the next entry.

The Window Title dialog-box entry lets you type in the name you want Windows to display in a Windows title box. If you omit the title, Windows will use the programs's name, minus the extension. In this case, type **DOS Directory TREE Command**.

The Optional Parameters dialog-box entry lets you type in the parameters you want Windows to place automatically in the program's command line. If you include a question mark (**?**) in the entry, Windows will display a dialog box prompting you to enter the desired command line. For TREE.COM, you might want to type in a specific disk-drive letter or the /F switch in the command line. You do not have to specify a value for this entry; however, in this case, type a question mark.

The Start-up Directory dialog-box entry lets you tell Windows the desired default directory that Windows should select when it executes your program. If you are running a word processing program, for example, you might want Windows to automatically select the directory \WORDPROC\LETTERS. In this case, leave the entry unused.

The Video Mode option lets you tell Windows whether the program uses text or graphics mode. Multiple Text refers to text based applications that use multiple video display pages. If you are not sure which entry to use, select Graphics/Multiple Text. Because TREE.COM is strictly a text based application, select Text mode.

The Memory Requirements dialog-box entry tells Windows the minimum amount of memory that must be present for the program to run. For most programs, leave this value unchanged. If more memory is present than the amount specified, Windows will let the program use it. This value simply specifies the amount of memory that must be available before Windows will let the program run. For TREE.COM, leave the value unchanged at 128K.

If your computer has extended memory available, the XMS Memory dialog-box entry lets you specify the minimum amount of extended memory that must be available before Windows will let the program run, as well as the maximum amount of extended memory

Windows will let the program use. If you set the maximum limit at -1, Windows will give the program access to all available extended memory.

Because Windows can run several programs simultaneously, it needs to prevent one program from attempting to access a device being used by another. The Directly Modifies option lets you grant the program exclusive access to the serial communications ports COM1 through COM4, as well as the keyboard. If you select the Keyboard option, Windows will provide the program exclusive access to the keyboard, disabling other program's predefined shortcuts or hot keys. If you are unsure about these options, do not select them. For TREE.COM, leave all options unused.

In Lesson 44 you will learn how to exchange information between applications by using the Windows Clipboard. When you are running a non-Windows program, you can copy the current screen contents into the Clipboard by using Alt-Prtsc.

The No Screen Exchange dialog box option lets you save memory by disabling Windows' ability to copy the current screen to the Clipboard. If you are unsure about this option, do not select it. For TREE.COM, leave the entry unused.

As you have learned, Windows lets you run several programs simultaneously, switching from one to another as your needs require. The Prevent Program Switch option lets you disable Windows' ability to switch from this program to another. For TREE.COM, leave this option unused.

As discussed, Windows automatically closes your screen and redisplays its active windows each time your application completes. In many cases, this won't allow you enough time to view the program's output. By disabling the Close Window on Exit option, you direct Windows to prompt the user to press a continuation key before Windows erases the program's screen. For TREE.COM, disable this option by removing the X from the box.

By default, Windows predefines several shortcut keys that perform important functions. For example, there are shortcut keys that allow you to switch from one window to another, invoke the Windows Task Manager, or copy the current screen image to the Clipboard. If one or more of these Windows key combinations conflicts with keyboard combinations in an application, you can reserve those keys for the program. When you reserve keys, you effectively restrict

Windows' shortcut definitions. For TREE.COM, do not reserve any keys. At this point, your PIF for TREE.COM should look like Figure 43.2.

To save the PIF, invoke the PIF Editor File menu and select the Save As option. The PIF Editor will display a dialog box already containing the file name TREE.PIF, as in Figure 43.3.

To save the file, press Enter or click on the OK option.

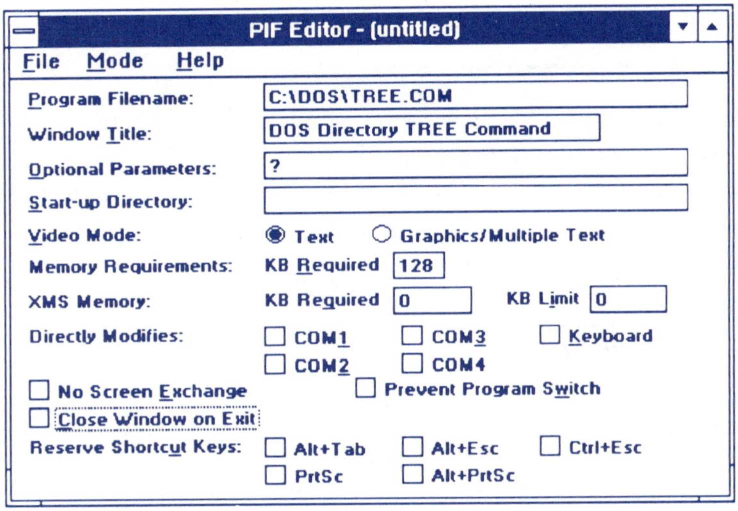

PIF Editor - (untitled)
File Mode Help
Program Filename: C:\DOS\TREE.COM
Window Title: DOS Directory TREE Command
Optional Parameters: ?
Start-up Directory:
Video Mode: Text Graphics/Multiple Text
Memory Requirements: KB Required 128
XMS Memory: KB Required 0 KB Limit 0
Directly Modifies: COM1 COM3 Keyboard
COM2 COM4
No Screen Exchange Prevent Program Switch
Close Window on Exit
Reserve Shortcut Keys: Alt+Tab Alt+Esc Ctrl+Esc
PrtSc Alt+PrtSc

Figure 43.2: *PIF for TREE.COM*

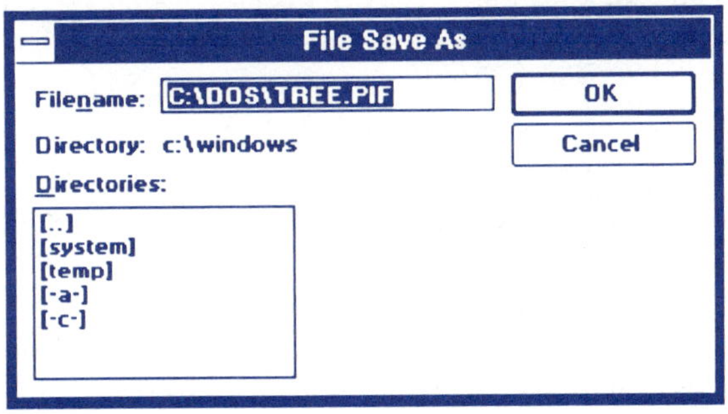

File Save As
Filename: C:\DOS\TREE.PIF OK
Directory: c:\windows Cancel
Directories:
[..]
[system]
[temp]
[-a-]
[-c-]

Figure 43.3: *PIF save dialog box*

How to Use a PIF

Once a PIF file exists, Windows will use it in one of two ways. First, when you invoke an EXE, COM, or BAT file, Windows will locate the corresponding PIF to determine the program's requirements. Second, if you select a PIF file using point and shoot, Windows will automatically execute the corresponding program.

Using TREE.PIF

Using the File Manager, open a directory window for the WINDOWS subdirectory and execute the file TREE.PIF. Windows will first display the dialog box in Figure 43.4, prompting you to type in the command line.

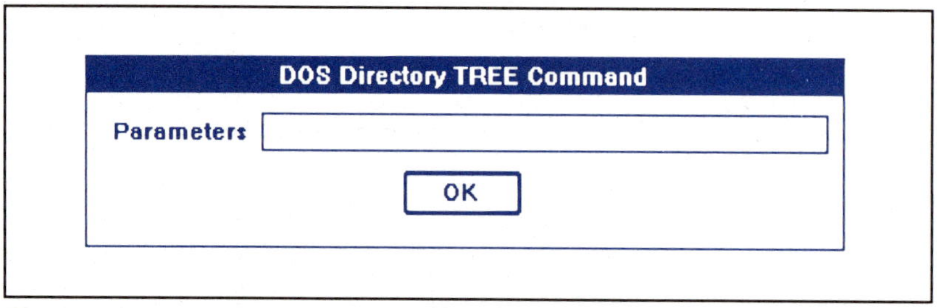

Figure 43.4: Command line dialog box for TREE.COM

If you type **/F** and press Enter, TREE.COM will display each directory and its files. When TREE.COM completes, Windows will prompt you to press any key to continue.

Using _DEFAULT.PIF

As discussed, if a program does not have its own PIF, Windows uses the default PIF. Most programs will run successfully with the default. Using the PIF editor File menu you can open the file _DEFAULT.PIF and change one or more settings. Many users, for example, will disable the Close Window on Exit option, forcing Windows to wait for a keystroke before erasing the program's screen.

How to Learn More about the PIF Editor

The PIF Editor provides extensive on-line help that explains each dialog-box option in detail. In addition, Lesson 63 examines the use of the PIF Editor for applications that run in Windows' 386 mode.

LESSON 44

Sharing Data Using the Windows Clipboard

Featuring

- Cutting and pasting data to and from the clipboard
- Saving and printing the current screen or window

THE CLIPBOARD IS PART OF THE FUNCTIONALITY OF Windows. It provides a temporary storage location for data being shared by two or more applications. (The Clipboard program—CLIPBRD.EXE—is a utility that lets you view the Clipboard's contents.) Several Windows applications have an Edit menu that provides Cut and Copy operations. Using these options, you can cut and paste (move) or copy (duplicate) selected text from the application into the Clipboard. Once the Clipboard contains text or a graphic image, another application can paste a copy of the Clipboard's contents into its own data area.

When you place information on the Clipboard, it remains there until you clear the clipboard, copy new information into the clipboard, close the Clipboard, or exit Windows.

How to Use the Clipboard

To become familiar with Clipboard, you will use it now to transfer a graphic image created with the Windows Paintbrush into a memo created with the Write word processor, to achieve the memo shown in Figure 44.1.

To begin, invoke the Write word processor from the Program Manager Accessories group and type the text shown in Figure 44.2.

Next, invoke the Paintbrush program from the Accessories group and create the map shown in Figure 44.3.

Next, using the Paintbrush Cut tool, highlight the image. Then, using the Edit menu, *copy the illustration* into the Clipboard, as shown in Figure 44.4.

Finally, select the Write window and position the cursor at the bottom of the memo. Invoke the Edit menu and choose Paste. Write will *paste the image* of the map into your memo as shown in Figure 44.5.

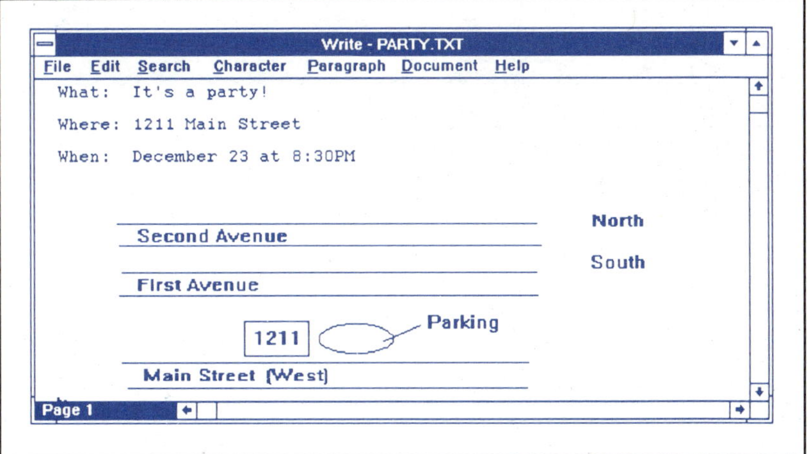

Figure 44.1: Combining text and graphics via the Clipboard

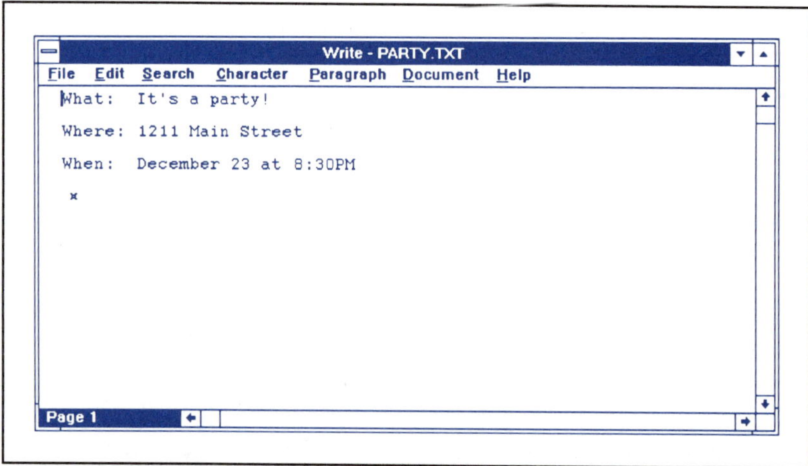

Figure 44.2: *Entering the memo's text using Write*

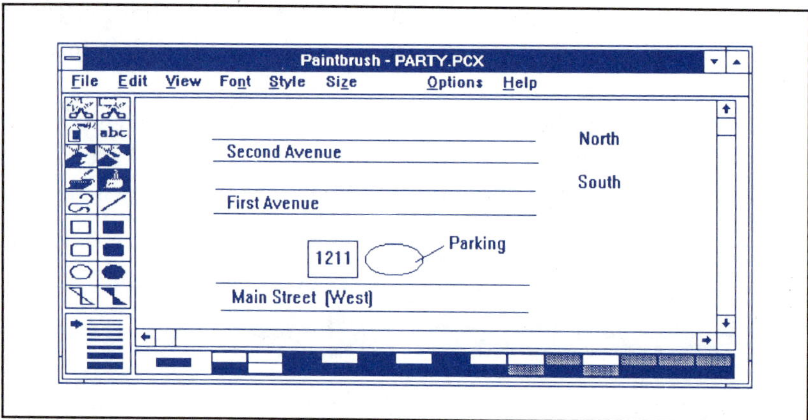

Figure 44.3: *Creating the memo's graphics using Paintbrush*

In this case, you used the Clipboard to share data between programs without having to invoke Clipboard from the Program Manager Main group.

How to Save Clipboard Images

Depending on your application, you may want to *save* the Clipboard's contents to a file. To do so, invoke the Clipboard program

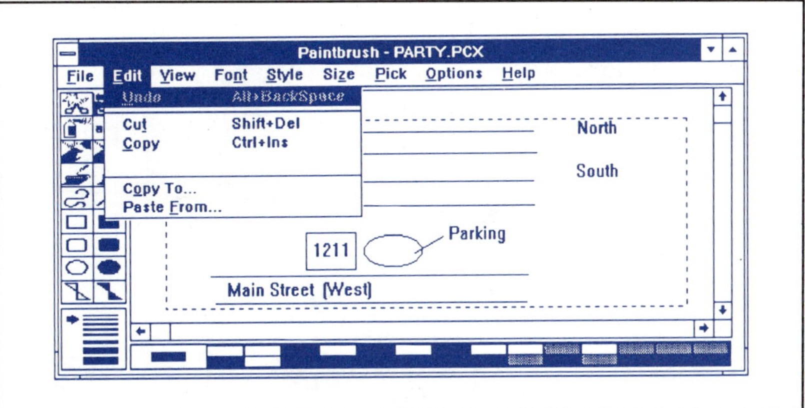

Figure 44.4: Copying a Paintbrush image to the Clipboard

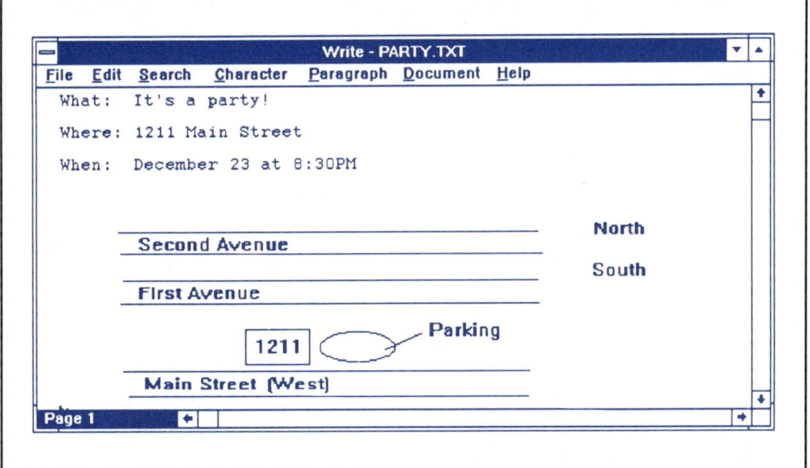

Figure 44.5: Pasting a graphic image from the Clipboard

from the Program Manager Main group. Windows will open a Window for the Clipboard, displaying a portion of its current contents, as in Figure 44.6.

Using the Clipboard's File menu, you can save the Clipboard's current contents. Clipboard files normally use the CLP extension. Most users, though, paste Clipboard images into their applications, such as Write or Paintbrush, using the application to save the image to

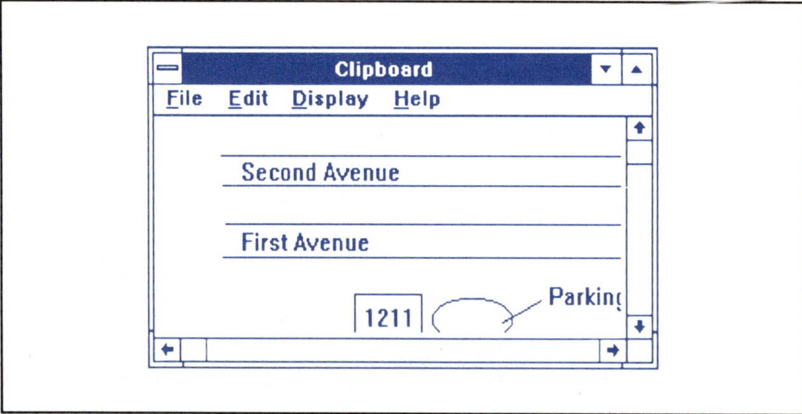

Figure 44.6: Windows' Clipboard

disk. Like all windows, you can move, size, or close the Clipboard window.

How to Save the Current Screen's or Window's Contents

Users call printed copies of their screen's contents a screen dump. In Windows, you can copy the contents of the screen to the Clipboard by pressing the PrtSc key. Once the Clipboard contains the screen image, you can paste its contents into a Write word-processing file or a Paintbrush file and *print* the screen dump using the application's File menu Print option.

To save the contents of the current window (as opposed to the entire screen), press Alt+PrtSc or Shift+PrtSc.

How to Learn More about Clipboard

Clipboard provides extensive on-line help for its commands and features. Using Help, you can learn how to cut and paste information to and from non-Windows programs, and how to view the Clipboard's contents in different formats.

LESSON 45

Using the Windows Task List to Select an Active Application

Featuring

- Quickly selecting and closing active windows
- Managing screen icons

IN LESSON 11 YOU INVOKED THE WINDOWS TASK LIST TO tile and cascade the active windows on your screen. Invoke the Clock, Calculator, and Notepad from the Program Manager Accessories group. To invoke the Task List you must double-click your mouse on the Windows desktop, or use the Ctrl+Esc keyboard combination. When you invoke the Task List, Windows will open a window listing current application windows and providing you with several capabilities, such as switching to or ending a specific application. The Task List is shown in Figure 45.1.

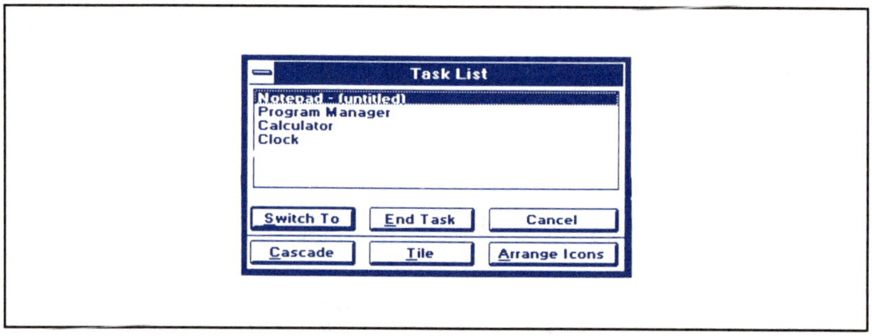

Figure 45.1: Windows' Task List

How to Switch Application Windows Using the Task List

The Windows Task List gives you a quick way to switch from one application window to another.

To select an active application from the Task List, aim your mouse pointer at the name of the desired application on the Task List and double-click.

To select an active application from the Task List using your keyboard, highlight the desired application's name and press Enter.

How to End a Program Using the Task List

The Windows Task List lets you quickly end a program, removing its window from the screen.

To end a program from the Task List using your mouse, aim the mouse pointer at the desired program's name within the Task List and single-click. When the desired file is highlighted, aim the mouse pointer at the End Task option and click.

To end a program from the Task List using your keyboard, use your arrow keys to highlight the desired program's name. Next, press the Tab key until Windows highlights the End Task option. Press Enter to end the program.

How to Cancel the Task List

If you invoke the Task List window and decide you don't want to perform an operation, click your mouse on the Cancel option or press Esc.

How to Arrange Icons Neatly

If you run several programs at the same time, it isn't uncommon for icons to be scattered all over your screen. Using the Task List window, you can clean up your screen by lining up all the icons across the bottom. To do so, invoke the Task List and select the Arrange Icons option.

PART IV

Customizing Windows

LESSON 46

Using Setup to Change Your System Configuration

Featuring

- Changing your hardware configuration
- Informing Windows about new software

WHEN YOU FIRST INSTALL WINDOWS, THE INSTALLATION program lets you define your video-display, keyboard, and mouse types, and specify whether you are connected to a local area network. If you add to or upgrade your hardware configuration after installing Windows, you will need to inform it of the new hardware. The Setup program lets you make such changes without having to re-install Windows.

How to Change Your Hardware Configuration

Invoke the Setup program from the Program Manager Main group. The Setup program will open a window displaying the current hardware configuration, as in Figure 46.1.

Using your mouse or Alt+O, invoke the Options menu shown in Figure 46.2.

The Change Systems Settings option lets you *change your hardware settings*. If you select this option, Setup places a window with 4 scroll bars over the old window, as in Figure 46.3.

To select a system option using a mouse, click on the scroll bar that corresponds to the desired option. Setup will expand the single option into a list of available selections for the current option, as shown in Figure 46.4.

Northgate Windows Setup
Options Help

Display:	EGA
Keyboard:	All AT type keyboards (84 - 86 keys)
Mouse:	Microsoft, or IBM PS/2
Network:	Network not installed
Swap file:	None

Figure 46.1: *Windows' hardware configuration*

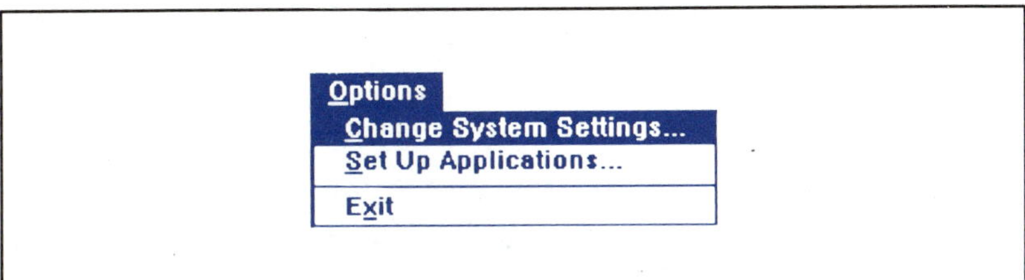

Figure 46.2: *Setup Options menu*

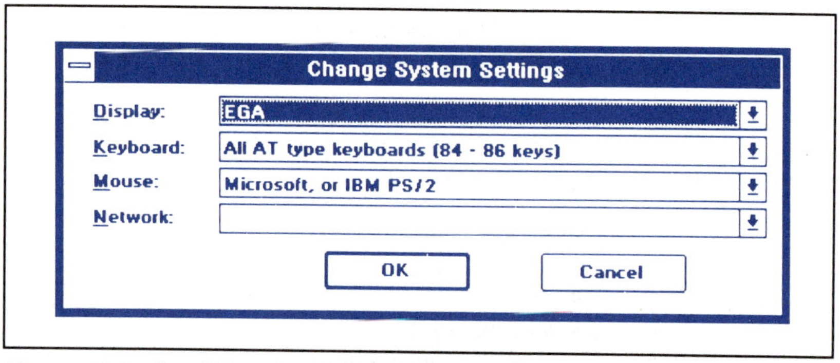

Figure 46.3: Scroll Bars for selecting system options

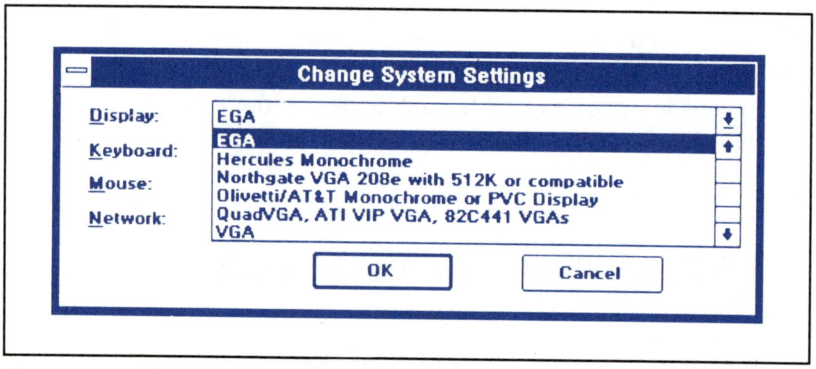

Figure 46.4: Expanding available selections

To select a system option using your keyboard, press the Tab key to highlight the desired option. Using your arrow keys, scroll through the list of available options. If you enter Alt+Down Arrow, Setup will expand the options as shown in Figure 46.4.

When you have selected your desired options, select the OK option or press Enter. Setup will display the window containing the current system configuration. Using the window's Control menu, you can close the window.

How to Add New Windows Software to a Group

If you purchase *new software* that runs under Windows, you will want to add it to either the Program Manager Windows Applications group or the Non–Windows Applications group. To do so, invoke the Setup Options menu and choose Set Up Applications. Setup will display the dialog box in Figure 46.5, prompting you for the drives you want it to search.

Using your mouse or keyboard arrow keys, you can scroll through the available drive letters, selecting the drive you desire. Next, select OK or press Enter to continue. Setup will search the drives specified, creating a window of applications it has found, as shown in Figure 46.6.

Using your mouse or keyboard, select the desired files from the Applications found list and Add them to the Setup for use list. When you have selected the desired applications, select the OK option. Setup will redisplay a window containing the current hardware options. Using the Window's Control menu, close the Setup program.

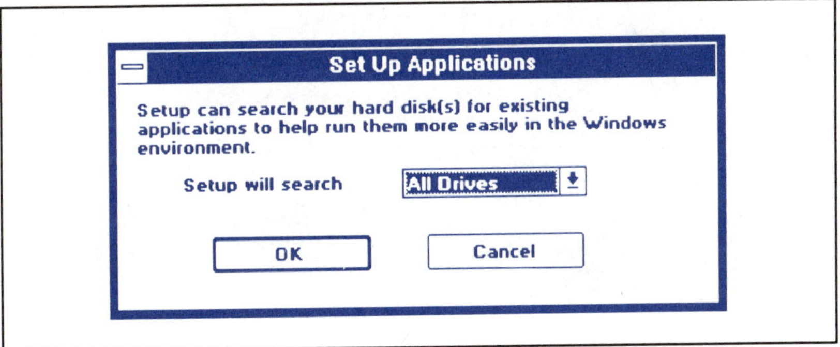

Figure 46.5: Search drives dialog box

Set Up Applications
Applications found on hard disk(s):
LINK Utility
LINK Utility
LINK Utility
Microsoft Basic
Microsoft C Compiler
Microsoft Macro Assembler
Microsoft Quick C
Add ->
<- Remove
Add All
Set up for use with Windows.
LINK Utility
C:\C600\BINB\link.exe
OK
Cancel

Figure 46.6: Applications found by Setup

LESSON 47

Customizing Your Screen Colors

Featuring

- The Windows Control Panel
- Predefined color schemes
- Custom color mixing

AS SHOWN IN LESSON 1, WINDOWS LETS YOU CUSTOMIZE your screen colors, letting you select the colors you find most pleasing and soothing to your eyes. Lessons 47 through 56 teach you how to customize Windows through the Windows Control Panel. Invoke the *Control Panel* from the Program Manager's Main group. The Control Panel will open a window that contains several customization icons, as in Figure 47.1.

Figure 47.1: Windows' Control Panel

Using your mouse you can double-click on any icon to select it. If you are using your keyboard, use your keyboard arrow keys to highlight an option and then press Enter.

How to Customize the Desktop's Colors

Select the Colors icon from the Control Panel by double-clicking. The Control Panel will open a window containing a scroll bar for existing *color schemes* and a sample desktop that illustrates the current color selections, as shown in Figure 47.2.

To help you customize your screen colors, Windows provides a collection of predefined color schemes you can select for your desired colors.

To select a predefined color scheme using your mouse, click on the down-arrow scroll button that appears below the Color Schemes prompt. The Control Panel will display the list of available color schemes shown in Figure 47.3.

As you click on each color scheme, the Control Panel will change the colors of the sample desktop, letting you preview them.

To select a predefined color scheme using your keyboard, use your keyboard arrow keys to browse through the available colors. As

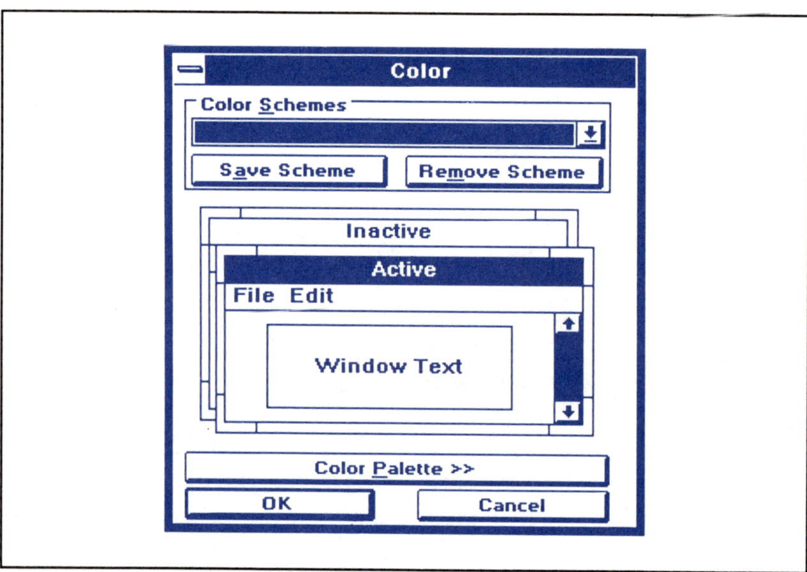

Figure 47.2: Color option window

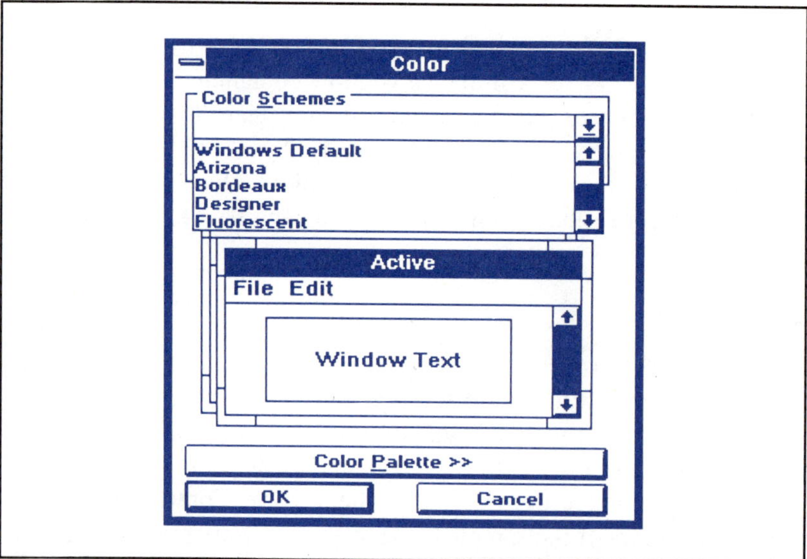

Figure 47.3: Available color schemes

you do, the Control Panel will change the colors of the sample desktop, letting you preview them. If you enter the Alt+Down Arrow keyboard combination, the Control Panel will expand the color schemes as shown in Figure 47.3.

If you find a color scheme you like, select the OK option or press Enter. If you don't find a scheme you like, select the Color Palette option. The Color window will double in size, displaying 48 predefined colors. You can now select individual colors for each desktop component, as in Figure 47.4.

The Screen Element scroll bar lets you select different desktop components such as Menu Bars, Menu Text, and the Windows Background. If you click on the scroll bar with your mouse, or enter Alt+Down Arrow, the Control Panel will let you scroll through the desktop components. If you are using your keyboard, use your arrow keys to scroll through the components.

Each time you display a different desktop component, the Control Panel will place a small frame around its current color.

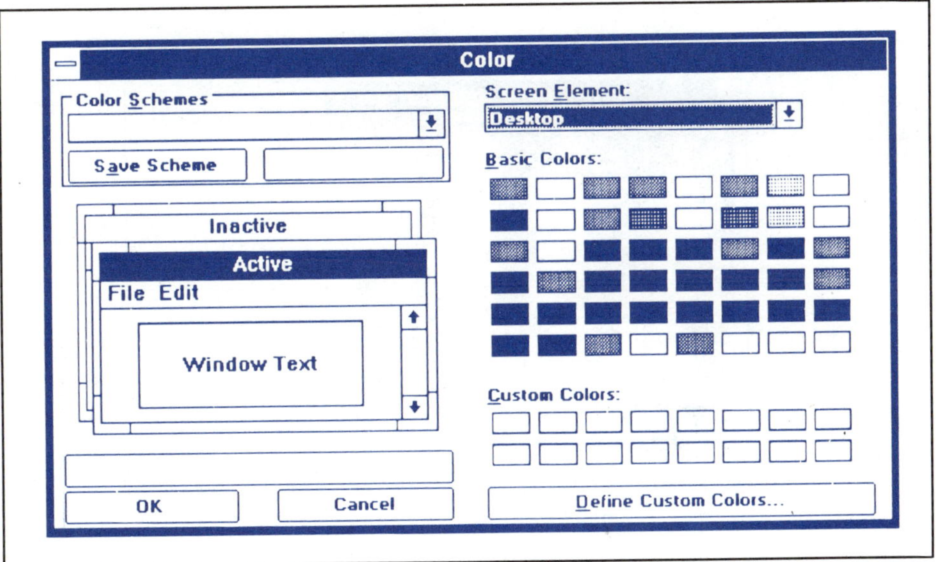

Figure 47.4: *Color window expansion*

To select a new component color using your mouse, aim the mouse pointer at the desired color and click.

To select a new component color using your keyboard, press the Tab key to select the color region. Next using your keyboard arrow keys, highlight the desired color and press the spacebar. As you select new component colors, the Control Panel will update the color of the sample desktop, letting you preview your selection.

How to Create Your Own Custom Colors

If you can't find a basic color that suits your needs, the Control menu lets you define 16 *custom colors* of your own. To create your own colors, select the Define Custom Colors option. Your window will display a color-mixing chart that you can use to create the desired shade (Figure 47.5).

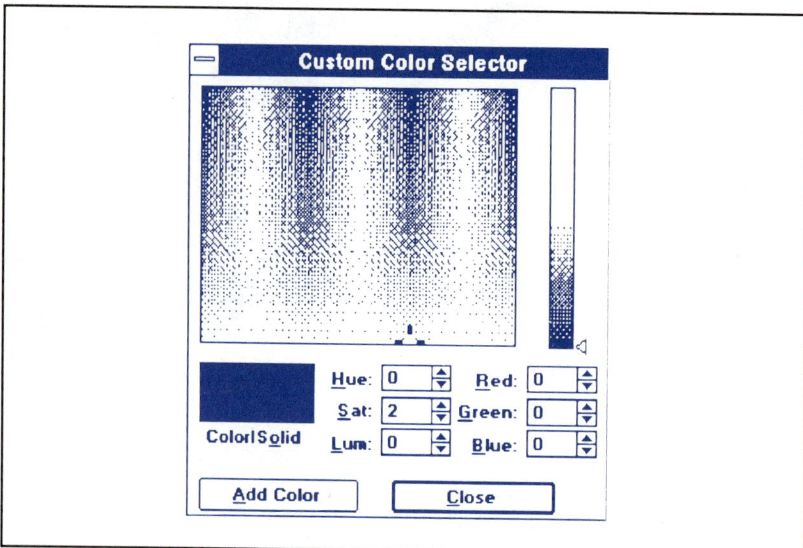

Figure 47.5: Custom color options

The Control Panel displays a crossbar cursor at the current color position. Using your mouse you can move the cursor around the available colors. As you do so, the Control Panel will change the values corresponding to the various options. Table 47.1 briefly describes the effect of each option.

Table 47.1: *Color Option Definitions.*

OPTION	PURPOSE
Hue	Defines the color's position in the color spectrum from 0 to 239.
Sat	Defines the hue's saturation or purity, where 0 is grey and 240 is pure color.
Lum	Defines the color's luminosity or brightness, where 0 is darkest and 240 is brightest.
Red	Defines the amount of red shade used to create the color, where 0 is none and 255 is the maximum.
Green	Defines the amount of green shade to create the color, where 0 is none and 255 is the maximum.
Blue	Defines the amount of blue shade to create the color, where 0 is none and 255 is the maximum.

If you are using your keyboard to define your colors, you must select each color option and type in the desired value. When you are satisfied with the color, select the Add Color option. The Control Panel will add your color to the first available Custom Color box. You can repeat this process to create additional colors. To return to the previous color screen, select the Close option.

LESSON 48

Managing Your Fonts

Featuring

- Adding new fonts
- Saving memory by removing unnecessary fonts

AS DISCUSSED, A FONT IS A GRAPHIC REPRESENTATION of a character or number. You can display text in a normal (roman), *italic*, or **bold** font. For example, the Windows Write word processor, discussed in Lesson 40, lets you make extensive use of different fonts in your documents. Windows groups fonts into *font sets*, which contain the same character representations in different sizes. Font sets are stored in files and normally have the extension FON. When you use the Windows Setup program to install a new printer, SETUP automatically copies the files from the Windows distribution floppy disk containing the font sets that your printer supports.

Many laser printers use built-in fonts or font cartridges, which Windows can access by using the printer's device driver. Each time you send a document to the printer, Windows checks to ensure the printer driver supports the selected fonts. If it does not, Windows substitutes a supported font, instead. For more specifics on printers and fonts, use the File Manager to print the file PRINTERS.TXT, which resides in the WINDOWS directory.

How to Add a New Font

If you purchase *additional font sets* from your printer's manufacturer or another third party vendor, you will need to install the font before Windows can use it. To do so, invoke the Control Panel from the Program Manager Main group and select the Fonts icon by double-clicking. The Control Panel will open a window containing a list of the available fonts, as well as options to add or delete fonts, as in Figure 48.1.

Using your keyboard arrow keys or mouse, take a moment to highlight each available font and view the samples. To add a new

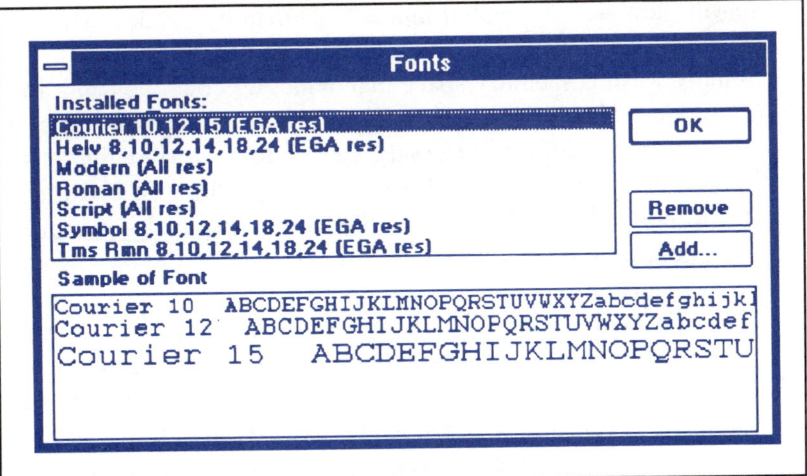

Figure 48.1: The Control Panel Fonts dialog box

font, select the Add button. The Control Panel will display the dialog box shown in Figure 48.2, prompting you to enter the name of the file containing the font set.

Type in the file name and press Enter.

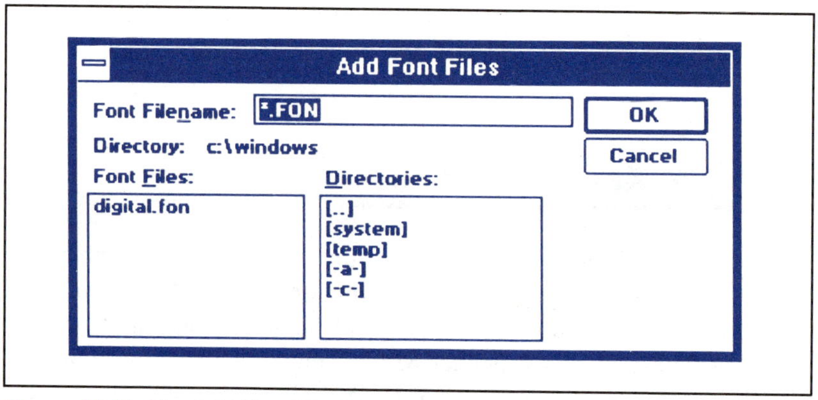

Figure 48.2: The Add Font File dialog box

When to Remove a Font

Every font that Windows installs requires memory. Depending on the font set, the actual amount of memory needed will differ. If Windows installs one or more fonts that you never use, the font is simply wasting memory space that Windows could be using for other programs. Using the Control Panel's Font dialog box, you can remove one or more unnecessary fonts. To *remove a font*, use your mouse or keyboard arrow keys to highlight the font and then select the Remove option. The Control Panel will display a confirmation dialog box, prompting you to confirm that you want to remove the font, as in Figure 48.3.

When you remove a font, Windows does not delete the font file from disk. Instead, Windows removes the font from its list of available fonts, which frees up memory. If you ever need the font in the future, you can simply add it as discussed earlier in this lesson. Note that Windows uses the Helvetica font (Helv) for dialog box text. Do *not* remove this font.

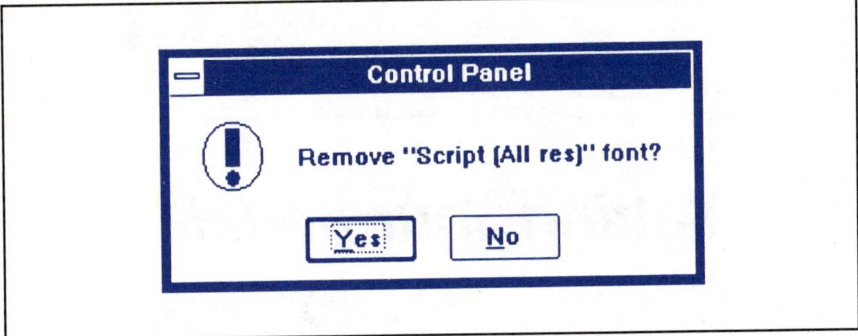

Figure 48.3: Remove font dialog box

LESSON 49

Setting Your Serial Communication Port Characteristics

Featuring

- Understanding serial and parallel devices
- Configuring your serial ports

COMPUTER HARDWARE COMPONENTS THAT ARE NOT physically contained within your computer's chasis, such as printers, mice, and modems, are called external devices. To communicate with (or send information to) external devices, you must have them connected to your computer. Depending on the number of wires used to connect the device to the computer (the actual wires are concealed inside a cable), a device is classified as either a *parallel* or a *serial device*. A parallel device receives 8 bits of data at one time, while a serial device only 1 bit. Most printers, for example, are parallel devices, whereas most modems and external mice are serial devices.

The connector at the back of your computer where you attach the cable that goes to the external device is called a port. Most computers have at least one parallel and one serial port. Figure 49.1 illustrates parallel and serial cables and ports.

Because most printers (often called line printers) are parallel, the parallel ports are given the names LPT1, LPT2 and so on, standing for Line Printer 1 and Line Printer 2. Likewise, because serial ports are often used for data communications, the ports are named COM1, COM2 and so on, standing for Communications Port 1 and Communications Port 2.

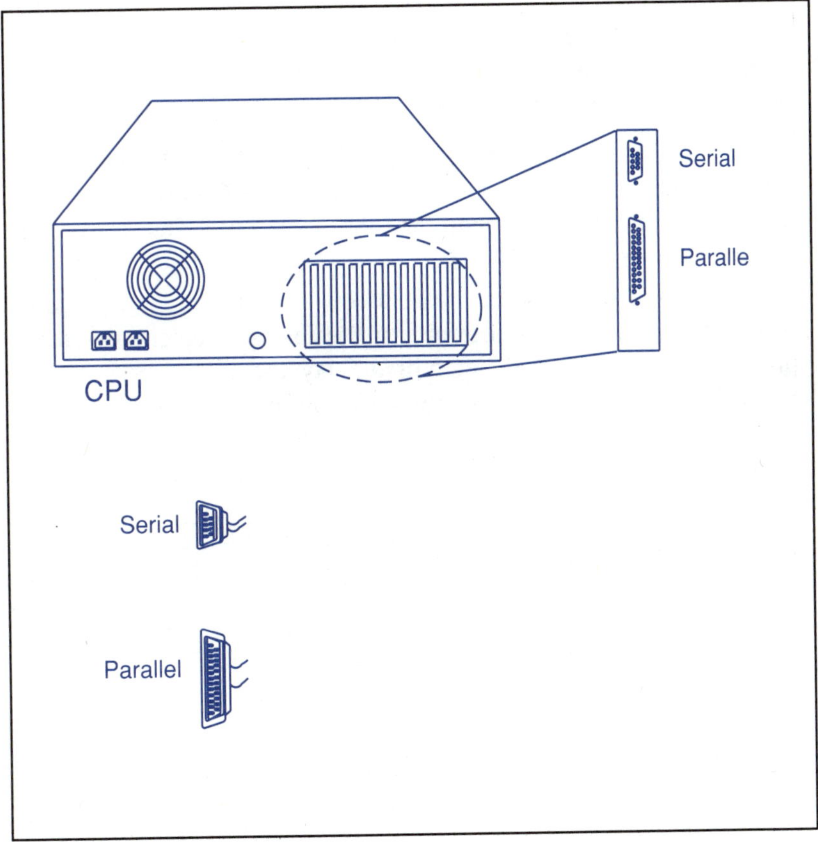

Figure 49.1: *Parallel and serial cables and ports*

When you connect an external device to a serial communications port, you must ensure that your computer is sending data to or receiving data from the port at the same speed setting and in the same format that the device is using. These speeds and settings are often called data-communications settings or parameters. If you purchase a new serial device, its documentation will tell you the correct settings. If you are using a modem to communicate with a remote computer, you must know the remote computer's data-communications settings before you begin. Lesson 41 discusses the Windows Terminal program, which allows you to access remote computers using your modem.

How to Assign Your Computer's Serial Port Settings

Invoke the Control Panel from the Program Manager Main group and double-click on the Ports icon. The Control Panel will open a window containing icons for the serial ports COM1 through COM4 as shown in Figure 49.2.

Using your mouse or keyboard arrow keys, highlight the desired serial port. Next, using your mouse or the Tab key, select the Settings option and the Control Panel will display the dialog box in Figure 49.3, specifying the data-communications parameters.

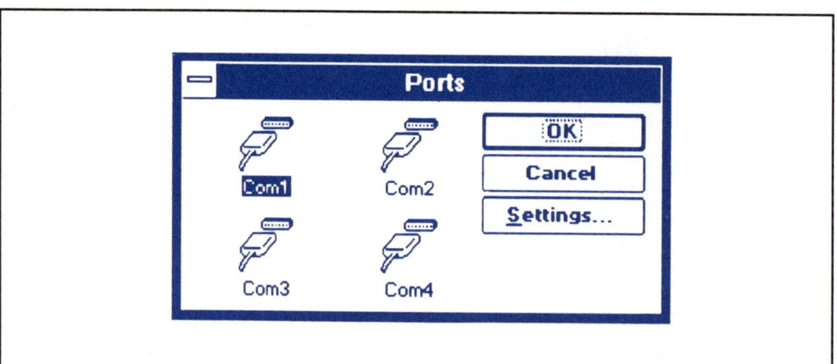

Figure 49.2: Control Panel Ports option box

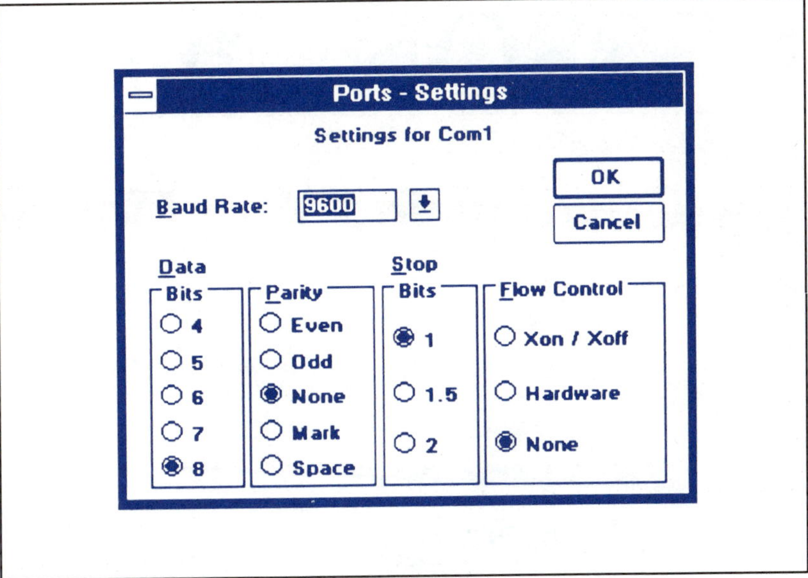

Figure 49.3: Serial data-communications parameters

To select a data-communications parameter using your mouse, aim the mouse pointer at the desired option and click.

To select a data-communications parameter using your keyboard, press the Tab key to select the desired group. Next, use your arrow keys to select the desired option.

When you have selected the desired settings, select the OK option or press Enter. The Control Panel will redisplay the window of ports giving you a chance to configure additional ports. Select the OK option or press Enter to continue.

LESSON 50

Customizing Your Mouse

Featuring

- Setting your mouse tracking speed
- Reversing mouse buttons

AS YOU BECOME MORE COMFORTABLE WITH USING YOUR mouse to traverse Windows' menus and dialog boxes, you can use the Windows Control Panel to improve your mouse's responsiveness. For instance, you can increase the speed at which the mouse pointer travels across your screen, or you can decrease the time Windows waits for the second click in a double-click operation. By adjusting these response speeds, you can make your mouse more comfortable to use.

How to Customize the Mouse

Invoke the Control Panel from the Program Manager Main group and double-click on the Mouse icon. The Control Panel will display the dialog box in Figure 50.1. To the left are the scroll bars that let you *adjust your mouse speed* while the left (L) and right (R) buttons specify the current *mouse select button*.

The Mouse Tracking Speed scroll bar lets you control the speed at which the mouse pointer moves (or tracks) across the screen when you move your mouse. Experiment with faster and slower speeds until you find a speed you are comfortable with.

The Double Click Speed option lets you set the speed Windows will use to recognize a double-click option. As you adjust the speed, double-click on the box containing the word TEST. If you double-click fast enough for the new speed, the box will toggle between white and black.

By default, Windows uses your left mouse button as the mouse-select button. The Swap Left/Right Buttons box lets you select the mouse's right button as the select button. If you select this option (by X-ing in the option box), Windows will immediately recognize the mouse's right button as the select button, ignoring the left button. Which button you use is simply a matter of preference.

Once you have made your mouse selections, click on the OK option, or press Enter.

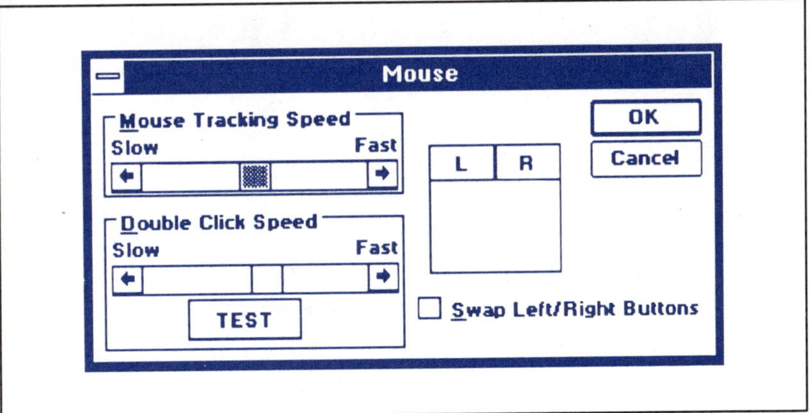

Figure 50.1: Mouse customization dialog box

LESSON 51

Customizing Your Desktop's Appearance

Featuring

- Displaying desktop patterns and wallpaper
- Designing your own background
- Defining icon grids

THE AREA OF YOUR SCREEN BEHIND THE OPEN WINDOWS is called the desktop. By default, Windows displays the desktop as a solid color. However, as you will learn in this lesson, you can use Windows' predefined patterns and graphic images to produce a wallpaper like backdrop for your desktop. In addition, you will learn how to create your own images, such as a company logo, for use as a desktop design. Also, using the Control Panel's Desktop dialog box, you can improve your screen's appearance by controlling where Windows places your icons.

How to Install a Predefined Desktop Design

Invoke the Control Panel from the Program Manager Main group and double-click on the Desktop icon. The Control Panel will open a dialog box containing the Desktop customization options, as in Figure 51.1.

The dialog box gives you two ways to assign designs to the desktop: *patterns and wallpaper*. A pattern is a simple design you can create with this dialog box. To help you get started, the Control Panel provides several predefined patterns that you can select or modify.

To select a pattern using your mouse, aim the mouse pointer at the downward scroll button and click. The dialog box will display a list of available patterns. To select a specific pattern, click on its name in the list.

To select a pattern using your keyboard, press the Tab key until the Pattern option is highlighted. Next, press the Alt+Down Arrow

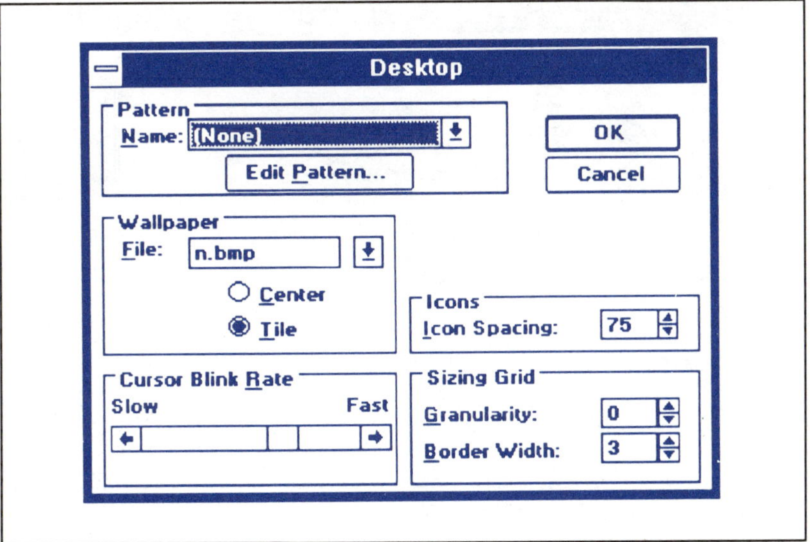

Figure 51.1: Desktop customization dialog box

keyboard combination to display the list of available pattern names. To select a specific pattern, use your arrow keys to highlight the desired name.

In this case, select the Spinner pattern and press Enter or select the OK option. The Control Panel will change the desktop's pattern as shown in Figure 51.2.

In addition to the predefined patterns, the Control Panel provides several very colorful wallpaper designs. To select a wallpaper design, invoke the desktop dialog box as before. Next, disable the Pattern display by selecting None for the pattern option. Using your mouse or your keyboard, expand the available wallpaper options. Note that each option has the BMP extension for bit-mapped files. Wallpaper images can be graphic images created with software programs like Paintbrush or even complex scanned images such as color photographs. In this case, select the Paper option. The Control Panel will assign a crinkled paper background to your desktop, as shown in Figure 51.3.

Take time to experiment with the wallpaper options until you find the one you like best.

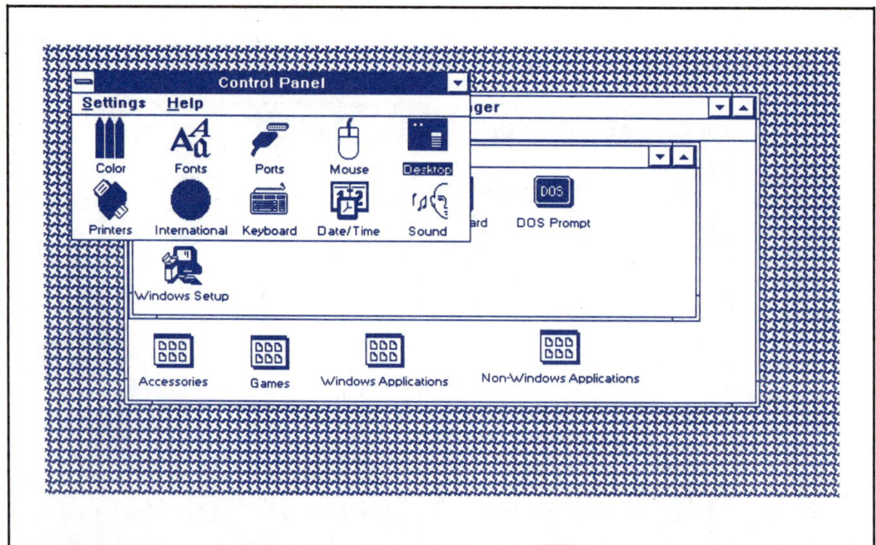

Figure 51.2: Assigning a desktop pattern

Figure 51.3: A wallpaper desktop design

How to Create Your Own Patterns

In addition to letting you select predefined patterns and wallpaper, the Desktop dialog box lets you *create your own patterns*, provided you have a mouse. To begin, invoke the Desktop dialog box and disable the Wallpaper display by selecting None as the wallpaper option. Next, choose any of the patterns (you can even choose None) and select the Edit option. The dialog box will display the pattern edit box in Figure 51.4.

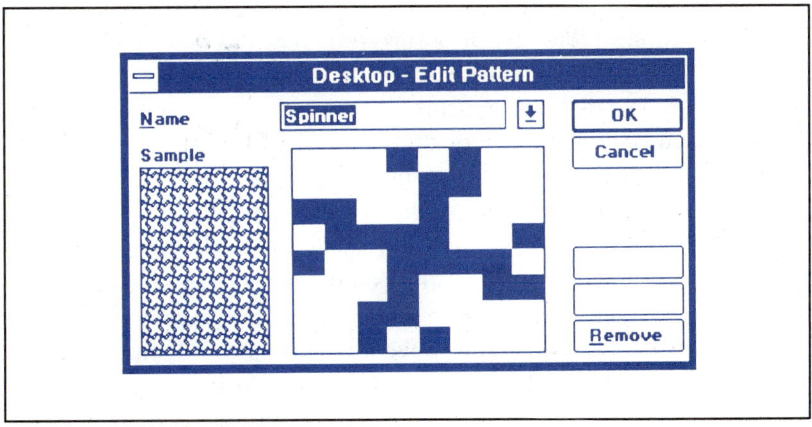

Figure 51.4: Edit Pattern dialog box

First, type in the name for the pattern. In this case, type **Stripes**, but do not press Enter. Next, using your mouse, toggle on or off the squares that make up the pattern by clicking on them. Try creating the striped pattern shown in Figure 51.5.

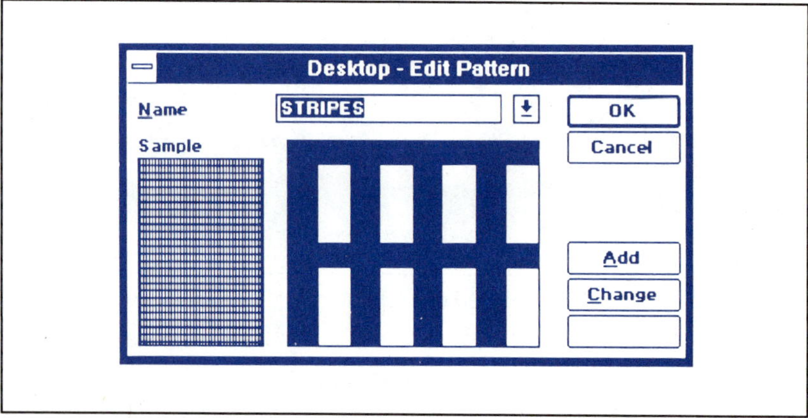

Figure 51.5: Creating a custom pattern

Select the Add option or press Enter to add the new pattern to the list. Then select OK or press Enter to direct the Control Panel to use your new pattern.

Other Desktop Customization Techniques

In addition to letting you define your desktop pattern, the Control Panel lets you set the cursor's blink rate, the spacing between icons, and icon positioning grids. To increase your cursor's blink rate, click on one of the cursor speed scroll arrows or press Alt+R and use your arrow keys to adjust the speed. The *Icon Spacing* option specifies (in pixels—the dots on the screen that make up characters and images) the minimum amount of space Windows will place between icons. Use your mouse to click on the up or down scroll arrows to change this value, or press Alt+I and type in the desired setting.

By default, each time you move a window or an icon, Windows leaves it at the location you specify. The Granularity option lets you create an invisible *grid*, to which Windows will always align icons and windows when you move them. The Granularity option lets you enter a value from 0 to 49. The value 0 disables the grid. The value 1 places the grid lines 8 pixels apart. The value 2 places the grid lines 16 pixels apart, and so on, in multiples of 8. Using your mouse you can increase and decrease the values by clicking on the up- and down-arrow buttons. If you are using a keyboard, press Alt+G and then type in the desired value.

Finally, the *Border Width* option lets you specify, in pixels, the width of the border that surrounds each window on your screen from 1 to 49, where 49 is the thickest possible border. As before, by clicking your mouse on the up- and down-arrow scroll buttons, you can increase and decrease the border width. If you are using a keyboard, press Alt+B and then type in the desired value.

LESSON 52

Changing Your Printer Configuration

Featuring

- Adding a new printer
- Selecting the Windows default printer

DURING THE INSTALLATION PROCESS, WINDOWS LETS you install one or more printers. If you purchase a new printer after installing Windows or want to change printer ports or the default printer, you will need to use the Control Panel to make your printer changes. Before you begin, however, use the Windows Notepad to examine the file PRINTERS.TXT. This file contains additional printer documentation not found in the Windows manual.

How to Add a New Printer

To inform Windows of a *new printer*, you must use the Control Panel to perform the following steps.

1. Install the proper printer-driver software, either from your Windows distribution disk or from a disk provided by your printer's manufacturer.
2. Assign the printer to a specific port.
3. Assign the printer settings specific to your printer.

In addition, you may choose to make the new printer the default printer that Windows uses for all printer operations.

To begin, invoke the Control Panel from the Program Manager Main group and double-click on the Printers icon. The Control Panel will open a dialog box that lets you select your printer configuration, as shown in Figure 52.1.

Select the Add Printer option, and the dialog box will expand to display a list of printers, as shown in Figure 52.2.

To add a new printer, click on the scroll bar that appears below the List of Printers option, or press Alt+L and use your keyboard arrow keys to highlight a printer name. To select a printer, double-click on the printer's name or highlight the name and press Enter. The Control Panel will display a dialog box prompting you to place the Windows Setup disk containing the printer driver into drive A and then to press Enter. When you do so, the Control Panel will copy the printer driver to your hard disk, displaying the new printer's name in the list of available printers.

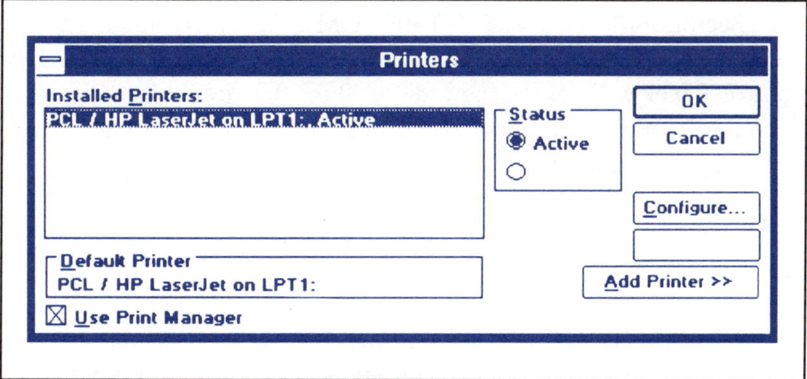

Figure 52.1: Printer configuration dialog box

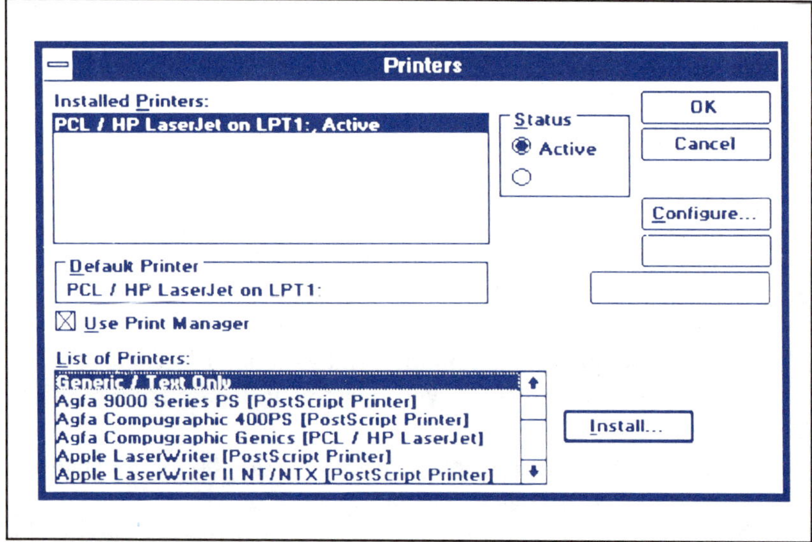

Figure 52:2: *Dialog box containing available printer list*

If your printer does not appear in the list of supported printers, there may be another printer in the list that is compatible with yours, or your printer may have a driver provided by the manufacturer. If this is the case, select Unlisted Printer and insert the disk with the driver. If neither of these is successful, contact your printer's manufacturer for details or the possibility of their sending you a Windows driver.

After you install the printer driver, you must assign the printer to a specific port, such as LPT1 or COM1. To do so, highlight the new printer's name and select the dialog box's Configure option. The Control Panel will open a new dialog box that lets you assign the printer to a port or remove the printer from the list of available printers, as in Figure 52.3.

Using your mouse or Alt+P, highlight the port the new printer will be attached to. Next, use your mouse or Alt+S to select the Setup option. The Control Panel will display a third dialog box containing options for the new printer driver, as shown in Figure 52.4.

Select the desired options and then choose the OK option. The Control Panel will return to the previous configuration dialog box. Again select the OK option and the original printer dialog box will appear.

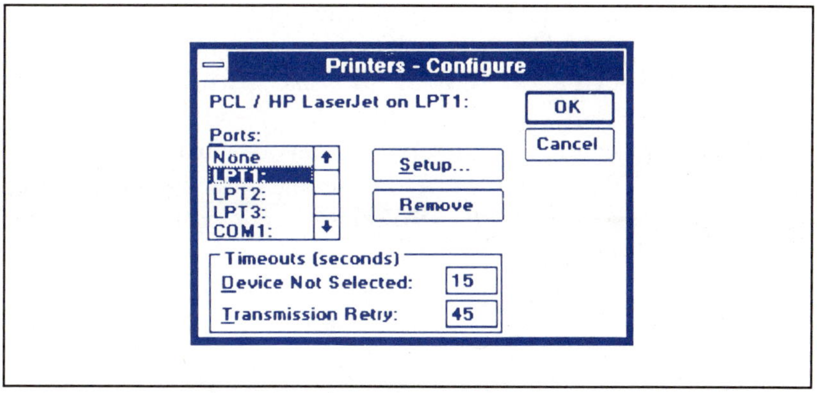

Figure 52.3: *Printer configuration dialog box*

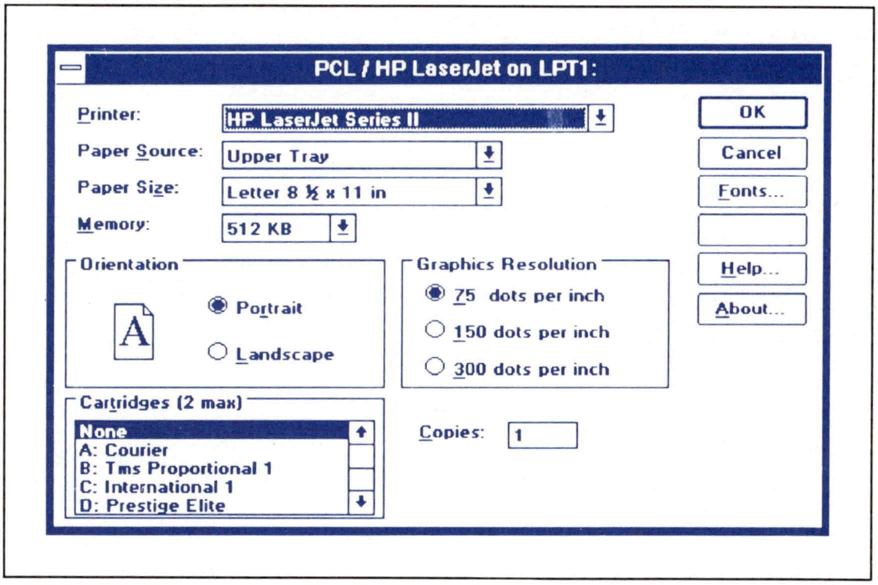

Figure 52.4: *Printer setup dialog box*

Next, if you want the new printer to be the port's default printer, you must select it as active. To do so, highlight the printer and click on the Active status, or press Alt+S and select active using your keyboard arrow keys.

If you have several printers attached to different ports, you will need to select one printer as the *Windows default printer*. To do so, decide which of the printers in the Installed Printers list you want to be the default and double-click on its name, or highlight it and press Alt+D. The dialog box will display the printer's name in the Default Printer box.

If you are configuring a serial printer attached to one of the ports COM1–COM4, you may need to set the ports communications settings as discussed in Lesson 49. Refer to your printer manual for the correct settings.

LESSON 53

Changing Windows' International Settings

Featuring

- Selecting international keyboard templates
- Selecting international date, time, and currency formats

WINDOWS HELPS INTERNATIONAL USERS MAXIMIZE productivity by allowing them to select their own character sets, keyboard templates, and country-specific date, time, and currency formats from the Control Panel. If your copy of Windows is already set properly, you can skip to Lesson 54.

How to Select International Settings

Invoke the Control Panel from the Windows Program Manager and double-click on the International icon. The Control Panel will display the dialog box shown in Figure 53.1, containing different international settings.

When you select a specific country from the Country option, the corresponding date, time, list-separator, number, and currency formats change automatically. To display the list of available countries, click your mouse on the down-arrow button, or press the Tab key to highlight the option and press Alt+Down Arrow.

The Language option provides a list of the supported languages that different applications use to sort information or perform character conversions. Using your keyboard or mouse, select the language that corresponds to your Country setting. The Keyboard option lets you select a particular country's keyboard template (or layout). The Measurement option lets you select the English or Metric system. Lastly, the List Separation option lets you specify which character is to be used to separate items in a list.

Most international users will customize only the Country and Keyboard settings, using the default date, time, and currency formats for whatever country is selected. If, however, you want to further customize these options, you can do so by selecting the Change button for the desired option. When you change an option's format, the Control Panel will display an additional dialog box. Figure 53.2, for example, displays the dialog box for the international-date format.

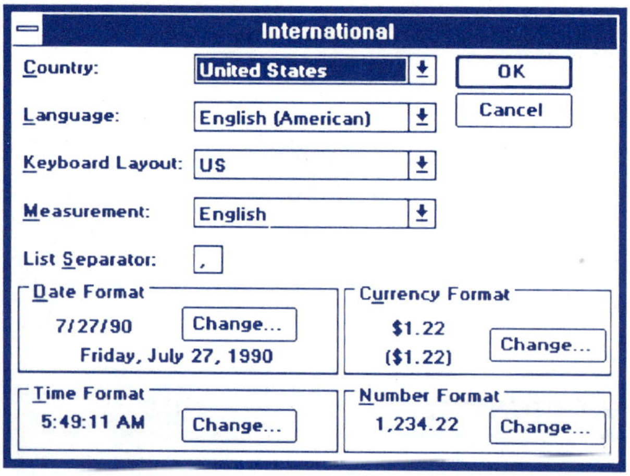

Figure 53.1: *International settings dialog box*

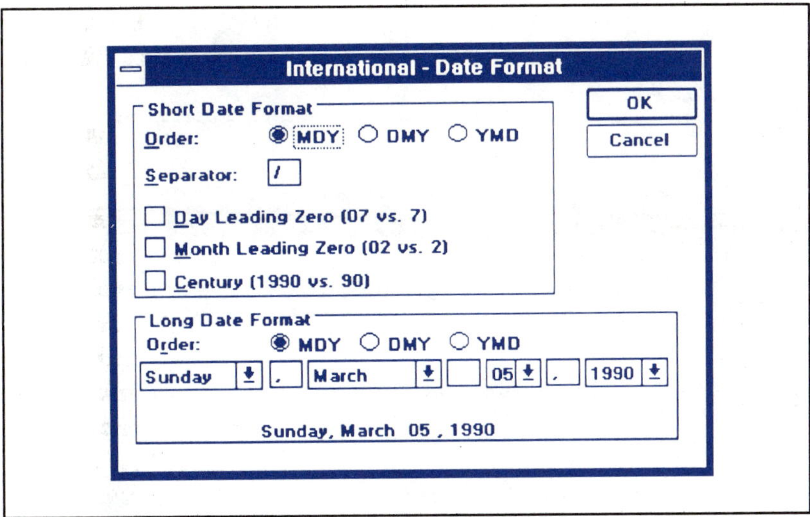

Figure 53.2: International-Date Format dialog box

After you have chosen your settings, select the OK option to return to the Control Panel.

LESSON 54

Getting the Fastest Response from Your Keyboard

Featuring

- Adjusting your keyboard's typematic rate

THE COMPUTER USUALLY ACCEPTS KEYBOARD INPUT much faster than most users can type it in. The one possible exception is when a user simply holds down a key to type the key repeatedly. The speed at which your keyboard responds when you hold down a specific key is called the keyboard's *typematic rate*. The Windows Control Panel lets you increase or decrease your keyboard's typematic rate to the speed that makes you most comfortable.

How to Set Your Keyboard's Typematic Rate

Invoke the Control Panel from the Program Manager Main group and double-click on the Keyboard option. The Control Panel will display a dialog box that lets you adjust the typematic rate, as shown in Figure 54.1.

To adjust your keyboard's typematic rate using your mouse, click on the right- and left-direction arrows to increase and decrease the rate.

To adjust your keyboard's typematic rate using your keyboard, press Alt+R and then use your keyboard's Right and Left Arrows to increase and decrease the rate.

After you change the typematic rate, select the Test Typematic box with your mouse or by pressing Alt+T. Hold down a key, such as **A**, making the letter repeat across the box. When you are satisfied with the response speed, select OK or press Enter.

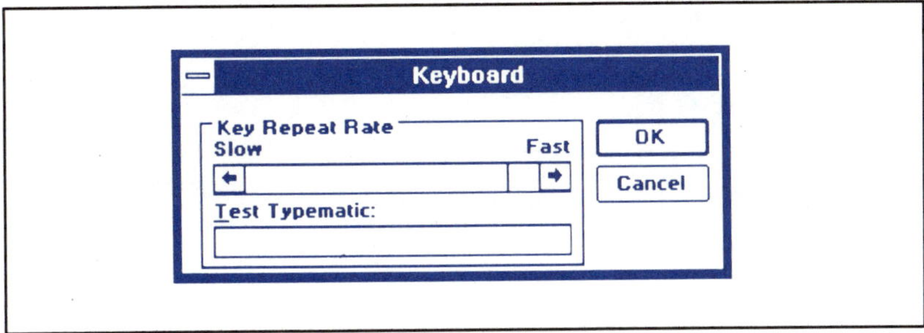

Figure 54.1: Keyboard typematic rate dialog box

LESSON 55

Setting Your System's Date and Time

Featuring

- Maintaining accurate file dates and time stamps

MOST COMPUTERS HAVE A BATTERY POWERED CLOCK that automatically keeps track of the current date and time. It is very important that you keep your system's date and time accurate. As you will recall, each time you change or create a file's contents, DOS dates and time-stamps the file, using the current system's date and time. If your system's date and time are incorrect, all of your files' dates and time stamps will be invalid.

If either your system's date or time is wrong, you can reset it using the DOS DATE or DOS TIME commands, but resetting the date or time is simpler using the Windows Control Panel.

How to Set Your System's Date and Time

Invoke the Control Panel from the Program Manager Main group and double-click on the Date/Time option. The Control Panel will display the dialog box shown in Figure 55.1, containing the system's current date and time.

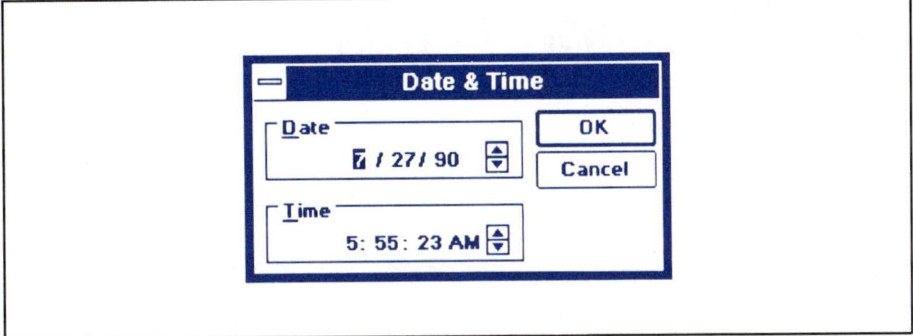

Figure 55.1: Date & Time dialog box

To set the system's date or time using your mouse, click the mouse pointer at the day-, month-, year-, or time-field and click. Next, click the mouse on the up- or down-arrow scroll button to increase or decrease the field's value.

To set the system's date or time using your keyboard, press Alt+D to select the date or Alt+T to select the time. Next, press the Tab key to advance to the appropriate field and type in the desired value.

When you have selected the correct date and time, select the OK option or press Enter.

LESSON 56

Enabling and Disabling Warning Beeps

Featuring

- The Control Panel Sound icon

AS YOU HAVE FOUND, WHEN WINDOWS DISPLAYS A DIALOG log box requesting information, you must either enter the information and select OK or Cancel the dialog box, before Windows lets you continue. If you attempt to perform a mouse operation outside of the dialog box, Windows ignores the operation and sounds a short tone to notify you of the error. If you find this tone annoying, the Control Panel lets you disable it. When you disable the sound, Windows will still ignore illegal operations, it just won't sound the tone.

How to Disable the Warning Beep

Invoke the Control Panel from the Program Manager Main group and double-click on the Sound icon. The Control Panel will open a dialog box that lets you enable or disable the warning sound, as shown in Figure 56.1.

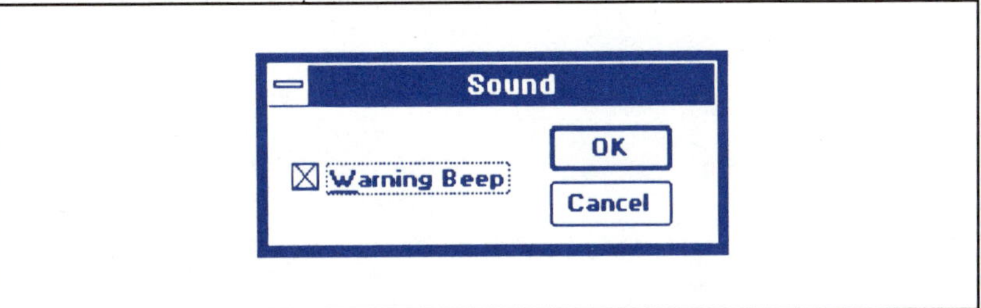

Figure 56.1: *Warning beep enable/disable dialog box*

To disable the warning beep, click on the option with your mouse or press the spacebar to remove the X from the box. Then select OK or press Enter. To re-enable the warning beep, simply repeat this process, replacing the X in the box.

PART V

Rounding Out the Program Manager

LESSON 57

Using the Print Manager

Featuring

- Displaying files in the print queue
- Changing the print order
- Controlling the print speed

AS YOU KNOW, EACH TIME YOU PRINT A FILE, WHETHER you are using the File Manager, the Write word processor, or even Paintbrush, Windows uses the Print Manager to oversee the file's printing. The Print Manager serves two functions. First, because the Print Manager oversees the actual printing of files, you are free to continue working on other projects while your files print. Second, because several Windows applications may attempt to print at the same time, the Print Manager works as a traffic cop, deciding which program uses the printer next. Each timc you print a file, the Print Manager checks to see if another program is using the printer. If the printer is available, the Print Manager begins printing your file. If the printer is busy, the Print Manager places your file in a list of files waiting for the printer, called the *print queue*. The Print Manager automatically places files into the queue in the order in which they arrive.

Most of the time, you can ignore the Print Manager icon, which appears on your screen when files print. In some cases, however, you may want to change the order of the files in the queue. You may want to print a shorter file before a longer, more time-consuming file, or you may want to temporarily suspend printing to change the paper stock in your printer. To perform these tasks, you need to access the Print Manager window.

How to Use the Print Manager

If the Print Manager icon is visible on the desktop (which means the Print Manager is running), double-click on it with your mouse, or press Alt+Tab until the icon is highlighted and then press Enter. If the Print Manager icon is not active, select the Program Manager Main group and invoke the Print Manager icon. The Print Manager will appear, displaying your printer's name and a list of the files currently queued for printing, as shown in Figure 57.1.

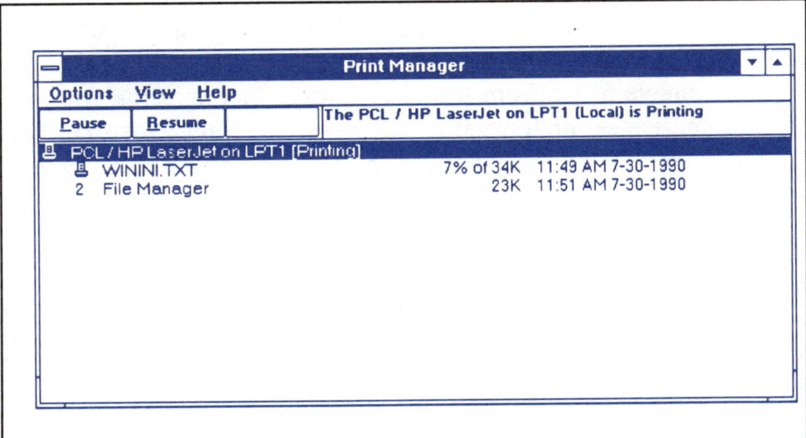

Figure 57.1: *Windows' Print Manager*

If your computer has more than one active printer or has access to network printers, the Print Manager may display the files in each queue separately.

By default, the Print Manager displays the name of the program printing the file, the name of the file to be printed, its size, and the time when the Print Manager placed it in the queue. For the file being printed, the Print Manager will display the percentage printed.

How to Change the Print Queue Order

If the Print Manager has queued several large files, and you need to print a short file immediately that is later in the queue, you can *change the default ordering*, moving your short file ahead of the others.

To move a file to a new location in the print queue using your mouse, drag the file to its desired location and release the mouse button.

To move a file to a new location in the print queue using your keyboard, highlight the file using your arrow keys. Next, hold down the Ctrl key and use the arrow key to move the highlight to the desired location. When you release the Ctrl key, the Print Manager will move the file.

To remove a file from the print queue, highlight the file and click on the Delete option with your mouse, or press Alt+D. The Print Manager will in turn display a confirmation dialog box to guard against inadvertent file deletion.

Temporarily Suspending and Resuming Printing

As discussed, there may be times when you need to suspend printing temporarily. To do so, invoke the Print Manager and click on the Pause option with your mouse or press Alt+P.

To resume printing, click on the Resume option or press Alt+R.

How to Change Your Printing Speed

The Print Manager's function is called a background task because it works behind the scenes, printing your files while you perform other tasks. To accomplish its work in the background, the Print Manager shares your computer's processor (CPU) with the other active Windows programs. In other words, the Print Manager runs for an instant, then a different Windows program runs, and then the Print Manager runs again. Because the exchange of information occurs so fast, your computer appears to be performing two tasks at the same time. Therefore, what appears to be your computer's performing several tasks simultaneously—multitasking—is actually an illusion.

Since the Print Manager exchanges control of the CPU with your other Windows applications, all operations are slower than they would be if they were running alone. If file printing is a priority to you, though, you can increase the amount of time the Print Manager uses the CPU with each exchange. Likewise, if you would rather have your applications run faster, and your files printed as time permits, you can decrease the Print Manager's CPU time allotment.

The Print Manager Options menu, shown in Figure 57.2, lets you select the desired priority.

The Low Priority option gives more computing time to your applications, causing files to print more slowly. Medium Priority shares processing time equally between the Print Manager and your active Windows programs. Lastly, High Priority results in faster printing, with a performance cost to your applications.

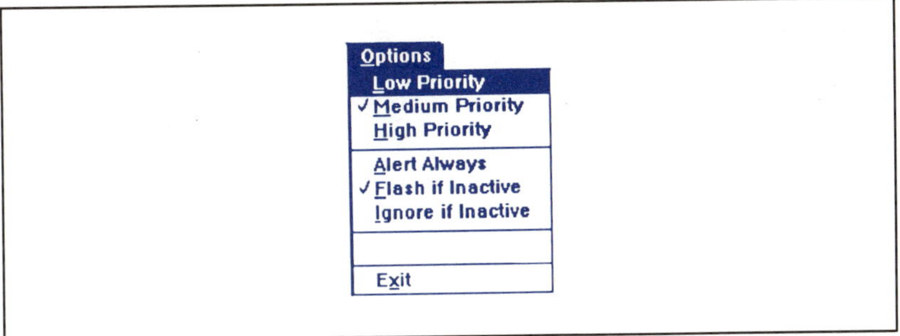

Figure 57.2: *The Print Manager Options menu*

How to Learn More about the Print Manager

The Print Manager provides extensive on-line help that can teach you how to use network printers and control Print Manager messages. Spend a few moments browsing through the available help topics.

LESSON 58

Temporarily Exiting Windows to DOS

Featuring

- Quick access to the DOS prompt

ALTHOUGH YOU CAN RUN MOST OF YOUR PROGRAMS and perform most of your file and directory manipulations within Windows, there may be times when you need to issue a few commands from the DOS prompt. Unfortunately, your need to access the DOS prompt normally occurs after you have opened several windows when exiting Windows would be very inconvenient. Fortunately, though, the Windows Program Manager lets you temporarily exit Windows so you can issue commands at the DOS prompt. When you later return from DOS to Windows, all of your active windows will be unchanged.

How to Exit Windows Temporarily

To exit Windows temporarily, invoke the Program Manager Main group and double-click on the DOS prompt icon. Your screen will clear and DOS will display its prompt, letting you issue commands. When you are ready to return to Windows, issue the EXIT command as follows, and Windows will redisplay your previously active windows.

C> EXIT

Important: Do not confuse exiting Windows temporarily with ending your Windows session altogether. When you end your Windows session, Windows makes sure you close and save all open files, and is removed from RAM memory. When you temporarily exit Windows, all your files remain open and Windows remains running in memory. If you were to turn off your computer at this point, you would risk losing or damaging the files you had opened during your Windows session. That is why it is very important to exit Windows formally before you turn off your machine.

LESSON 59

Creating Your Own Program Groups

Featuring

- Creating a new program group
- Adding programs to an existing group
- Deleting programs and groups

THROUGHOUT THIS BOOK, YOU HAVE USED THE PROGRAM Manager Main and Accessories groups to execute programs quickly by using point and shoot. As the number of Windows and non-Windows applications grows, you eventually may want to create your own program groups to better organize your programs. As you will learn in this lesson, the Program Manager makes it easy for you to create or delete groups, assigning the programs you want to each.

How to Create a New Program Group

In this lesson you will *create a new program group* called Demo that will contain Windows' Clock and Calculator programs. You can use the steps presented to create other new groups—say Budget or Spreadsheet—to store your most commonly used programs. To begin, use your mouse or Alt+F to invoke the Program Manager File menu, which is shown in Figure 59.1.

Select the File menu New option and the Program Manager will display a dialog box prompting you to select a Program Group or a Program Item, as in Figure 59.2.

The New Program Group option lets you create a new program group, such as Demo. The New Program Item option lets you *add new programs* or new documents to a current group. In this case, select the Program Group option and the Program Manager will display a dialog box prompting you to enter the group's description, which will appear in the group's Title Bar and below the group icon. The dialog box also prompts you to enter the group's file name. In this case, type in Demo and DEMO.GRP as shown in Figure 59.3.

When you press Enter or select the OK option, the Program Manager will create and display an empty group named Demo. You now may add programs or documents (Program Items) to the group using the File Manager New option. In this case, add the Windows Clock program using the Program Item Properties group, as shown in Figure 59.4.

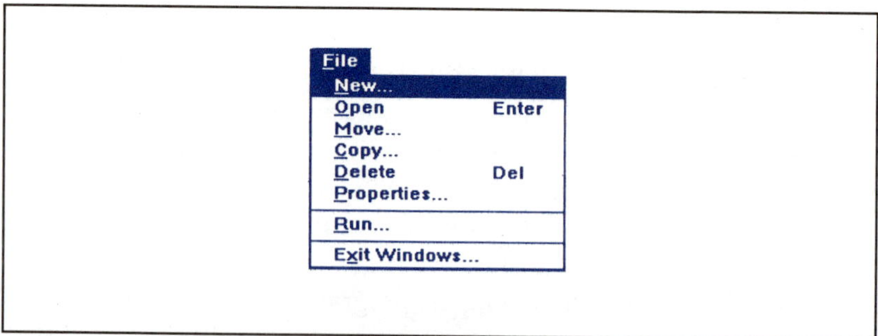

Figure 59.1: Program Manager File menu

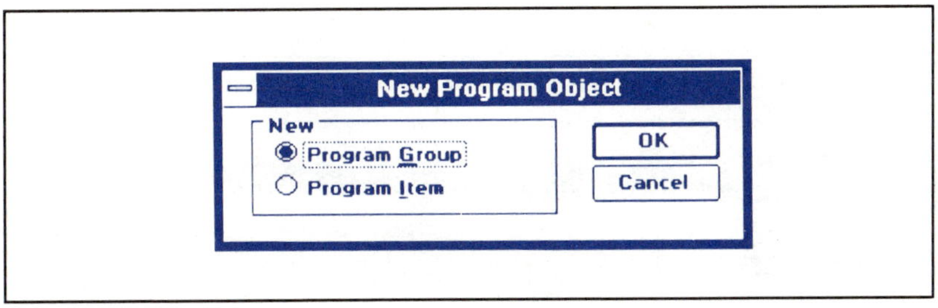

New Program Object
New
Program Group
Program Item
OK
Cancel

Figure 59.2: *New Program Object dialog box*

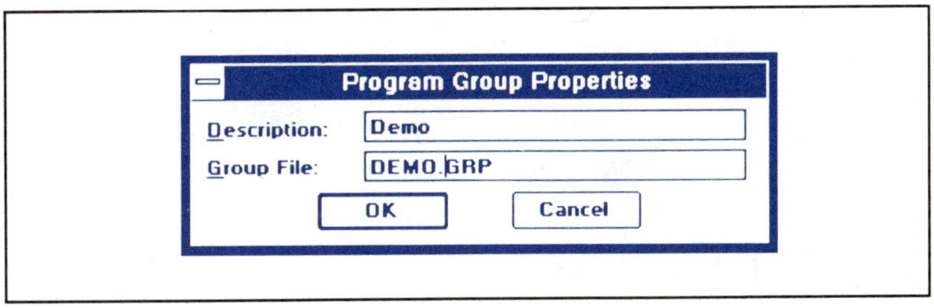

Program Group Properties
Description: Demo
Group File: DEMO.GRP
OK
Cancel

Figure 59.3: *Program Group Properties dialog box*

Program Item Properties
Description: Clock
Command Line: C:\WINDOWS\CLOCK.EXE
OK
Cancel
Browse...
Change Icon...

Figure 59.4: *Adding the Windows Clock to the Demo group*

When you select the OK option or press Enter, the Program Manager will add the Clock icon to the Demo group, as seen in Figure 59.5.

Again using the Program Item Properties dialog box, add the Windows Calculator (CALC.EXE) to the Demo group. Once a program is in a group, you can run it using point and shoot. Use the Demo group's Control menu to close the group's window. The Program Manager will display the Demo group's icon at the bottom of its window, next to the other available groups.

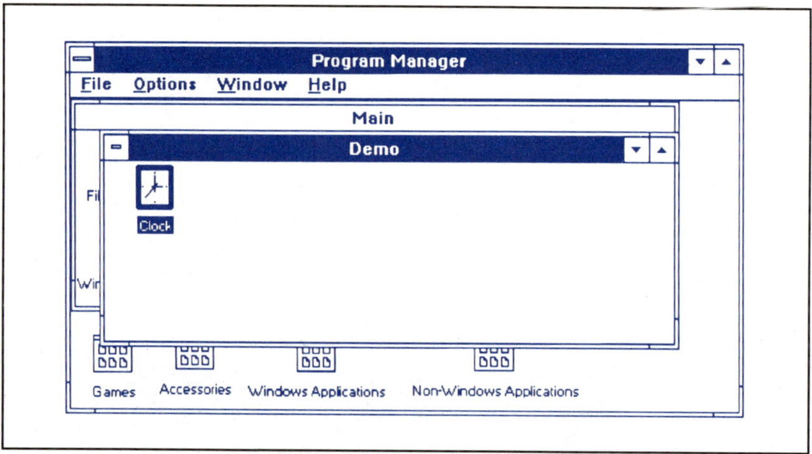

Figure 59.5: *Displaying the Clock icon in the Demo group*

How to Delete a Program Group

Just as you can create program groups and add programs to them, you can also *delete a group* or one or more of its programs. To begin, select the newly created Demo group and highlight the Calculator icon. Next, select the Program Manager's File menu Delete option using your mouse, or press the Del key. The Program Manager will display the dialog box shown in Figure 59.6, asking you to confirm that you want to remove the Calculator program from the group.

Select Yes to delete the Calculator.

If you want to delete an entire group, iconize the group and highlight the icon. Next, select the Program Manager Delete option

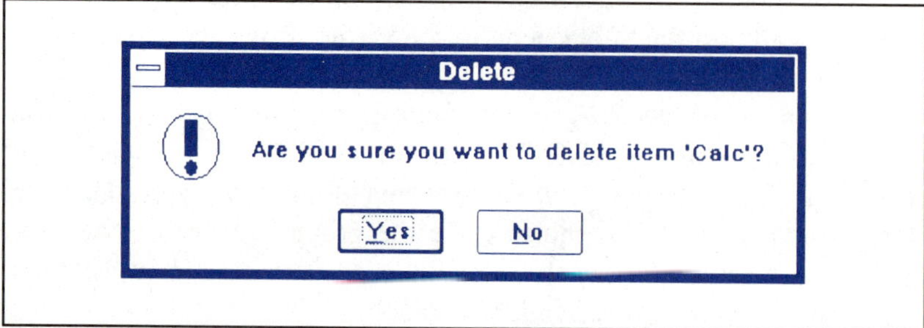

Figure 59.6: *Program item Delete dialog box*

or press the Del key. The Program Manager will display another dialog box asking you to verify you want to remove the group, as seen in Figure 59.7.

Select the Yes option to remove the group.

Note that if you inadvertently delete a group, you can rebuild it by following the steps shown earlier in this lesson. Deleting a group does not delete its individual files from your disk.

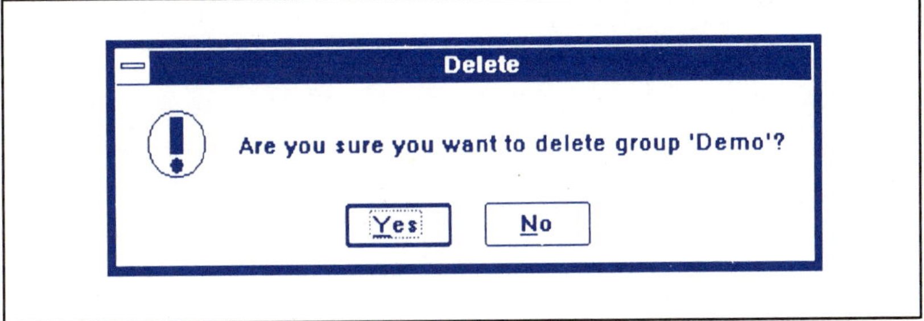

Figure 59.7: Delete group dialog box

PART VI

Running Other Applications

LESSON 60

Using Windows' Different Modes of Operation

Featuring

- When to use Real mode
- When to use Standard mode
- When to use 386 Enhanced mode

IN LESSON 2 YOU LEARNED THAT, DEPENDING ON YOUR available hardware, Windows runs in one of three modes: Real, Standard, or 386 Enhanced. Table 60.1 briefly summarizes the hardware requirements for each mode.

Table 60.1: *Hardware Requirements for Windows' Three Modes of Operation.*

HARDWARE	MEMORY	MODE
8088	640K	Real
80286 (or higher)	1 Mb	Standard
80386 (or higher)	2 Mb	386 Enhanced

Throughout this book, we have examined Windows without regard for the current mode, but for most applications, Windows behaves identically in each mode. The most significant difference between each mode relates to Windows' multitasking capabilities. As you have learned, multitasking is the illusion that your computer is performing two or more tasks at the same time.

All three Windows modes let you multitask Windows applications (i.e., programs specifically written for use under Windows that run within a window). If you are running non-Windows programs, however, Windows' Real and Standard modes let you run only one non-Windows application at a time. To run several non-Windows programs simultaneously, you must use Windows' 386 Enhanced mode. When you run several non-Windows programs in 386 Enhanced mode, each program gets its own screen. You can switch between the programs by pressing Alt+Esc.

When to Use Real Mode

If you are using an IBM PC or PC compatible with an 8088 processor, or if your PC AT has only 640K of RAM, Windows will automatically run in *Real mode*. Under Real mode, Windows will let you multitask your Windows applications only. You can also start one DOS or non-Windows program in Real mode. If you start a non-Windows program, though, Windows will swap (or write to disk) the current memory contents that contain the active windows, freeing up memory for the DOS program. When the DOS program ends, Windows will restore its previous memory contents from disk.

If you are trying to run an older Windows program under version 3.0, and the program fails, you may be able to run the program in Real mode. If you are using a system that normally uses Standard or 386 Enhanced mode, you can force Windows to use Real mode by including the /R switch when you invoke Windows, as shown here.

```
C:\> WIN /R
```

When to Use Standard Mode

Standard mode is the default mode for computers with the 80286 processor, such as the IBM PC AT, or 80386 and 80486 computers that have less than 2 Mb of RAM. Like Real mode, Windows' Standard mode lets you multitask Windows applications and run one DOS or non-Windows program. The primary difference between the Real and Standard modes is that Standard lets Windows take full advantage of your computer's extended memory. By doing so, Windows can load more programs into memory without having to swap programs to disk, which is a slow process.

Until updates for all existing Windows programs are available, you may encounter a program that must run in Standard as opposed to 386 Enhanced mode. To start Windows in Standard mode, you must invoke Windows using the /S switch shown here.

C:\> WIN /S

When to Use 386 Enhanced Mode

If you are using a 80386 or 80486 computer with 2 or more Mb of RAM, you can use Windows' most powerful operating mode, *386 Enhanced*. As discussed, 386 Enhanced mode lets you multitask not only Windows applications, but non-Windows programs as well.

In addition, 386 Enhanced mode provides a powerful memory management technique called virtual memory, which combines space on your disk with your computer's RAM to run programs that are larger than the available memory. Using virtual memory, Windows can bring portions of a program into memory as needed, instead of loading an entire program and possibly having to swap another program out to disk.

Using the PIF editor's 386 Enhanced options, you can control the amount of processing time each non-Windows program receives, as well as the resources the program can use.

Although Standard mode is the default for 80386 and 80486 computers that have less then 2 Mb of RAM, you can force Windows to run in 386 Enhanced mode if your 80386 or 80486 system has at least 1 Mb. To do so, use the /3 switch as shown here.

C:\> WIN /3

Although Windows will then run in 386 Enhanced mode, if your system has less than 2 Mb of RAM, Windows will run more slowly than in Standard mode.

LESSON 61

Getting the Most from Your System's RAM

Featuring

- Understanding conventional, extended, and expanded memory
- Using a RAM drive to store temporary files
- Improving system performance using a disk cache

IBM PC's AND PC COMPATIBLES USE A COMBINATION OF three different kinds of memory. To begin, all PC's use up to 640K of *conventional* Random Access Memory (RAM). When you start your computer, DOS is loaded into conventional memory. Depending on your CONFIG.SYS entries and the DOS version, the amount of conventional memory that DOS consumes will differ. Because programs are becoming larger and more powerful, many have difficulty running in only 640K. Thus, users often install add-on boards insidc their computers to increase the available memory. The two types of add-on memory are extended and expanded memory boards.

Understanding Extended Memory

Extended memory lets the 80286 (IBM PC AT), 80386, and 80486 access RAM beyond 1Mb. The 8088 (IBM PC) does not support extended memory. To use extended memory, you must install device-driver software that lets programs take advantage of the memory. Windows provides the HIMEM.SYS extended-memory device driver which you can install in your DOS CONFIG.SYS file. Use the following command string.

DEVICE = HIMEM.SYS

Most Windows programs are designed to make full use of your extended memory when you use Standard or 386 Enhanced mode.

Understanding Expanded Memory

Although most IBM PC's have only 640K of RAM, the PC can actually use up to 1Mb of memory. *Expanded memory* uses hardware and software to increase the PC's memory-addressing capabilities. You can place several megabytes of expanded memory into your computer. The expanded memory software selects an unused block of memory between the PC's 640K boundary and its 1Mb-limit. It then exchanges the contents of the expanded memory that reside above the PC's 1Mb-limit in and out of the block as the memory is required. Programs designed to take advantage of expanded memory reside in expanded RAM only partially. The software moves different parts of the program into the exchange block in lower memory as they are required.

To access your computer's expanded memory, you must install an expanded-memory driver. This is done by placing the driver name in CONFIG.SYS. Most hardware manufacturers provide a driver on disk when you purchase an expanded memory board.

If you are running Windows in Real mode, your Windows programs can take advantage of expanded memory. If you are running in Standard or 386 Enhanced mode, use the extended memory instead to improve your system's performance, if possible.

Some applications require expanded memory. If you have a "386" computer that you are not running in 386 Enhanced mode, use the EMM386.SYS device driver to simulate expanded memory by using your extended memory.

How to Install and Use a RAM Drive

A *RAM drive* is an electronic disk drive that lets you use a portion of your computer's memory to simulate a disk drive. RAM drives behave similarly to hard disks, with the exception that when you turn off your computer's power or reboot, all information in the RAM drive is lost. Because RAM drives reside in your computer's fast electronic memory, they are much faster than mechanical disk drives. This makes RAM drives a convenient place to store temporary files.

To create a RAM drive, you must install the RAMDRIVE.SYS device driver in your CONFIG.SYS file. RAMDRIVE.SYS resides in your WINDOWS subdirectory. Its format is as follows.

DEVICE = C:\WINDOW\RAMDRIVE.SYS [DiskSize SectorSize DirectoryEntries [/E or /A]]

The strings in brackets are optional. The DiskSize option specifies the desired size of the RAM drive in kilobytes from 10 to 4096. The SectorSize option specifies the size of each RAM-drive sector in bytes. Use one of the following sizes: 128, 256, 512, or 1024.

Every DOS disk has a root directory, from which all other directories grow. The DirectoryEntries option specifies the maximum number of file and subdirectory entries the RAM drive's root directory can store, from 2 to 1024.

If your system has extended or expanded memory available, you can use the additional memory to hold the RAM drive. The /E option directs RAMDRIVE.SYS to place the RAM drive in extended memory. The /A option places the RAM drive in expanded memory. If you don't specify either option, RAMDRIVE.SYS places the RAM drive in conventional memory.

The following CONFIG.SYS entry for example, creates a 360K RAM drive in extended memory.

DEVICE = :\WINDOWS\RAMDRIVE.SYS 360/E

RAM drives provide a convenient storage location for temporary files. Remember, though, if your computer loses power, the RAM drive's contents will be lost. As you work with its applications, Windows periodically creates its own temporary files. When Windows creates a temporary file, it searches the DOS environment for an entry named TEMP. Windows uses TEMP to determine where it should create its own temporary files. If you use RAMDRIVE.SYS to create a RAM drive, you can issue a SET command to assign TEMP to point to the RAM drive. Assuming your RAM drive uses the drive letter D, place the following entry in your AUTOEXEC.BAT file.

```
SET TEMP=D:\
```

Because RAM drives are much faster than mechanical drives, Windows can create the temporary files much faster, improving its performance.

How to Reduce Slow Disk Operations Using SMARTDRV.SYS

Compared to your computer's very fast electronic components, such as the CPU or RAM, your mechanical disk drive operates very slowly. If you can reduce the number of slow disk-drive operations that Windows must perform, your programs will run faster, in turn making you more productive. If your computer has either extended or expanded memory, you can use Windows' SmartDrive *disk-cache* software to reduce disk operations.

When SmartDrive is active, it saves into RAM a copy of the most recent information Windows has read or written. Should a program need to access the information a second time, SmartDrive can get the information directly from RAM, instead of having to access the slower hard disk.

Because SmartDrive doesn't have unlimited space, it stores only as much of your recently accessed information as it can. If the information you need is in memory, SmartDrive will use it. If the information is not present, SmartDrive must read it from disk. Depending on the various types of programs you are running, the amount of information SmartDrive will locate in memory will differ. In most cases, however, SmartDrive will boost your system's performance.

To install SmartDrive, you must type a **DEVICE=** cntry in the file CONFIG.SYS. The format of the SMARTDRV.SYS device driver is as follows.

DEVICE=C:\WINDOWS\SMARTDRV.SYS
[NormalCache MinimumCache [/A]]

The brackets indicate optional items. The NormalCache entry specifies the size (in kilobytes) of the SmartDrive cache or storage region when Windows is not running. The size value can range from 128K to 8192K (8Mb). If you don't specify a value, the default is 256K.

Depending on the Windows mode you are using, Windows may reduce the cache size to access more memory for use by programs. The MinimumCache entry defines the smallest size in kilobytes that Windows can reduce the cache to. If you don't specify a value, Windows can reduce the cache to a minimum of 256K bytes.

Lastly the /A switch informs the SMARTDRV.SYS driver that the cache will reside in expanded memory.

The following CONFIG.SYS entry installs SmartDrive in extended memory with a 1024K (1Mb) disk cache.

DEVICE=C:\WINDOWS\SMARTDRY.SYS

If you have expanded or extended memory, you should install a SmartDrive cache.

LESSON 62

Configuring Your System for Windows' Three Modes of Operation

Featuring

- Configuring a Real mode CONFIG.SYS
- Creating a CONFIG.SYS to maximize Standard and 386 Enhanced modes

DEPENDING ON THE HARDWARE CONFIGURATION OF YOUR computer, Windows will run in one of three modes: Real, Standard or 386 Enhanced. Depending on your mode of operation, you can place different values in your CONFIG.SYS file to improve your system's performance.

Real Mode CONFIG.SYS Entries

Real mode is Windows' slowest mode of operation for two reasons. First, in Real mode Windows does not have enough memory to load several programs efficiently into memory for simultaneous execution. Windows must repeatedly swap programs to and from your hard disk to make room in memory for other programs. Second, if you are running in Real mode, you are probably using an 8088 processor, which is many times slower than 80286 and 80386 processors. The bottom line is, if you need to run Windows in Real mode, you should take steps to configure your system for optional performance.

If your system has expanded memory, Windows will use it not only for program storage, but also for a RAM-drive or SmartDrive disk cache, as discussed in Lesson 61. If your system supports SmartDrive, you should use it.

Make sure you have the FILES= entry in your CONFIG.SYS file set to at least **30**. If you can't use the SmartDrive disk cache, set the BUFFERS= entry to **20**. If you can use SmartDrive, though, you can reduce BUFFERS= to **5**.

The following illustrates a Real mode CONFIG.SYS for a system that does not have expanded memory.

```
FILES=30
BUFFERS=20
```

Next, this CONFIG.SYS illustrates a Real mode CONFIG.SYS for a system supporting expanded memory.

```
FILES=30
BUFFERS=5
DEVICE=C:\DOS\XMAEM.SYS
DEVICE=C:\WINDOWS\SMARTPRV.SYS 1024 /A
```

This CONFIG.SYS file assumes the name of the expanded memory device driver is EMAEM.SYS. The name of your driver may differ. Note that the file installs the expanded-memory driver before SMARTDRV.SYS.

Standard Mode and 386 Enhanced Mode CONFIG.SYS Entries

As discussed in Lesson 61, Windows' Standard and 386 Enhanced modes support extended and expanded memory. If your memory board supports both memory techniques, use extended memory for best performance. To use extended memory with Windows, you must install the HIMEM.SYS extended-memory manager in your CONFIG.SYS file. The format of HIMEM.SYS is as follows.

DEVICE = C:\WINDOWS\HIMEM.SYS [/HMAMIN = m] [/NUMHANDLES = n] [/SHADOW:on/off] [/MACHINE:Name]

The entries in brackets are optional. The /HMAMIN switch specifies the minimum number of kilobytes of high memory area (HMA) memory an application must use before HIMEM.SYS will allow the application to access high memory. The default value is 0K. You can specify a value from 0K to 63K. Windows uses this switch only in Standard mode.

Each time a program requests additional extended memory, the HIMEM.SYS returns a handle or index to a memory location that satisfies the request. The /NUMHANDLES option specifies the number of handles that can be in use at one time. Windows uses the handles internally to access the extended memory. The default value is 32. You can specify a value from 1 to 128. Each handle requires 6 bytes of memory. Windows uses this switch only in Standard mode.

Your computer is shipped with special read-only memory (ROM) chips that contain built-in, machine-dependent functions that perform video output and other functions. Because ROM is slower than RAM, some machines copy (or shadow) the ROM code into a faster region of RAM. On systems that have less than 384K of extended memory, HIMEM.SYS attempts to disable the shadow RAM to reserve memory space for Windows and other programs. The /SHADOW option lets you control how HIMEM.SYS uses shadow RAM. If you specify **/SHADOW:ON**, HIMEM.SYS will leave shadow memory enabled, regardless of the amount of extended memory. If you use **/SHADOW:OFF**, HIMEM.SYS will disable shadow RAM.

When HIMEM.SYS is loaded into memory, it determines the machine type and process accordingly. If you are using an Acer 1100 computer, however, you must tell HIMEM.SYS about your computer type using the switch as follows: **/MACHINE:Acer1100**.

The following CONFIG.SYS entry installs HIMEM.SYS using its default settings.

DEVICE:C:\WINDOWS\HIMEM.SYS

After you have installed HIMEM.SYS, you can create a RAM drive that uses extended memory and the SmartDrive disk cache as discussed in Lesson 61. The following CONFIG.SYS file illustrates a possible configuration for Standard or 386 Enhanced mode in a system with extended memory.

```
FILES=30
BUFFERS=5
DEVICE=C:\WINDOWS\HIMEM.SYS
DEVICE=C:\WINDOWS\RAMDRIVE.SYS 256 /E
DEVICE=C:\WINDOWS\SMARTDRV.SYS
```

LESSON 63

Using Windows' 386 Enhanced Mode Features

Featuring

- 386 Enhanced mode PIF options

AS DISCUSSED, WINDOWS' 386 ENHANCED MODE LETS you multitask both Windows and non-Windows programs. Most non-Windows programs were not developed to run within a window, nor were they designed to share memory with other programs or contend with other programs for resources such as the printer, keyboard, and screen. To multitask these programs, Windows must constantly monitor and control the operations each program is trying to perform. To assist Windows in controlling non-Windows programs, you need to create a PIF for each such program by using the PIF Editor's Advanced Options for 386 Enhanced mode.

How to Create 386 Enhanced Mode PIFs

Invoke the PIF Editor from the Program Manager Accessories group. The PIF Editor will open a window, as discussed in Lesson 43. Using your mouse or Alt+M, invoke the Mode menu and select the 386 Enhanced option. Next, select the dialog box's Advanced option. The PIF Editor will display its Advanced options dialog box, shown in Figure 63.1.

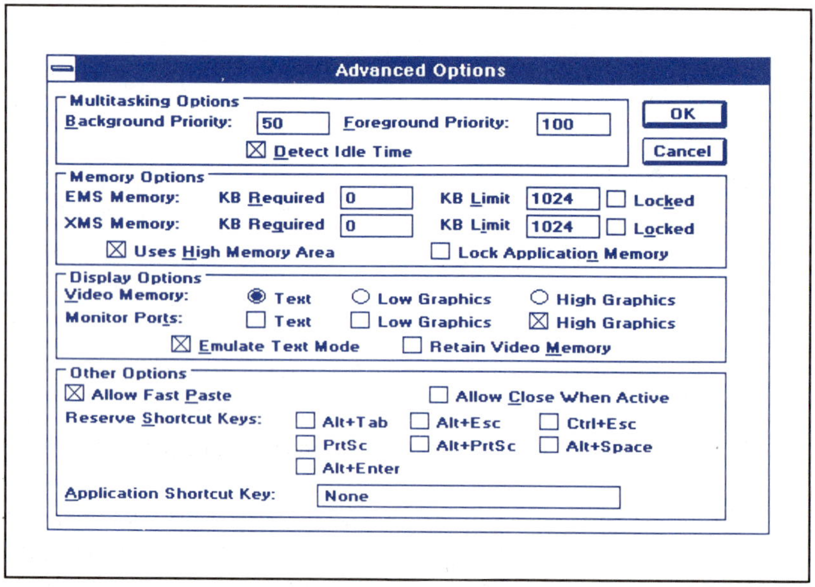

Figure 63.1: *The PIF Editor's Advanced options*

As you can see, several of the options are identical to those already discussed in Lesson 43. The new options relate specifically to multitasking.

Understanding the Multitasking Options

When Window multitasks, it quickly exchanges control of the processor between applications. By default, every program receives an equal share of the processor's time. Depending on your application, there may be times when you want a critical program to complete its task sooner or run faster than others. To do so, you increase the program's priority. The Advanced options dialog box lets you assign a priority for programs running in the background (not the active window) and a different priority for programs run in the foreground (the active window). You can assign priority values from 0 to 1000, where 0 is the lowest priority and 1000 is the highest.

The program's priority determines the percentage of processing time it receives in relation to the other programs. Assume, for example, that you have three programs running with the priorities 50, 100, and 500. Windows will calculate each program's percentage of processor time as follows.

Program A, with Priority 50:
50 ÷ (50 + 100 + 500) = 50 ÷ 650 = **8% (approx.)**

Program B, with Priority 100:
100 ÷ (50 + 100 + 500) = 100 ÷ 650 = **15% (approx.)**

Program C, with Priority 500:
500 ÷ (50 + 100 + 500) = 500 ÷ 650 = **77% (approx.)**

For most applications, the default priorities are satisfactory. If you have a special application that needs to process quickly, though (such as a communications program that runs in the background), you may need to increase its priority.

The Detect Idle Time option directs Windows to release sharable resources for use by other programs when this program becomes idle, as it does when waiting for keyboard input, for example. For best system performance, always leave this option selected.

Understanding the Memory Options

In 386 Enhanced mode, Windows supports extended (XMS) and expanded (EMS) memory. The KB Required option tells Windows the amount of extended or expanded memory (in kilobytes) that must be available before the program can run. The KB Limit option restricts the amount of extended or expanded memory the program can access. The value 0 prevents the program from accessing any extended or expanded memory. The Locked option prevents Windows from swapping the program's high memory to disk, which it does to let a second program use the memory temporarily. Selecting this option restricts Windows' memory management flexibility and will reduce overall system performance. The performance of the program that has locked the memory may or may not improve.

The first 64K of extended memory is called the high memory area (HMA). Leave this option selected to let applications access the HMA if it is available.

Understanding the Display Options

The Video Memory option tells Windows how the program initially uses the video display mode. Each video mode requires Windows to reserve a different amount of memory. Table 63.1 briefly describes each option.

The Video option specifies the program's starting video mode. If the program later selects a higher video mode, Windows will try to allocate additional memory. If insufficient memory is available for allocation, all or part of the application's display may be lost. To prevent this problem, select the highest possible video mode the program may need to access.

Some programs perform their video output by accessing special hardware ports within your computer. For Windows to execute these programs successfully, it monitors their use of the hardware ports.

Table 63.1: *Video Memory Options.*

VIDEO OPTION	MEMORY REQUIREMENTS
Text	Directs Windows to set aside enough memory to display the application in text mode. This may require up to 16K.
Low Graphics	Directs Windows to set aside enough memory to display the application in low resolution graphics. This may require up to 32K.
High Graphics	Directs Windows to set aside enough memory to display the application in high resolution graphics. Depending on the current video mode, this may require up to 128K.

The three options direct Windows to monitor the hardware ports for a specific video mode. If an application does not display its output correctly when it initially runs, or when Windows reselects the program as active, use the hardware ports option to monitor the ports.

The Emulate Text Mode lets Windows display an application's output very quickly by emulating Text mode as opposed to using Graphics mode. For most Windows applications, you should leave this option selected. If Windows displays a program's text as garbled, select this option.

If you are running a program that changes from one video mode to another, Windows will adjust the program's video memory allocation. But if the program later needs to change to a higher video mode and there is not enough memory, the program may lose all or a portion of its display. The Retain Video Memory option lets you prevent Windows from changing a program's video memory allocation when the program changes video modes.

How to Use the PIF's Other Options

As you have learned, Windows lets you exchange information between applications using the Clipboard. Some non-Windows applications cannot paste information as fast as Windows can provide it. If a program has difficulty pasting information, remove the Allow Fast Paste option and Windows will paste information at a slower rate. The Allow Close When Active option lets Windows end a session while the program is running. Although this option lets you close Windows quickly, closing an active program may result in lost data if it has open files. If the program does not use DOS file handles, do not select this option.

Changing a Program's Settings before It Runs

If you execute a program that does not have a PIF, Windows uses the default PIF. If you need to customize a program's characteristics, you can create a PIF for the application as just discussed. And, if you select an application's Control menu and choose the Settings option, Windows will display the dialog box in Figure 63.2, which lets you change the program's settings.

Using this dialog box, you can instruct Windows either to run the program in a window or to use the entire screen, or set the program's priority. The Tasking Options Exclusive option lets you suspend other programs while this program is running. The Background option lets you direct Windows to run this program in the background while you are using another program. This option is best suited for programs that don't require user interaction.

When you are running a program from the DOS prompt and the program hangs (preventing you from ending or continuing it), you must normally restart your system, using Ctrl+Alt+Del. However, if you have several active programs running and one fails, restarting your computer is not a good solution. If you can invoke the program's Control menu and select the Terminate option, Windows will end the hanging program only. If the program has open files, the information may be lost, but at least other programs' data will be saved.

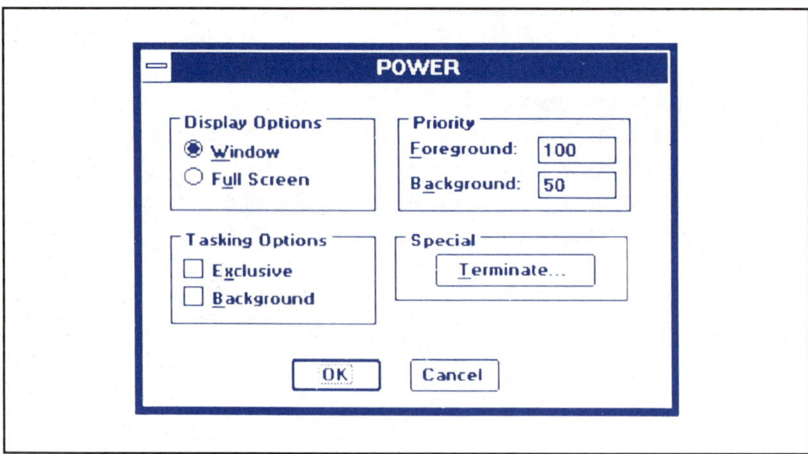

Figure 63.2: Program control dialog box

LESSON 64

Understanding Windows' Initialization Files

Featuring

- Using WINSTART.BAT
- Understanding WIN.INI and SYSTEM.INI

AS YOU HAVE LEARNED, WINDOWS LETS YOU CUSTOMIZE your screen colors, mouse, keyboard, color settings, and other options. When you select these options, Windows stores them in one of two initialization files. By examining the contents of these files, you can learn a great deal about Windows and how to improve your system's performance.

Understanding WINSTART.BAT

Each time you start Windows in 386 Enhanced mode, it searches the subdirectory containing your Windows files for a batch file named

WINSTART.BAT. If the file exists, Windows executes the commands it contains. If there are certain programs you want Windows to execute automatically and you are using 386 Enhanced mode, place the commands in WINSTART.BAT, just as you would any batch file.

Understanding WIN.INI

WIN.INI is the Windows initialization file that contains your screen and hardware preferences. When you modify your system using the Windows Control Panel, Windows places your preferences in the file WIN.INI. Using the Windows Notepad, you can edit the file or print its contents. In most cases, though, you will never have to edit WIN.INI. The two possible exceptions are the LOAD and RUN entries.

The RUN option lets you specify programs you want Windows to execute automatically each time it starts. Unlike WINSTART.BAT, which runs only in 386 Enhanced mode, you can use the WIN.INI RUN entry to execute a program in any Windows mode. The following entry, for example, directs Windows to run the Windows Clock program each time the system starts.

RUN = CLOCK.EXE

The LOAD option, on the other hand, directs Windows to load a specified program as an icon. The following entry, for example, loads the Windows Calendar program as an icon when Windows begins.

LOAD = CALENDAR.EXE

To help you better understand WIN.INI, Windows provides the file WININI.TXT on your disk. Use the Notepad to print this file.

Understanding SYSTEM.INI

In addition to the file WIN.INI, Windows includes a file called SYSTEM.INI. Windows uses this file to store hardware-driver information and to record the location of the Windows temporary swap file. Using the Windows Notepad you can view or print this file's contents. Most user's will never have to change SYSTEM.INI. However, to provide you with more information on its entries, Windows includes the file SYSINI.TXT, which contains details on all SYSTEM.INI entries. Use the Notepad to print this file, too.

A Word of Warning

The files WIN.INI and SYSTEM.INI are critical to the operation of Windows. If you make an inadvertent edit, you may prevent Windows from starting. Do not make changes to these files until you fully understand all of their functions.

APPENDIX A

Installing Windows

APPENDIX A

Installing Windows

INSTALLING WINDOWS IS VERY STRAIGHTFORWARD IF you know one or two secrets. To begin, you must have at least 6Mb of available disk space and the Windows Setup disks. Next, make a list of the following:

The directory where you want Windows to reside. Normally **C:\WINDOWS**.

The type of computer you are using: 8088 (IBM PC), 80286 (PC AT), 80386, or 80486.

Your monitor type: CGA, EGA, VGA and so on.

Your mouse type, if you are using a mouse. If you don't know, use the Microsoft mouse option.

Your keyboard type. Normally an 82-key or 101-key enhanced keyboard.

The language the keyboard should support. Normally **US**.

The network type and version if you are connected to a local area network.

Your printer type and the port the printer is connected to, such as LPT1 or COM1.

Once your list is complete, place Windows Disk 1 into drive A and type **A:SETUP** as shown here.

C:\> A:SETUP

The Windows installation will display an introductory screen explaining the process. Read the screen and press Enter to continue the installation, or key F1 for additional information about the installation.

The Windows installation will prompt you to enter the directory you want the Windows files to reside in. The default subdirectory is WINDOWS. Press Enter to select the default directory name.

Next, the installation will display what it has determined your current hardware configuration to be. Using your list of hardware components, verify that each setting is correct. If a setting is not correct, use your keyboard arrow keys to highlight the desired setting and press Enter. Windows will display a list of possible values for the setting, which you can scroll through using your arrow keys. When you identify the correct value, press Enter to select it. After all the settings are correct, select the No Changes option and press Enter to continue the installation.

The installation will now begin copying files from floppy disks to your hard disk. When you need to insert a new disk, the installation will display a message on the screen, requesting you to insert a specific disk number. Place the specified disk in drive A and press Enter to continue.

After the installation has copied several files to your hard disk, the screen's appearance will change, and SETUP will display a screen containing your first Windows dialog box. If your system has a mouse, you can use your mouse for the remainder of the installation.

A dialog box is a window containing one or more options or a prompt for you to type in specific information. In this case, the dialog box has preselected (an X indicates a selected option) the three possible options. The *Set Up Printers* option lets you tell Windows your printer type (or types, if you have multiple printers) and each printer's port. The *Set Up Applications* option directs Windows to search your disk for commonly used programs and to configure each to simplify its use. Lastly, the *Read On-line Documentation* option directs Windows to invoke its Notepad editor to let you read the latest additions to the Windows documentation.

To remove a selected option using your mouse, aim the mouse pointer at the option and click.

To remove a selected option with your keyboard, use your keyboard arrow keys to highlight the option. Then press the spacebar to toggle the selection on or off.

Most users should leave all three options selected. To continue the installation, press Enter or click on OK with your mouse.

The installation will continue copying files to your hard disk, prompting you to insert disks as needed.

Next, SETUP will display a dialog box informing you that it intends to update your AUTOEXEC.BAT and CONFIG.SYS files. If you understand the current entries in these files, you might want to review SETUP's intended changes before they are made. Otherwise, let SETUP make the changes by pressing Enter or clicking on the Continue option.

SETUP will then display a dialog box telling you it has modified CONFIG.SYS and AUTOEXEC.BAT and that it saved each file's previous contents in the files CONFIG.OLD and AUTOEXEC.OLD. Press Enter or click your mouse on the OK option to continue.

SETUP will display a dialog box that lets you select your printer type. Use your keyboard arrow keys to scroll through the list of available printers until you locate yours. When your printer is highlighted, press Enter.

Depending on your printer type, Windows may need you to insert the Windows disk containing the drivers for your printer. By default, Windows assigns the printer to the parallel port LPT1. If the printer is attached to a different port, press Alt+C or click your mouse on the Configure option, and SETUP will display a dialog box that lets you select the correct port.

Repeat this process to install each printer connected to your system. You may need to press the Tab key several times to advance the highlight back to the list of available printers. After you have installed your printer (or printers), press the Tab key until the OK option is highlighted and press Enter, or simply click on the OK option with your mouse.

SETUP will display a new dialog box asking you which disks you want it to search for commonly used programs. Be sure the All Drives option is highlighted and press Enter or click on the OK option with your mouse. SETUP will begin searching your disk for known applications. Depending on the type of application, SETUP will let you add the application either to the group of programs that run in a window (the Windows Applications group) or to the group of commonly used DOS programs that don't run in a window (the Non-Windows Application group). You can still run non-Windows applications using Windows. When SETUP locates applications for the groups, it will display the list of application names in a dialog box, letting you add each program individually to the group. If several program names are listed, select the Add All option by pressing the Tab key to highlight the option and then pressing Enter, or by clicking on the option with your mouse. Next, select the OK option to continue. SETUP will continue by building one or more program groups on your screen.

SETUP then invokes the Windows Notepad editor, letting you view the contents of the file README.TXT. This file contains the latest Windows documentation that is not found in your manual. Using your keyboard arrow keys, scroll through the file's contents.

Finally, use Alt+F4 to close the Notepad window. SETUP will display its final dialog box, telling you the Windows installation is complete and giving you the option of rebooting your computer (to restart Windows) or returning to DOS. Remove the Windows disk from drive A and press Enter to restart your computer. When your computer reboots, turn to Lesson 1. You are now ready to start using Windows!

Index

A

B

D

E

F

G

H

I

J

K

L

M

N

O

P

R

S

T

U

V

W

X

Selections from The SYBEX Library

OPERATING SYSTEMS

The ABC's of DOS 4
Alan R. Miller
275pp. Ref. 583-2
This step-by-step introduction to using DOS 4 is written especially for beginners. Filled with simple examples, *The ABC's of DOS 4* covers the basics of hardware, software, disks, the system editor EDLIN, DOS commands, and more.

ABC's of MS-DOS (Second Edition)
Alan R. Miller
233pp. Ref. 493-3
This handy guide to MS-DOS is all many PC users need to manage their computer files, organize floppy and hard disks, use EDLIN, and keep their computers organized. Additional information is given about utilities like Sidekick, and there is a DOS command and program summary. The second edition is fully updated for Version 3.3.

DOS Assembly Language Programming
Alan R. Miller
365pp. 487-9
This book covers PC-DOS through 3.3, and gives clear explanations of how to assemble, link, and debug 8086, 8088, 80286, and 80386 programs. The example assembly language routines are valuable for students and programmers alike.

DOS Instant Reference SYBEX Prompter Series
Greg Harvey
Kay Yarborough Nelson
220pp. Ref. 477-1, 4 3/4" × 8"
A complete fingertip reference for fast, easy on-line help:command summaries, syntax, usage and error messages. Organized by function—system commands, file commands, disk management, directories, batch files, I/O, networking, programming, and more. Through Version 3.3.

DOS User's Desktop Companion SYBEX Ready Reference Series
Judd Robbins
969pp. Ref. 505-0
This comprehensive reference covers DOS commands, batch files, memory enhancements, printing, communications and more information on optimizing each user's DOS environment. Written with step-by-step instructions and plenty of examples, this volume covers all versions through 3.3.

Encyclopedia DOS
Judd Robbins
1030pp. Ref. 699-5
A comprehensive reference and user's guide to all versions of DOS through 4.0. Offers complete information on every DOS command, with all possible switches and parameters -- plus examples of effective usage. An invaluable tool.

Essential OS/2 (Second Edition)
Judd Robbins
445pp. Ref. 609-X
Written by an OS/2 expert, this is the guide to the powerful new resources of the OS/2 operating system standard edition 1.1 with presentation manager. Robbins introduces the standard edition, and details multitasking under OS/2, and the range of commands for installing, starting up, configuring, and running applications. For Version 1.1 Standard Edition.

Essential PC-DOS (Second Edition)
Myril Clement Shaw
Susan Soltis Shaw
332pp. Ref. 413-5
An authoritative guide to PC-DOS, including version 3.2. Designed to make experts out

of beginners, it explores everything from disk management to batch file programming. Includes an 85-page command summary. Through Version 3.2.

Graphics Programming Under Windows

Brian Myers
Chris Doner

646pp. Ref. 448-8

Straightforward discussion, abundant examples, and a concise reference guide to graphics commands make this book a must for Windows programmers. Topics range from how Windows works to programming for business, animation, CAD, and desktop publishing. For Version 2.

Hard Disk Instant Reference SYBEX Prompter Series

Judd Robbins

256pp. Ref. 587-5, 4 3/4" × 8"

Compact yet comprehensive, this pocket-sized reference presents the essential information on DOS commands used in managing directories and files, and in optimizing disk configuration. Includes a survey of third-party utility capabilities. Through DOS 4.0.

The IBM PC-DOS Handbook (Third Edition)

Richard Allen King

359pp. Ref. 512-3

A guide to the inner workings of PC-DOS 3.2, for intermediate to advanced users and programmers of the IBM PC series. Topics include disk, screen and port control, batch files, networks, compatibility, and more. Through Version 3.3.

Inside DOS: A Programmer's Guide

Michael J. Young

490pp. Ref. 710-X

A collection of practical techniques (with source code listings) designed to help you take advantage of the rich resources intrinsic to MS-DOS machines. Designed for the experienced programmer with a basic understanding of C and 8086 assembly language, and DOS fundamentals.

Mastering DOS (Second Edition)

Judd Robbins

722pp. Ref. 555-7

"The most useful DOS book." This seven-part, in-depth tutorial addresses the needs of users at all levels. Topics range from running applications, to managing files and directories, configuring the system, batch file programming, and techniques for system developers. Through Version 4.

MS-DOS Advanced Programming

Michael J. Young

490pp. Ref. 578-6

Practical techniques for maximizing performance in MS-DOS software by making best use of system resources. Topics include functions, interrupts, devices, multitasking, memory residency and more, with examples in C and assembler. Through Version 3.3.

MS-DOS Handbook (Third Edition)

Richard Allen King

362pp. Ref. 492-5

This classic has been fully expanded and revised to include the latest features of MS-DOS Version 3.3. Two reference books in one, this title has separate sections for programmer and user. Multi-DOS partitons, 3 1/2-inch disk format, batch file call and return feature, and comprehensive coverage of MS-DOS commands are included. Through Version 3.3.

MS-DOS Power User's Guide, Volume I (Second Edition)

Jonathan Kamin

482pp. Ref. 473-9

A fully revised, expanded edition of our best-selling guide to high-performance DOS techniques and utilities—with details on Version 3.3. Configuration, I/O, directory structures, hard disks, RAM disks, batch file programming, the ANSI.SYS device driver, more. Through Version 3.3.

Programmers Guide to the OS/2 Presentation Manager

Michael J. Young

683pp. Ref. 569-7

This is the definitive tutorial guide to writing programs for the OS/2 Presentation Manager. Young starts with basic architecture, and explores every important feature including scroll bars, keyboard and mouse interface, menus and accelerators, dialogue boxes, clipboards, multitasking, and much more.

Programmer's Guide to Windows (Second Edition)

David Durant
Geta Carlson
Paul Yao

704pp. Ref. 496-8

The first edition of this programmer's guide was hailed as a classic. This new edition covers Windows 2 and Windows/386 in depth. Special emphasis is given to over fifty new routines to the Windows interface, and to preparation for OS/2 Presentation Manager compatibility.

Understanding DOS 3.3

Judd Robbins

678pp. Ref. 648-0

This best selling, in-depth tutorial addresses the needs of users at all levels with many examples and hands-on exercises. Robbins discusses the fundamentals of DOS, then covers manipulating files and directories, using the DOS editor, printing, communicating, and finishes with a full section on batch files.

Understanding Hard Disk Management on the PC

Jonathan Kamin

500pp. Ref. 561-1

This title is a key productivity tool for all hard disk users who want efficient, error-free file management and organization. Includes details on the best ways to conserve hard disk space when using several memory-guzzling programs. Through DOS 4.

Up & Running with Your Hard Disk

Klaus M Rubsam

140pp. Ref. 666-9

A far-sighted, compact introduction to hard disk installation and basic DOS use. Perfect for PC users who want the practical essentials in the shortest possible time. In 20 basic steps, learn to choose your hard disk, work with accessories, back up data, use DOS utilities to save time, and more.

Up & Running with Windows 286/386

Gabriele Wentges

132pp. Ref. 691-X

This handy 20-step overview gives PC users all the essentials of using Windows -- whether for evaluating the software, or getting a fast start. Each self-contained lesson takes just 15 minutes to one hour to complete.

COMPUTER LITERACY

The ABC's of the IBM PC and Compatibles (Second Edition)

Joan Lasselle
Carol Ramsay

167pp. Ref.370-8

This attractively illustrated, clear and simple book guides complete beginners through every step necessary to become familiar with their PC and put it to work. Assumes no prior knowledge of computers.

UTILITIES

Mastering the Norton Utilities

Peter Dyson

373pp. Ref. 575-1

In-depth descriptions of each Norton utility make this book invaluable for beginning and experienced users alike. Each utility is described clearly with examples and the text is organized so that readers can put Norton to work right away. Version 4.5.

Mastering PC Tools Deluxe

Peter Dyson

400pp. Ref. 654-5

A complete hands-on guide to the timesaving—and "lifesaving"—utility programs in Version 5.5 of PC Tools Deluxe. Contains concise tutorials and in-depth discussion of every aspect of using PC Tools—from high speed backups, to data recovery, to using Desktop applications.

Mastering SideKick Plus

Gene Weisskopf

394pp. Ref. 558-1

Employ all of Sidekick's powerful and expanded features with this hands-on guide to the popular utility. Features include comprehensive and detailed coverage of time management, note taking, outlining, auto dialing, DOS file management, math, and copy-and-paste functions.

Up & Running with Norton Utilities

Rainer Bartel

140pp. Ref. 659-6

Get up and running in the shortest possible time in just 20 lessons or "steps." Learn to restore disks and files, use UnErase, edit your floppy disks, retrieve lost data and more. Or use the book to evaluate the software before you purchase. Through Version 4.2.

Up & Running with PC Tools Deluxe 6

Thomas Holste

180pp. Ref.678-2

Learn to use this software program in just 20 basic steps. Readers get a quick, inexpensive introduction to using the Tools for disaster recovery, disk and file management, and more.

COMMUNICATIONS

Mastering Crosstalk XVI (Second Edition)

Peter W. Gofton

225pp. Ref. 642-1

Introducing the communications program Crosstalk XVI for the IBM PC. As well as providing extensive examples of command and script files for programming Crosstalk, this book includes a detailed description of how to use the program's more advanced features, such as windows, talking to mini or mainframe, customizing the keyboard and answering calls and background mode.

Mastering PROCOMM PLUS

Bob Campbell

400pp. Ref. 657-X

Learn all about communications and information retrieval as you master and use PROCOMM PLUS. Topics include choosing and using a modem; automatic dialing; using on-line services (featuring CompuServe) and more. Through Version 1.1b; also covers PROCOMM, the "shareware" version.

Mastering Serial Communications

Peter W. Gofton

289pp. Ref. 180-2

The software side of communications, with details on the IBM PC's serial programming, the XMODEM and Kermit protocols, non-ASCII data transfer, interrupt-level programming and more. Sample programs in C, assembly language and BASIC.

NETWORKS

The ABC's of Local Area Networks

Michael Dortch

212pp. Ref. 664-2

This jargon-free introduction to LANs is fur current and prospective users who see general information, comparative options, a look at the future, and tips for effective LANs use today. With comparisons of Token-Ring, PC Network, Novell, and others.

The ABC's of Novell Netware

Jeff Woodward

282pp. Ref. 614-6

For users who are new to PC's or networks, this entry-level tutorial outlines each basic element and operation of Novell. The ABC's introduces computer hardware and software, DOS, network organization and security, and printing and communicating over the netware system.

Mastering Novell Netware

Cheryl C. Currid
Craig A. Gillett

500pp. Ref. 630-8

This book is a thorough guide for System Administrators to installing and operating a microcomputer network using Novell Netware. Mastering covers actually setting up a network from start to finish, design, administration, maintenance, and troubleshooting.

Networking with TOPS

Steven William Rimmer

350pp. Ref. 565-4

A hands on guide to the most popular user friendly network available. This book will walk a user through setting up the hardware and software of a variety of TOPS configurations, from simple two station networks through whole offices. It explains the realities of sharing files between PC compatibles and Macintoshes, of sharing printers and other peripherals and, most important, of the real world performance one can expect when the network is running.

WORD PROCESSING

The ABC's of Microsoft Word (Third Edition)

Alan R. Neibauer

461pp. Ref. 604-9

This is for the novice WORD user who wants to begin producing documents in the shortest time possible. Each chapter has short, easy-to-follow lessons for both keyboard and mouse, including all the basic editing, formatting and printing functions. Version 5.0.

The ABC's of WordPerfect

Alan R. Neibauer

239pp. Ref. 425-9

This basic introduction to WordPefect consists of short, step-by-step lessons—for new users who want to get going fast. Topics range from simple editing and formatting, to merging, sorting, macros, and more. Includes version 4.2

The ABC's of WordPerfect 5

Alan R. Neibauer

283pp. Ref. 504-2

This introduction explains the basics of desktop publishing with WordPerfect 5: editing, layout, formatting, printing, sorting, merging, and more. Readers are shown how to use WordPerfect 5's new features to produce great-looking reports.

The ABC's of WordPerfect 5.1

Alan R. Neibauer

352pp. Ref. 672-3

Neibauer's delightful writing style makes this clear tutorial an especially effective learning tool. Learn all about 5.1's new drop-down menus and mouse capabilities that reduce the tedious memorization of function keys.

Advanced Techniques in Microsoft Word (Second Edition)

Alan R. Neibauer

462pp. Ref. 615-4

This highly acclaimed guide to WORD is an excellent tutorial for intermediate to advanced users. Topics include word processing fundamentals, desktop publishing with graphics, data management, and working in a multiuser environment. For Versions 4 and 5.

Advanced Techniques in MultiMate

Chris Gilbert

275pp. Ref. 412-7

A textbook on efficient use of MultiMate

for business applications, in a series of self-contained lessons on such topics as multiple columns, high-speed merging, mailing-list printing and Key Procedures.

Advanced Techniques in WordPerfect 5

Kay Yarborough Nelson

586pp. Ref. 511-5

Now updated for Version 5, this invaluable guide to the advanced features of WordPerfect provides step-by-step instructions and practical examples covering those specialized techniques which have most perplexed users—indexing, outlining, foreign-language typing, mathematical functions, and more.

The Complete Guide to MultiMate

Carol Holcomb Dreger

208pp. Ref. 229-9

This step-by-step tutorial is also an excellent reference guide to MultiMate features and uses. Topics include search/replace, library and merge functions, repagination, document defaults and more.

Encyclopedia WordPerfect 5.1

Greg Harvey
Kay Yarborough Nelson

1100pp. Ref. 676-6

This comprehensive, up-to-date WordPerfect reference is a must for beginning and experienced users alike. With complete, easy-to-find information on every WordPerfect feature and command -- and it's organized by practical functions, with business users in mind.

Introduction to WordStar

Arthur Naiman

208pp. Ref. 134-9

This all time bestseller is an engaging first-time introduction to word processing as well as a complete guide to using WordStar—from basic editing to blocks, global searches, formatting, dot commands, SpellStar and MailMerge. Through Version 3.3.

Mastering DisplayWrite 4

Michael E. McCarthy

447pp. Ref. 510-7

Total training, reference and support for users at all levels—in plain, non-technical language. Novices will be up and running in an hour's time; everyone will gain complete word-processing and document-management skills.

Mastering Microsoft Word on the IBM PC (Fourth Edition)

Matthew Holtz

680pp. Ref. 597-2

This comprehensive, step-by-step guide details all the new desktop publishing developments in this versatile word processor, including details on editing, formatting, printing, and laser printing. Holtz uses sample business documents to demonstrate the use of different fonts, graphics, and complex documents. Includes Fast Track speed notes. For Versions 4 and 5.

Mastering MultiMate Advantage II

Charles Ackerman

407pp. Ref. 482-8

This comprehensive tutorial covers all the capabilities of MultiMate, and highlights the differences between MultiMate Advantage II and previous versions—in pathway support, sorting, math, DOS access, using dBASE III, and more. With many practical examples, and a chapter on the On-File database.

Mastering WordPerfect

Susan Baake Kelly

435pp. Ref. 332-5

Step-by-step training from startup to mastery, featuring practical uses (form letters, newsletters and more), plus advanced topics such as document security and macro creation, sorting and columnar math. Through Version 4.2.

Mastering WordPerfect 5

Susan Baake Kelly

709pp. Ref. 500-X

The revised and expanded version of this definitive guide is now on WordPerfect 5 and covers wordprocessing and basic desktop publishing. As more than 200,000 readers of the original edition can attest, no tutorial approaches it for clarity and depth of treatment. Sorting, line drawing, and laser printing included.

Mastering WordPerfect 5.1

Alan Simpson

1050pp. Ref. 670-7

The ultimate guide for the WordPerfect user. Alan Simpson, the "master communicator," puts you in charge of the latest features of 5.1: new dropdown menus and mouse capabilities, along with the desktop publishing, macro programming, and file conversion functions that have made WordPerfect the most popular word processing program on the market.

Mastering WordStar Release 5.5

Greg Harvey
David J. Clark

450pp. Ref. 491-7

This book is the ultimate reference book for the newest version of WordStar. Readers may use Mastering to look up any word processing function, including the new Version 5 and 5.5 features and enhancements, and find detailed instructions for fundamental to advanced operations.

Microsoft Word Instant Reference for the IBM PC

Matthew Holtz

266pp. Ref. 692-8

Turn here for fast, easy access to concise information on every command and feature of Microsoft Word version 5.0 -- for editing, formatting, merging, style sheets, macros, and more. With exact keystroke sequences, discussion of command options, and commonly-performed tasks.

Practical WordStar Uses

Julie Anne Arca

303pp. Ref. 107-1

A hands-on guide to WordStar and MailMerge applications, with solutions to comon problems and "recipes" for day-to-day tasks. Formatting, merge-printing and much more; plus a quick-reference command chart and notes on CP/M and PC-DOS. For Version 3.3.

Understanding Professional Write

Gerry Litton

400pp. Ref. 656-1

A complete guide to Professional Write that takes you from creating your first simple document, into a detailed description of all major aspects of the software. Special features place an emphasis on the use of different typestyles to create attractive documents as well as potential problems and suggestions on how to get around them.

Understanding WordStar 2000

David Kolodney
Thomas Blackadar

275pp. Ref. 554-9

This engaging, fast-paced series of tutorials covers everything from moving the cursor to print enhancements, format files, key glossaries, windows and MailMerge. With practical examples, and notes for former WordStar users.

Visual Guide to WordPerfect

Jeff Woodward

457pp. Ref. 591-3

This is a visual hands-on guide which is ideal for brand new users as the book shows each activity keystroke-by-keystroke. Clear illustrations of computer screen menus are included at every stage. Covers basic editing, formatting lines, paragraphs, and pages, using the block feature, footnotes, search and replace, and more. Through Version 5.

WordPerfect 5 Desktop Companion SYBEX Ready Reference Series

Greg Harvey
Kay Yarborough Nelson

1006pp. Ref. 522-0

Desktop publishing features have been added to this compact encyclopedia. This title offers more detailed, cross-referenced entries on every software features including page formatting and layout, laser printing and word processing macros. New users of WordPerfect, and those new to Version 5 and desktop publishing will find this easy to use for on-the-job help.

WordPerfect Instant Reference SYBEX Prompter Series

Greg Harvey
Kay Yarborough Nelson

254pp. Ref. 476-3, 4 3/4" × 8"

When you don't have time to go digging through the manuals, this fingertip guide offers clear, concise answers: command summaries, correct usage, and exact keystroke sequences for on-the-job tasks. Convenient organization reflects the structure of WordPerfect. Through Version 4.2.

WordPerfect 5 Instant Reference SYBEX Prompter Series

Greg Harvey
Kay Yarborough Nelson

316pp. Ref. 535-2, 4 3/4" × 8"

This pocket-sized reference has all the program commands for the powerful WordPerfect 5 organized alphabetically for quick access. Each command entry has the exact key sequence, any reveal codes, a list of available options, and option-by-option discussions.

WordPerfect 5.1 Instant Reference

Greg Harvey
Kay Yarborough Nelson

252pp. Ref. 674-X

Instant access to all features and commands of WordPerfect 5.0 and 5.1, highlighting the newest software features. Complete, alphabetical entries provide exact key sequences, codes and options, and step-by-step instructions for many important tasks.

WordPerfect 5 Macro Handbook

Kay Yarborough Nelson

488pp. Ref. 483-6

Readers can create macros custom-tailored to their own needs with this excellent tutorial and reference. Nelson's expertise guides the WordPerfect 5 user through nested and chained macros, macro libraries, specialized macros, and much more.

WordPerfect 5.1 Tips and Tricks (Fourth Edition)

Alan R. Neibauer

675pp. Ref. 681-2

This new edition is a real timesaver. For on-the-job guidance and creative new uses, this title covers all versions of WordPerfect up to and including 5.1—streamlining documents, automating with macros, new print enhancements, and more.

WordStar Instant Reference SYBEX Prompter Series

David J. Clark

314pp. Ref. 543-3, 4 3/4" × 8"

This quick reference provides reminders on the use of the editing, formatting, mailmerge, and document processing commands available through WordStar 4 and 5. Operations are organized alphabetically for easy access. The text includes a survey of the menu system and instructions for installing and customizing WordStar.

SPREADSHEETS AND INTEGRATED SOFTWARE

1-2-3 for Scientists and Engineers

William J. Orvis

341pp. Ref. 407-0

Fast, elegant solutions to common problems in science and engineering, using Lotus 1-2-3. Tables and plotting, curve fitting, statistics, derivatives, integrals and differentials, solving systems of equations, and more.

The ABC's of 1-2-3 (Second Edition)

Chris Gilbert
Laurie Williams

245pp. Ref. 355-4

Online Today recommends it as "an easy

and comfortable way to get started with the program." An essential tutorial for novices, it will remain on your desk as a valuable source of ongoing reference and support. For Release 2.

The ABC's of 1-2-3 Release 2.2

Chris Gilbert
Laurie Williams

340pp. Ref. 623-5

New Lotus 1-2-3 users delight in this book's step-by-step approach to building trouble-free spreadsheets, displaying graphs, and efficiently building databases. The authors cover the ins and outs of the latest version including easier calculations, file linking, and better graphic presentation.

The ABC's of 1-2-3 Release 3

Judd Robbins

290pp. Ref. 519-0

The ideal book for beginners who are new to Lotus or new to Release 3. This step-by-step approach to the 1-2-3 spreadsheet software gets the reader up and running with spreadsheet, database, graphics, and macro functions.

The ABC's of Excel on the IBM PC

Douglas Hergert

326pp. Ref. 567-0

This book is a brisk and friendly introduction to the most important features of Microsoft Excel for PC's. This beginner's book discusses worksheets, charts, database operations, and macros, all with hands-on examples. Written for all versions through Version 2.

The ABC's of Quattro

Alan Simpson
Douglas J. Wolf

286pp. Ref. 560-3

Especially for users new to spreadsheets, this is an introduction to the basic concepts and a guide to instant productivity through editing and using spreadsheet formulas and functions. Includes how to print out graphs and data for presentation. For Quattro 1.1.

The Complete Lotus 1-2-3 Release 2.2 Handbook

Greg Harvey

750pp. Ref. 625-1

This comprehensive handbook discusses every 1-2-3 operating with clear instructions and practical tips. This volume especially emphasizes the new improved graphics, high-speed recalculation techniques, and spreadsheet linking available with Release 2.2.

The Complete Lotus 1-2-3 Release 3 Handbook

Greg Harvey

700pp. Ref. 600-6

Everything you ever wanted to know about 1-2-3 is in this definitive handbook. As a Release 3 guide, it features the design and use of 3D worksheets, and improved graphics, along with using Lotus under DOS or OS/2. Problems, exercises, and helpful insights are included.

Lotus 1-2-3 Desktop Companion SYBEX Ready Reference Series

Greg Harvey

976pp. Ref. 501-8

A full-time consultant, right on your desk. Hundreds of self-contained entries cover every 1-2-3 feature, organized by topic, indexed and cross-referenced, and supplemented by tips, macros and working examples. For Release 2.

Lotus 1-2-3 Instant Reference Release 2.2 SYBEX Prompter Series

Greg Harvey
Kay Yarborough Nelson

254pp. Ref. 635-9, 4 3/4" × 8"

The reader gets quick and easy access to any operation in 1-2-3 Version 2.2 in this handy pocket-sized encyclopedia. Organized by menu function, each command and function has a summary description, the exact key sequence, and a discussion of the options.

TO JOIN THE SYBEX MAILING LIST OR ORDER BOOKS
PLEASE COMPLETE THIS FORM

NAME ______________________ COMPANY ______________________

STREET ______________________ CITY ______________________

STATE ______________________ ZIP ______________________

☐ PLEASE MAIL ME MORE INFORMATION ABOUT **SYBEX** TITLES

ORDER FORM (There is no obligation to order)

PLEASE SEND ME THE FOLLOWING:

TITLE	QTY	PRICE
______________	_____	_____
______________	_____	_____
______________	_____	_____
______________	_____	_____
TOTAL BOOK ORDER	_____	$_____

SHIPPING AND HANDLING PLEASE ADD $2.00 PER BOOK VIA UPS _____

FOR OVERSEAS SURFACE ADD $5.25 PER BOOK PLUS $4.40 REGISTRATION FEE _____

FOR OVERSEAS AIRMAIL ADD $18.25 PER BOOK PLUS $4.40 REGISTRATION FEE _____

CALIFORNIA RESIDENTS PLEASE ADD APPLICABLE SALES TAX _____

TOTAL AMOUNT PAYABLE _____

☐ CHECK ENCLOSED ☐ VISA
☐ MASTERCARD ☐ AMERICAN EXPRESS

ACCOUNT NUMBER ______________________

EXPIR. DATE _______ DAYTIME PHONE ______________

CUSTOMER SIGNATURE ____

CHECK AREA OF COMPUTER INTEREST:

☐ BUSINESS SOFTWARE

☐ TECHNICAL PROGRAMMING

☐ OTHER: ______________________

OTHER COMPUTER TITLES YOU WOULD LIKE TO SEE IN PRINT:

____

____

THE FACTOR THAT WAS MOST IMPORTANT IN YOUR SELECTION:

☐ THE SYBEX NAME

☐ QUALITY

☐ PRICE

☐ EXTRA FEATURES

☐ COMPREHENSIVENESS

☐ CLEAR WRITING

☐ OTHER ______________________

OCCUPATION

☐ PROGRAMMER

☐ SENIOR EXECUTIVE

☐ COMPUTER CONSULTANT

☐ SUPERVISOR

☐ MIDDLE MANAGEMENT

☐ ENGINEER/TECHNICAL

☐ CLERICAL/SERVICE

☐ BUSINESS OWNER/SELF EMPLOYED

☐ TEACHER

☐ HOMEMAKER

☐ RETIRED

☐ STUDENT

☐ OTHER: ______________

CHECK YOUR LEVEL OF COMPUTER USE

☐ NEW TO COMPUTERS

☐ INFREQUENT COMPUTER USER

☐ FREQUENT USER OF ONE SOFTWARE PACKAGE:

NAME ______________________________

☐ FREQUENT USER OF MANY SOFTWARE PACKAGES

☐ PROFESSIONAL PROGRAMMER

OTHER COMMENTS:

____

____

____

____

____

____

____

PLEASE FOLD, SEAL, AND MAIL TO SYBEX

SYBEX, INC.
2021 CHALLENGER DR. #100
ALAMEDA, CALIFORNIA USA
94501

SEAL

SYBEX Computer Books are different.

Here is why . . .

At SYBEX, each book is designed with you in mind. Every manuscript is carefully selected and supervised by our editors, who are themselves computer experts. We publish the best authors, whose technical expertise is matched by an ability to write clearly and to communicate effectively. Programs are thoroughly tested for accuracy by our technical staff. Our computerized production department goes to great lengths to make sure that each book is well-designed.

In the pursuit of timeliness, SYBEX has achieved many publishing firsts. SYBEX was among the first to integrate personal computers used by authors and staff into the publishing process. SYBEX was the first to publish books on the CP/M operating system, microprocessor interfacing techniques, word processing, and many more topics.

Expertise in computers and dedication to the highest quality product have made SYBEX a world leader in computer book publishing. Translated into fourteen languages, SYBEX books have helped millions of people around the world to get the most from their computers. We hope we have helped you, too.

PIF Editor - (untitled)

File Mode Help

Program Filename:

Window Title:

Optional Parameters:

Start-up Directory:

Video Mode: Text Graphics/Multiple Text

Memory Requirements: KB Required 128

XMS Memory: KB Required 0 KB Limit 0

Directly Modifies: COM1 COM3 Keyboard

COM2 COM4

No Screen Exchange Prevent Program Switch

Close Window on Exit

Reserve Shortcut Keys: Alt+Tab Alt+Esc Ctrl+Esc

PrtSc Alt+PrtSc

File

New

Open...

Save

Save As...

Exit

Mode

✓ Standard

386 Enhanced

Help

Index

Keyboard

Commands

Procedures

Standard Options

386 Enhanced Options

Advanced Options

Using Help

About PIF Editor...